Expressing Critical Thinking through Disciplinary Texts

Also available from Bloomsbury

Academic Writing and Genre, by Ian Bruce
Academic Writing in a Second or Foreign Language, edited by Ramona Tang
Acquiring Metaphorical Expressions in a Second Language, by Chris Mengying Xia
On Writtenness, by Joan Turner
Reflective Language Teaching, by Thomas S. C. Farrell

Expressing Critical Thinking through Disciplinary Texts

Insights from Five Genre Studies

Ian Bruce

BLOOMSBURY ACADEMIC
LONDON • NEW YORK • OXFORD • NEW DELHI • SYDNEY

BLOOMSBURY ACADEMIC
Bloomsbury Publishing Plc
50 Bedford Square, London, WC1B 3DP, UK
1385 Broadway, New York, NY 10018, USA
29 Earlsfort Terrace, Dublin 2, Ireland

BLOOMSBURY, BLOOMSBURY ACADEMIC and the Diana logo are trademarks of
Bloomsbury Publishing Plc

First published in Great Britain 2020
This paperback edition published in 2022

Copyright © Ian Bruce, 2020

Ian Bruce has asserted his right under the Copyright, Designs and
Patents Act, 1988, to be identified as Author of this work.

All rights reserved. No part of this publication may be reproduced or transmitted
in any form or by any means, electronic or mechanical, including photocopying,
recording, or any information storage or retrieval system, without prior
permission in writing from the publishers.

Bloomsbury Publishing Plc does not have any control over, or responsibility for, any
third-party websites referred to or in this book. All internet addresses given in this
book were correct at the time of going to press. The author and publisher regret
any inconvenience caused if addresses have changed or sites have ceased to
exist, but can accept no responsibility for any such changes.

A catalogue record for this book is available from the British Library.

A catalog record for this book is available from the Library of Congress.

ISBN: HB: 978-1-3501-2789-0
PB: 978-1-3501-9308-6
ePDF: 978-1-3501-2791-3
eBook: 978-1-3501-2790-6

Typeset by Deanta Global Publishing Services, Chennai, India

To find out more about our authors and books visit www.bloomsbury.com and
sign up for our newsletters.

To Carolyn

Contents

List of tables	viii
Preface	ix

1	Critical thinking: Definitions, origins, controversies	1
2	Investigating the expression of critical thinking through writing	15
3	Expressing critical thinking in the university essay	47
4	Expressing critical thinking in PhD Discussion chapters	69
5	Expressing critical thinking in research article literature reviews	91
6	Expressing critical thinking in corporate disclosure communication	111
7	Expressing critical thinking in journalistic commentary	129
8	Expressing critical thinking through writing	145

Appendices	163
Notes	178
References	180
Index	197

Tables

2.1	Approaches to Text Classification	27
2.2	Genre Knowledge	40
2.3	A Model for Cognitive Genres in Academic Prose	42
3.1	Relations Framing Critical Statements: English Literature Essays	56
3.2	Relations Framing Critical Statements: Sociology Essays	56
4.1	Frequencies of Use of the Schema: 'Point Support Evaluation'	76
4.2	Coherence Relations Framing Critical Statements in the Evaluation	81
4.3	Use of Hedges and Attitude Markers in Critical Statements	84
5.1	Swales' 'Create a Research Space' (CARS) Move Structure	95
5.2	Move Structure in the Introductions of the Applied Linguistics Texts	99
5.3	Move Structure in the Introductions of the Psychology-related Texts	100
5.4	Sample of Attitude Markers in one Move 1b Occurrence: Applied Linguistics Texts	102
5.5	Sample of Attitude Markers in one Move 1b Occurrence: Psychology Texts	103
5.6	Attitude Markers in Applied Linguistics Text 6	104
5.7	Numbers of Occurrences of the Concession Contraexpectation Relation in the Applied Linguistics Texts	105
5.8	Numbers of Occurrences of the Concession Contraexpectation Relation in the Psychology Texts	106
6.1	Move Structure of the Fund Manager Commentary Genre	120
Appendix A	Sociology Essays from the BAWE Corpus	163
Appendix B	English Literature Essays from the BAWE Corpus	165
Appendix C	Example of the Analysis: English Essay 7	167
Appendix D	Source Theses of Discussion Chapters	169
Appendix E	Crombie's Interpropositional Relations	170
Appendix F	The Sample of Fund Manager Commentary Texts	172

Preface

This book came about because of my work in three areas: teaching university courses, doctoral supervision and genre research. In each area, a central requirement is for writers to express critical thinking through the texts that they must create. In exploring how writers fulfil this requirement, I bring together in this book five published studies in which I used genre analysis to identify how critical thinking is expressed in texts from different domains. Turning these studies into a book has involved revisiting and re-evaluating their findings and considering their commonalities and differences as well as the wider contextual influences of the different academic and professional domains to which the genres belong.

I begin the book by reviewing theory and research from two areas, those of 'critical thinking' and 'genre studies'. In Chapter 1, I examine the historical origins of, and different approaches to, conceptualizing critical thinking as well as the different ways in which it has been taught. In Chapter 2, I review previous studies that have examined how critical thinking is expressed through written texts, most of which have focused on the use of a single linguistic feature and have used corpus methods. I then argue that the use of genre as an analytical framework provides a more holistic, multivariable approach to this type of research. In developing this approach, I review different theories of genre and outline the particular genre model that I use in my investigations. In each of the following five chapters (Chapters 3–7), I use this model to examine how critical thinking is expressed in a particular academic or professional genre. In the final chapter, drawing together the findings of these studies, I propose key principles that emerge about how critical thinking is communicated through text.

In addition to my research focus on how critical thinking is expressed through texts, I have also tried to provide some suggestions about how the findings of these studies can be used pedagogically by those tasked with teaching academic, research and professional writing. To this end, I include a section towards the end of four of the genre studies where I relate the findings to the teaching of writing and, in particular, teaching how critical thinking is expressed through writing. In a section in the final chapter, I draw these pedagogic implications threads together, summarizing the ideas and principles discussed in previous chapters.

This book is not the final word on how critical thinking is expressed through writing, nor is it the final word on how this should be taught. However, I hope that the approach that I take and the insights and suggestions that I offer will contribute to the ongoing discourse that relates to this challenging pedagogical issue.

1

Critical thinking

Definitions, origins, controversies

1.0 Overview

My overall aim in this book is to explore how critical thinking is communicated through written text. While most books that deal with the subject of critical thinking are concerned with how it is formulated, and draw on the disciplines of philosophy, logic or rhetoric, my focus here is on understanding how critical thinking is expressed through the written texts of different disciplines. As a framework for this enquiry, I use genre analysis and bring together the findings of five previously published studies to provide insights into the textual means employed.

In this chapter, I establish the context of the book, first, by defining the key terms that I use, second, by briefly considering the origins of critical thinking in Western scholarship and science, and third, by discussing the different approaches to the teaching of critical thinking. In Chapter 2, I outline the genre model that I use as an analytical framework to investigate how critical thinking is expressed through specialist writing from different disciplines. In Chapters 3, 4 and 5, I explore how critical thinking is expressed in academic writing, specifically in undergraduate essays, PhD discussion chapters and research article (RA) literature reviews. In Chapter 6, I examine its expression in an example of business writing, the online genre of the fund manager commentary (FMC), and in Chapter 7, I explore how it is expressed in journalistic opinion writing, exemplified in a political commentary column from *The Guardian* newspaper. Finally in Chapter 8, I review the discussions and findings of the previous five chapters. I consider how they contribute further to understanding how critical thinking is expressed through writing and how this may be taught by writing instructors.

1.1 Definitions

To establish a definitional framework for the following chapters, I begin by introducing the key terms that are used, those of *critical thinking, enacting criticality, text* and *discourse*. The concepts related to these terms are presented briefly here and discussed again in greater detail at the beginning of Chapter 2. For the purposes of this book, the term 'critical thinking' is used to describe an evaluation made within any field of human activity about some aspect, object or behaviour of that field according to the 'standards of judgment of that field' (Swales & Feak, 2012, p. 328). This definition accords with the ideas of McPeck (1981), who states: 'the criteria for the use of scepticism are supplied by the norms and standards of the field under consideration' (pp. 7–8). The adjunct term 'enacting criticality' refers to the actual process of the communication (transmission and reception among interlocutors) of such an evaluative judgement. A core idea in the definitions of McPeck (1981) and Swales and Feak (2012) underpins the approach to critical thinking taken here, which is: when expressing critical thinking, writers (or speakers) communicate evaluative judgements on some aspect of their particular area of specialist activity according to the values and standards of the discipline, profession or area of activity within which the evaluation occurs. In Western societies, critical thinking is usually regarded as a central element of engagement with any field of specialist human activity, such as academic scholarship, research, professional practice, business, manufacturing, art, sport, entertainment or politics. It is seen as essential to the development and refinement of the knowledge, skill, product, service or other outcome of the specialist field within which it occurs.

Following this definitional approach, an underlying requirement for any credible enactment of criticality is for an interlocutor to be an insider within, or possess a certain threshold level of knowledge about the field of activity within which a judgement is being made. In relation to academic subjects, the philosopher Hirst (2009) calls this type of disciplinary insider knowledge the logical grammar of a subject, or as he states, 'the logical grammar of its key concepts' (p. 37), which I suggest involves the epistemology and specialist knowledge of a particular subject discipline. Brookfield (2012) further defines this type of fundamental insider knowledge as 'the building blocks of knowledge that every student of that subject needs to know in order to be regarded as well versed in it' (p. 28). Brookfield goes on to say that 'what counts as content grammar is determined by scholars and institutions and [is] often codified by professional associations in standards and lists of best practices' (p. 28). However, since the focus of this book is on how critical thinking is expressed through written text (as part of the larger process of enacting criticality), the terms 'text' and 'discourse' are also central to this definitional framework.

Text, as Widdowson (2004) states, is 'the linguistic trace of a discourse process' (p. 69). Thus, text here is taken to mean the words on the page, which may be a written document or the written transcription of a spoken monologue or dialogue. Discourse, on the other hand, refers to the interpretations that relate to a text, involving the transmission and reception of ideas among interlocutors. Therefore, while a written text is the linguistic medium through which ideas are encoded and decoded, creating discourse involves the application to the text of socially constructed knowledge, interpretive frameworks and personal strategies along with a working knowledge of the different elements of the linguistic system used. Here discourse is seen as involving both social and cognitive processes within which texts may play a central and integral role. Where specialist written texts are involved, enacting criticality occurs among interlocutors (writers and readers) engaged in co-constructing discourse within particular disciplinary contexts.

Thus, the central idea that underpins the approach to critical thinking of this book is that enacting criticality is a contextually situated, discursive process, involving a wide range of types of knowledge that may include disciplinary, social, procedural and linguistic elements. Therefore, in exploring the genres discussed in Chapters 3 to 7, it is important that the theoretical approach used to examine the written expression of critical thinking is able to account for, and integrate the elements of, both the actual text and the discursive intentions and meanings that relate to the creation and interpretation of the text. In addressing this need for an encompassing theoretical approach, Chapter 2 outlines the genre model used to examine the different categories of texts of the subsequent chapters. However, to first establish a context for these investigations of expressing critical thinking through writing, Section 1.2 briefly considers the historical origins of critical thinking in Western scholarship and science.

1.2 Critical thinking in Western scholarship

The idea of expressing critical thinking through argumentation and reasoning, and the need for educated people to enact criticality when engaging with knowledge or scientific discovery are concepts that have a long history in Western scholarship – concepts that began with the approaches to philosophy and the theories of rhetoric, dialectic and logic of ancient Greece and Rome. In this section, I attempt to illustrate, very briefly, the historical development of the concept of exercising critical thinking through reference to a small number of landmark works.

During the classical period, theories advanced for the discovery of knowledge consisted of rules or patterns for deductive reasoning, such as the 'syllogism'.[1] Closely related to the theories of knowledge discovery of this era were proposals for principled approaches to the oral evaluation and communication of knowledge, specifically 'rhetoric' and 'dialectic'. For example, Aristotle's famous work *Rhetoric* provided a set of rules for persuasive speech-making. Similarly, dialectic, as a type of oral debate, was made popular by Plato in the *Socratic Dialogues*, its purpose being to establish the truth of a matter by following a prescribed set of principles as an approach to resolving a disagreement. Separate approaches for exclusively written communication emerged later during the early medieval period. Then the selective and pragmatic use of classical principles called 'rhetorica nova' was applied to a wide range of written texts, including letters, legal documents, sermons and verse. At this stage, the idea that written texts may be structured differently from spoken texts also began to be considered. This development is exemplified by Thomas Aquinas in the thirteenth century in his work *Summa Theologica*, which employed empirical reasoning and systematicity in addressing counter-arguments in religious debates.

During the Renaissance, the ideas and publications of the scientists and philosophers of the sixteenth and seventeenth centuries represented changing orientations towards the discovery of knowledge and how newly discovered knowledge should be reported. In his work *Novum Organum*, the English philosopher/politician Francis Bacon (1561–1626) proposed that knowledge discovery should involve qualitative observations of nature that provide a basis for establishing natural laws or principles. In seventeenth-century England, meetings of groups of scientists in London from about 1645 led to the formation of the Royal Society. Drawing on ideas from published works of Francis Bacon, the members of the Royal Society proposed 'empiricism' as a basis for enquiry in all areas of science. In conjunction with this new scientific approach, the members also sought a suitable theory of communication for the reporting and dissemination of scientific findings, a theory that moved away from the deductive routines of traditional, persuasive rhetoric. The figure within the Royal Society who was most influential in developing this plain, direct form of communication – the New Rhetoric (NR) – was John Locke (1632–1704), who proposed that argument should be based on factual content and supported induction as a means for presenting proof or evidence.

However, Bacon's ideas about the centrality of observation to knowledge discovery differed from those of the French philosopher Descartes (1596–1650), who proposed that knowledge is solely developed by means of human reasoning. In his work *Discourse on the Method*, Descartes proposes four principles for systematically evaluating knowledge, sometimes referred to as 'principles of systematic doubt', according to which reasoning about anything begins with doubt or scepticism. As a result, ideas about critical thinking or scepticism also came to be considered to be an integral part of the processes of the discovery of knowledge and its communication.

The critical approach to knowledge of British empiricism was further extended in the eighteenth century by the Scottish philosopher David Hume (1711–76), who was a strong empiricist who also belonged to the 'sceptical' philosophical tradition. Hume argued that human knowledge was based on what is observable, but also that humans had inbuilt capacities to form conceptions and make deductions about empirically observed knowledge. Later, in the early nineteenth century, empiricism as a basis for scientific investigation further evolved into the positivist approach, and was extended into the human sciences by the French philosopher Auguste Comte (1798–1857), who also emphasized the importance of the relationship between theory and empirical observation in order to gain a greater understanding of the world: 'If it is true that every theory must be based upon observed facts, it is equally true that facts cannot be observed without the guidance of some theories' (Comte, 1974, p. 27). Thus, from the ideas of Comte, the combination of inductive and deductive reasoning that characterizes 'positivism' or the 'scientific method' emerged. Some elements of this approach can also be seen in the writings of the German philosopher and physicist Ernst Mach (1838–1916) and the American philosopher and logician Charles Peirce (1839–1914).

In the philosophy of science in the early part of the twentieth century, there was a strong focus on theory-internal elements of critical/analytical thinking, involving the stringent application of logic to propositions as part of the development of scientific theory. This emerged when a number of philosophers of science (the Vienna Circle) developed a theory of scientific discovery termed 'logical positivism'. This theory emerged from the ideas of Frege (1848–1925), Russell (1872–1970) and Wittgenstein (1889–1951). Following this approach, rules of logic are applied to the analysis of scientific propositions, such as in Russell's 'logical atomism' whereby '[t]he truth or falsity of complex statements might, it seemed, be assessed by the truth or falsity of their most simple (empirical) atomic constituents' (Oldroyd, 1986, p. 221).

The ideas of logical positivism of the members of the Vienna circle were challenged by Karl Popper (1902–94), who was less interested in the meaningfulness of the propositions expressed within scientific theories than in the efforts of scientists to test their theories. His idea of 'falsification' was that scientists should test their hypotheses by carrying out empirical work with the ultimate goal of examining the extent to which they are wrong: 'Scientific theories were not the digest of observations, but that they were interventions – conjectures boldly put forward for trial, to be eliminated if they clashed with observations' (Popper, 1963, p. 46). Following Popper's approach, scientific predictions are expressed as 'falsifiable' statements so that they can be tested empirically. If a theory, once tested by the examination of the appropriate empirical evidence, could not be falsified, it could be said to be 'corroborated'. Thus, Popper's influence on science was his emphasis on the critical scrutiny of theories and the rigour in approaches to the empirical work that sought to prove or disprove them.

In the social sciences, the Critical Theory School emerged from the Institute for Social Research, established in 1923 at the University of Frankfurt. Critical theorists claimed that previous approaches to research, such as positivism, ignored political and social issues, and they proposed that research in the social sciences (differing from that of the physical sciences) should fulfil social agendas in order to benefit the whole of society. The Critical Theory approach eventually became associated with particular research methods: action research (the investigation of professional practice for the purpose of improvement) and critical discourse analysis (ideology critique).

The second half of the twentieth century saw more radical challenges to theories of science and knowledge discovery. Thomas Kuhn (1924–96), an American physicist and philosopher, focused on the social dimensions of scientific enquiry. In his work *The Structure of Scientific Revolutions* (1962), Kuhn suggested that the history of scientific thought is actually one of discontinuities, and that any scientific method used for the discovery of knowledge is an artefact of the constraints placed around it by the practitioners of a particular scientific community, which he termed a 'paradigm'. Another philosopher of science, Paul Feyerabend (1924–94), whose book *Against Method* (first published in 1975) emphasized, even more than Kuhn, the time- and context-situatedness of scientific ideas, raises the issue that 'progress' is often only made when current, received, scientific understandings are challenged by new ideas or theories that, by contrast, appear irrational – that is, outside of the current paradigm. Other theorists, such as those working in the field of the sociology of science (e.g. Gilbert & Mulkay, 1984; Latour & Woolgar, 1986; Knorr Cetina, 1999), have also argued that what is held to be scientific knowledge is the product of the thinking and values of historical periods, discourse communities and institutional environments within which such knowledge is developed, with these contextual elements influencing the ontological and epistemological views of researchers.

Thus, a thread that runs through Western theories of reasoning and knowledge discovery has been the emphasis placed on the scrutiny and critique of new knowledge, with different principled approaches to how new knowledge is validated being proposed during different historical periods. While earlier eras sought to articulate universal laws and principles that related to the discovery and communication of knowledge, a significant theme that emerged during the latter half of the twentieth century was recognition of the influences of historical, cultural, social and institutional contexts on the research methods of science and on how the process of scientific inquiry evolved. During this era, those writing about the philosophy and sociology of science began to challenge any idea of uniformity of method and structure, emphasizing the 'situatedness' of both scientific research and its reporting in texts. Situatedness refers to the influences of cultures, societies, discourse communities and institutions and their particular research methodologies on knowledge creation and on critical or evaluative thinking, which may differ according to context.

1.3 Operationalizing and teaching critical thinking

The brief historical overview of the previous section describes ongoing attempts throughout history to conceptualize approaches to analytical and critical thinking as a basis for undertaking both scientific investigations and knowledge communication. Given the underlying role and importance of these critical/ analytical traditions in Western scholarship and science, modern governments and educational institutions have long placed value on students developing the ability to formulate and communicate evaluative judgements – to express critical thinking through spoken and written texts in ways that are considered to be both intellectually sound and academically appropriate. This view of the importance of the development of critical thinking skills is often articulated as a core competency in state or national educational curricula, such as those of the province of British Columbia in Canada and the Republic of Singapore.

The importance of critical thinking is also identified in the mission statements of Western schools and universities. For example, the first core value of the University of Cambridge under the heading of 'Education' is 'the encouragement of a questioning spirit'. Similarly, Harvard's undergraduate college claims in its mission statement that it 'encourages students ... to rejoice in discovery and in critical thought'. Therefore, because critical thinking is identified as such an important fundamental academic attribute, it is often argued that it should be taught directly to students in schools and universities. However, when it comes to articulating what critical thinking is, how it is learned and how it should be taught, there is a considerable diversity of approaches. This section provides a brief outline of contemporary views and controversies about the pedagogical approaches to the development of critical thinking skills in students seeking to participate in higher education, with a particular focus on teaching critical thinking through writing.

Despite apparent widespread agreement on the importance of critical thinking in education (and especially in higher education), there are significant differences among educators in both how they define critical thinking and how they propose that it should be taught. Brookfield (2012) suggests that there are five intellectual traditions that are drawn upon for the teaching of critical thinking: analytic philosophy and logic, natural science, pragmatism, psychoanalysis and critical theory. He suggests that the most influential approach is that of analytic philosophy and logic, which appears to be about 'the mechanics of putting arguments together and taking them apart' (p. 33). This approach has its origins in classical philosophy and rhetoric, which were briefly considered in the previous section. The second tradition is the teaching of critical thinking based on the precepts of natural science, an approach that draws on empiricism and the tradition of hypothesis formulation and testing. As seen in the previous section of this chapter, this approach has a long history beginning with the sixteenth-century scientists of the Royal Society, nineteenth-century positivists, and logical positivism and Popper's principle of falsifiability in the twentieth century. Brookfield suggests that there are also critical thinking courses based on American pragmatism 'which constantly questions the tacit assumptions of earlier interpretations of the past' (West, 1982, p. 20). In addition, he suggests that courses on critical thinking in the fields of social work, nursing and education may draw on the tradition of psychoanalysis and psychotherapy, and that the critical theory approach of the Frankfurt school is employed in courses concerned with ideology critique, such as in the areas of education and critical discourse analysis. What emerges from Brookfield's overview is that ideas about what critical thinking is, and how it should be taught, come from a number of philosophical and scientific traditions, and that there is no common source or canon of knowledge that informs its teaching.

While also acknowledging, like Brookfield, the diversity of the theoretical origins of critical thinking and how it is conceptualized, Davies and Barnett (2015) attempt to identify the types of pedagogical focus that arise from these different intellectual traditions; they categorize them within three broad approaches. The first is the 'critical thinking movement', whose pedagogy has the aim of developing critical thinking skills as a 'reflective basis for decision making and judgment calls' (p. 11). Ennis (1989) defines this approach as 'reflective and reasonable thinking that is focused on deciding what to believe or do' (p. 45). This approach to teaching critical thinking has its origins in analytic philosophy and logic, and tends to predominate in the types of formative courses that governments and universities demand, such as in freshman critical thinking and writing and rhetoric courses. The second broad pedagogical approach that Davies and Barnett identify is 'the criticality movement', which includes a focus on developing the critical thinking dispositions of students. Like the previously mentioned 'thinking skills' approach, it is concerned not only with the judgements that students form but also with the interactions in which they engage. This involves developing student critical thinking dispositions arising in relation to self, to others and to the world, and it sees critical thinking as involving reflection and action: 'This is a sense of "critical thinking" that extends beyond the individual and his or her cognitive states and dispositions to the individual's participation in society as a critically engaged citizen in the world' (Davies & Barnett, 2015, p. 16). The third approach is the 'critical pedagogy movement' with a focus on participating critically in society, such as in understanding and resisting power relations in institutions and in the wider society. According to Davies and Barnett (2015), the aim of this approach is 'not simply educating for critical thinking or even enabling individuals to embody a critical spirit, but educating for *radical* transformation of society as well' (p. 20). They suggest that, in addition to developing skills and dispositions, it also involves incitement to action. Specifically, critical pedagogy aims to educate students to identify and take action against inequitable power structures of institutions and undemocratic tendencies in society, such as manifest in the power and influence exerted by large corporations.

While critical thinking is taught in introductory courses in philosophy and logic, it is also a focus of courses concerned with the teaching of writing, usually academic writing. In this field, Atkinson (1997) claims that attempts to define critical thinking are based on two broad definitions. The first is the application of logic to argument, a definitional approach that sees critical thinking as a well-defined, rational, transparent teachable set of behaviours related to argumentation and problem-solving. This definitional approach accords with Brookfield's view of the approach of courses based on analytic philosophy and logic, with its focus on argumentation and Davies and Barnett's classification of pedagogy that focuses on 'thinking skills'. Atkinson proposes that a second definitional approach that is used in some writing courses sees critical thinking as social practice – an organic part of a particular academic culture that differs according to the ontology and epistemology of each discipline. According to this view, exercising critical thinking is a behaviour that is largely tacitly acquired rather than overtly taught and learned. Supporters of this view also contend that academic thinking behaviours specific to one particular disciplinary context do not necessarily transfer into other contexts. This definitional approach appears to draw upon later twentieth-century theories that emphasize the situatedness of intellectual and scientific inquiry within specific cultures, disciplines and institutions, and would appear to relate to Davies and Barnett's criticality movement.

Atkinson (1997) suggests that these two different approaches to defining critical thinking give rise to two different approaches to its actual teaching in writing courses. One approach he terms the 'teachable skills' approach, which draws on the logical argument definition of critical thinking, and the other he terms the 'cognitive apprenticeship' approach, which draws on a social practice definition. Traditionally, writing and rhetoric courses (and also introductory critical thinking courses taught within philosophy programmes) have promoted the first, the teachable skills approach. Such instruction is concerned with the development of a set of fairly abstract, cognitive skills relating to argumentation, skills that are not specifically bound to any particular context. It was thought that the training of writers in the use of a set of generalizable reasoning and problem-solving skills may be transferred later into disciplinary contexts (e.g. Ennis, 1989; Glaser, 1984; Halpern, 1998, 2001). However, a number of studies refute the idea that students who are overtly trained in these allegedly generalizable skills will transfer their use into specific domains and disciplines. Much of this body of research is brought together in the extensive, meta-analysis of Huber and Kuncel (2016) who, on the basis of their findings, 'argue against investing additional time and resources in teaching *domain-general* critical thinking' (p. 460). Moreover, in relation to the teaching of academic writing, I argue that there are two fundamental problems with this particular approach.

First, in relation to the 'teachable skills' approach to critical thinking for teaching academic and professional writing, much of the pedagogic advice about critical thinking offered relates to the analysis or development of an overt, persuasive argument in a text, often about a common issue (such as an environmental problem). The problem with such advice is that, although much academic writing does relate to the development and presentation of an overall case (an argument in a broad sense), it seems that the types of rhetorical purpose involved rarely involve overt, persuasive argumentation. I found this to be the case in a study of proficient university essay writing in two different disciplines: sociology (as an example of social science writing) and English literature (as an example of humanities writing) using student texts taken from the *British Academic Written English* (BAWE) Corpus (Bruce, 2010a, 2015a, 2016) – see Chapter 3 in this volume. The findings from these studies suggest that developing a case (an argument, in a very broad sense) within an extended piece of academic writing involves the marshalling of a range of textual resources involving intermeshing rhetorical purposes, purposes that are specific to a disciplinary context. Therefore, it appears that subject content, writer orientation and the textual resources used in the development of a complex case will differ in the writing of different disciplines.

Second, when reading and processing disciplinary texts, the capacity to exercise critical thinking relates to a reader's levels of background knowledge about a particular text that they encounter, such as described by Hirst's (2009) concept of the 'logical grammar' of a subject discipline. For example, in order to formulate a critical judgement in relation to the subject content of a text in a disciplinary context, a reader already needs to have a considerable amount of knowledge of the ontology, epistemology and specialist content of the discipline, as well as prior knowledge of the particular genre or type of text and the role that the genre plays in communicating knowledge within that discipline. Readers need 'domain-specific knowledge [which] includes understanding methodological principles and competence to engage in norm-regulated practices that are at the core of reasonable judgments in those specific contexts' (Facione, 1990, p. 10).

The teachable skills approach to critical thinking has been challenged by a number of theorists and researchers, such as those reviewed by Ramanathan and Kaplan (1996), who conclude that 'the transfer and general applicability of critical thinking/reasoning skills [across domains] is at best a debatable one', and that the incorporation of critical thinking into writing 'is situated and context/discipline-dependent' (p. 242). The latter point reflects a view that resonates with the later 'academic literacies' movement's views on the discipline-specificity of knowledge and skills that relate to academic writing (Lea & Street, 1998, 2006). As I see it, the principal difficulty with the teachable skills approach is that it does not problematize sufficiently the notion of the expert writer who is a member of a disciplinary discourse community; that is, someone who has the specialist knowledge and skills needed to exercise critical thinking appropriately within that community. For example, an expert community member, when writing or reading an academic text situated within that community, brings to the task a consummate level of disciplinary knowledge and knowledge of prior texts, which, when taken together, enable full communication and participation as an experienced member of that community. On the other hand, a novice student member of the same disciplinary community reading the same text will have, at best, only a developing knowledge of the subject content of the discipline, and its research methodologies, genres and textual traditions.

As an alternative to the teachable skills approach, Atkinson (1997) proposes a pedagogy based on the cognitive apprenticeship definition of critical thinking, a pedagogy that is based loosely on the type of training that takes place in vocational apprenticeships, described by Collins, Brown and Newman (1989) as 'modelling, coaching and fading', an approach that has much in common with the Community of Practice approach to instruction of Lave and Wenger (1991). Essentially, the idea here is that novice members of an academic (or professional) community learn its practices and thinking behaviours by working with more experienced members of the community, observing and internalizing their practices, participating themselves under the guidance of experts, and then gradually participating more autonomously within an academic community and being subject to its feedback-providing and reviewing processes.

While the cognitive apprenticeship approach appears to account more satisfactorily for the complex issue of critical thinking and disciplinarity, mastering such knowledge and skills in an educational setting requires developing an understanding of the complex layers of disciplinary content knowledge, meta-knowledge and the conventionalized approaches to its communication. Similarly, research that investigates these types of knowledge requires theoretical orientations and the tools necessary to deconstruct disciplinary texts and their related discursive interpretations. For example, if texts are, as Widdowson states, 'the linguistic trace of a discourse process' (2004, p. 69), I would argue that the expression of critical thinking is, therefore, inextricably embedded within the disciplinary discourses that attach to a particular text. Therefore, deconstructing both the organizational and linguistic features of disciplinary texts, along with other discursively-influenced elements that realize the individualized expression of the writer (such as when communicating critical thinking), requires recourse to analytical approaches whereby not only the textual forms but also the local discursive intentions are able to be identified and deconstructed.

Therefore, the overall purpose of this book is that it seeks, in a small way, to uncover some understanding of how critical thinking is expressed in a range of academic and professional genres, focusing specifically on 'the textual trace of the discourse process' (2004, p. 69). The previously published studies drawn upon in Chapters 3 to 7 employ a particular approach to genre analysis (outlined in Chapter 2 following) in order to uncover those generic elements used to express critical thinking in academic and professional genres. The hope is that the findings may be of interest to those involved in theorizing, researching and teaching academic and professional writing, and, in particular, the dimension of critical thinking in such writing.

1.4 Conclusion

This chapter has been concerned with defining and tracing the origins of what is often called critical thinking. The chapter establishes that the application of critical thinking to the methods of discovery and reporting of knowledge has been seen to be central to Western research and scholarship, and to be a key attribute to be developed in the education of novice academics and researchers. However, it emerges that definitions of critical thinking and approaches to teaching this skill vary according to the intellectual traditions from which they originate. Also, such definitions and their related instructional approaches have not traditionally accounted for ontological and epistemological differences among disciplines, and how such differences shape the communication of scholarly and scientific knowledge. To explore this area further, subsequent chapters of this book examine the expression of critical thinking through five written genres from different disciplines: three academic and two professional genres. Specifically, what each of these chapters aims to do is explore disciplinary texts and their discursive meanings as a way of broadening understandings of critical thinking and how it is expressed.

Chapter 2 provides further discussion of the definitional framework used in this book and also proposes a theory for the analysis of specific genres or categories of text, a theory that will be employed in the studies reported in subsequent chapters.

2

Investigating the expression of critical thinking through writing

2.0 Introduction

In this chapter, I propose the use of a genre model as an analytical framework to examine extended written texts in terms of the resources that they employ to express critical thinking. In the first section of the chapter, I revisit and discuss further the key concepts introduced in Chapter 1, those of critical thinking, enacting criticality, text and discourse. This discussion will include consideration of the types of knowledge and operation that may be included in any theoretical framework used to examine texts in a comprehensive way. In the second section of the chapter, I review previous studies that have examined written texts for some aspect of the expression of critical thinking, most of which have focused on the use of a single linguistic feature, or features belonging to one particular discursive or linguistic category. I consider how these studies define critical thinking, their analytical methods and the textual features on which they focus. In the third section, I begin to consider the use of genre analysis for this type of research, reasoning that it provides a more multidimensional, holistic approach to analysing texts, including analyses that try to uncover how critical thinking is expressed textually. In this section, I also review three key theories of genre, considering what they operationalize in terms of textual and discursive knowledge. This review leads to a critique of genre theory in the fourth section. In that section, I focus on the lack of construct validity arising from the diversity of approaches and issues relating to the types of knowledge that existing theories of genre operationalize. To address these issues of operationalization, in the fifth and final section of the chapter, I present my 'social genre' and 'cognitive genre' model (Bruce, 2008a), which provides the theoretical and analytical framework that I used in the studies reported in the following five chapters.

2.1 Revisiting key terms and concepts[1]

In Chapter 1, I defined critical thinking as an evaluation made within any field of human activity about some aspect, object or behaviour of that field according to the 'standards of judgment of that field' (Swales & Feak, 2012, p. 328). Building on the ideas of McPeck (1981) and others, this definition emphasizes the situatedness of critical thinking, the idea that an expression of critical thinking is shaped by the specialist knowledge and discursive practices of the discipline, profession or area of expertise to which it relates and within which it occurs. This notion of the situatedness of disciplinary knowledge and its communication emerges in Chapter 1 in the ideas and theories of philosophers and sociologists during the second half of the twentieth century, who were concerned with examining and theorizing the nature of scientific knowledge (Feyerabend, 1975; Gilbert & Mulkay, 1984; Knorr Cetina, 1999; Kuhn, 1962; Latour & Woolgar, 1986). The argument for examining critical thinking in disciplinary contexts is also supported by the considerable literature that critiques educational approaches to critical thinking as a homogenous, interdisciplinary skill, including the empirical studies summarized in the meta-analysis of Huber and Kuncel (2016).

In Chapter 1, I also introduced the term 'enacting criticality' to describe the process of the communication (transmission and reception among interlocutors) of an evaluative judgement. I proposed that this is essentially a cognitive process that occurs within the minds of interlocutors engaged in co-constructing discourse. It is a process that is shaped by a wide range of socially motivated influences, and may employ types of knowledge and practices specific to the field within which the expression of an evaluative judgement takes place. However, it is important to state here that most of the text-external aspects of the discourse process of enacting criticality fall outside of the scope of the studies of this volume, which focus intensely on the textual trace of this discourse process. Examining the more visible social dimensions of this discourse process (such as through linguistic ethnography) is an important area of enquiry, and one that could potentially be combined with the genre framework used in the studies reported here. However, since the focus here is on the means used to express critical thinking through published texts, it is important to establish a framework for examining such texts and their salient, discourse-influenced elements in order to describe these in ways that are systematic and principled. Therefore, in Chapter 1, the terms 'text' and 'discourse' were introduced and proposed as central to this framework.

As I mentioned in Chapter 1, text, according to Widdowson, is 'the linguistic trace of a discourse process' (2004, p. 69), or as Foucault says, 'What discourse is in its material reality as a thing pronounced or written' (1984, p. 109). Thus, text here is taken to mean the words on the page, which may be a written document or the written transcription of a spoken monologue or dialogue. Texts are found in specific contexts, and they are the use of language for a particular purpose. Widdowson says that texts are 'an actual use of language as distinct from a sentence which is an abstract unit of linguistic analysis' (2007, p. 4). A text may be as small as a phrase on a public sign or as large as a novel by Tolstoy. The actual physical location of many everyday texts often offers clues for their discursive interpretation. For example, a text on a public notice or sign that we encounter when travelling abroad, which is encoded in a language that we do not understand, may still be interpreted by associating it with its context and with any accompanying symbols or other graphic information. Thus, a public notice in Japanese, even if it were written in the Latin alphabet (*romaji*) as '*Kitsuen Kinshi*', will have no meaning to a non-Japanese speaker when encountered without a context. However, if the sign is located in a public place, such as on the platform of a railway station, and the words are accompanied by a graphic of a smoking cigarette overlaid by a prohibited symbol, it is possible for a non-Japanese speaker to arrive at the correct discursive interpretation of the text.

Therefore, discourse, as defined in Chapter 1, is the interpretation that arises from a text. Widdowson (2007) says 'the term discourse is taken here to refer both to what a text producer meant by a text and what a text means to the receiver' (p. 7). Van Dijk (1998, p. 194) adds that discourse involves a 'specific communicative event ... [involving] a number of social actors, typically in speaker/writer and hearer/reader roles in a specific setting (time, place, circumstances) and based on other context features'. Discourse, therefore, refers to the social and cognitive operations that surround, and give meaning to text. Enacting discourse, when either encoding a text (as a writer or speaker) or decoding a text (as a reader or listener), involves at the very least the application to the text of socially constructed knowledge, personal strategies and interpretive frameworks along with a working knowledge of linguistic and/or other semiotic systems.

In relation to academic contexts, Hyland (2009) defines discourse as 'ways of thinking and using language which exist in the academy' (p. 1). However, he points out that approaches to defining and analysing discourse vary on a cline ranging from textual approaches, where discourses are investigated by close examination of the texts that they relate to, such as by means of genre analysis, corpus analysis or multimodal analysis, through to approaches that are less concerned with the analysis of texts than with the larger physical and social contexts within which language use takes place. A similar definitional distinction is proposed by Gee (2011) who uses ' the term Discourse with a capital "D"' to refer the analysis of social contexts and 'discourse with a little "d" to mean language in use or stretches of oral or written language in "texts"' (p. 36).

While not ignoring language use in texts, consideration of the larger context appears to be the research focus of those working in critical discourse analysis and sociolinguistics. In exemplifying the approach of critical discourse analysts, who are concerned with ideology critique, Van Dijk (1997) says that the 'concept of discourse' has 'three main dimensions (a) language in use (b) the communication of beliefs (cognition), and (c) interaction in social situations' (p. 2). However, in a later work, Van Dijk (2008) cautions that the term discourse does not itself equate to an ideology or an institutionalized mode of thinking:

> Sometimes 'discourse is used in a more generic sense ... for instance, when we speak of 'medical discourse', 'political discourse', or indeed of 'racist discourse'.... Although it is often used in that way, we do not *understand* by 'discourse' a philosophy, ideology, social movement or social system, as in the phrases 'the discourse of liberalism' or 'the discourse of modernity', unless we actually refer to collections of talk and text. (p. 104)

Similarly, Alvesson and Karreman (2000), when considering different approaches to discourse analysis, caution against '[i]nclinations to "jump over" language use in a social context and make broader statements about discourse at an aggregate level (Grand or mega-Discourse)' (p. 1145), and suggest that the label of discourse, when used at this level, should be replaced by a term such as ideology. Continuing this argument, these authors propose that conceptualizing 'Discourses' in this overarching way, such as is done by Foucault and other poststructuralist writers, 'should be grounded and shown – rather than [merely] postulated' (p. 1147).

Working in the field of sociolinguistics, Blommaert (2005) similarly defines discourse as 'language-in-action' and suggests that 'investigating it requires attention both to language and to action' (p. 2). Blommaert is anxious to analyse discourse in more than just linguistic terms. He states that in his analysis he includes 'conceptions of discourse that could be called fully "non-linguistic"', and says that discourse 'comprises all forms of meaningful semiotic activity seen in connection with social, cultural, and historical patterns and developments of use' (p. 3). Thus, more context- or action-focused approaches to discourse analysis, such as in critical discourse analysis or sociolinguistics, attempt to identify the discourse that relates to communication in a particular domain in terms of configurations of knowledge, communicative elements and behaviours that characterize 'ways of thinking and using language' in that domain (Hyland, 2009, p. 2). It seems, therefore, that the differences of approach in the different definitions of discourse appear to relate to the object of the analytical approach; that is, whether the focus of the analysis centres principally on the text itself or on the discursive activity that lends meaning to the text.

However, the challenge that faces any approach to discourse analysis is to ensure that any analysis of instances of 'language and action' within a specific domain involves an adequate and comprehensive operationalization of all of the elements of the particular discursive and textual knowledge and the practices involved. For example, in analysing the enactment of discourse through the artefact of a written text, such an operationalization needs to acknowledge that the text writer and reader draw upon personalized knowledge and strategies that potentially include the following: content knowledge related to the larger disciplinary context; knowledge of the immediate communicative context including the social or interactional setting (such as the positioning of a writer in relation to his/her audience); abstract procedural or organizational knowledge (often relating to more general rhetorical purposes); and systemic linguistic knowledge. While I acknowledge here that texts as a type of semiotic, of themselves, do not constitute discourse, I propose that they are *stable, analysable, material artefacts* of important aspects of the discourses within which they play a central communicative role. Thus, the principal research interest here is in the particular resources used to enact criticality through texts, with texts seen as 'the linguistic trace of a discourse process' (Widdowson, 2004, p. 69).

In further considering the relationship between discourse and text, it is useful to think about some of the differences between spoken and written texts and how the use of linguistic systems in conjunction with their related discursive processes may vary between the two modalities. In a spoken interaction, such as in a conversation, meaning is managed in real time through interactional feedback between interlocutors and the use of paralinguistic clues, which may include the physical setting and its related activity, facial expressions, tone of voice and other body language of the speakers involved. Thus, when enacting discourse through face-to-face conversations in everyday real-world contexts, language users tend use strategies that draw upon these types of knowledge in order to communicate successfully. In the case of an extended spoken monologue, such as a political speech or a university lecture, some contextual and paralinguistic clues are still available to the audience to aid interpretation, and such monologues may be enacted somewhat like a long single turn in a conversation. On the other hand, the production of an extended written text for an unseen audience involves an actual, a hypothetical or an imagined reader. In addition, because the writer (unlike a speaker in a conversation) cannot use paralinguistic cues and interactional feedback to mediate meaning, such a text requires organizational patterns, which may include a complex series of macro- and micro-level choices. Although there may still be the possibility of some extra-textual, multimodal resources (such as images, symbols or, in the case of electronic text, hyperlinks), organizational knowledge tends to play a more significant role in the staging of extended written texts to facilitate their processing and comprehension. In considering these types of knowledge, Miller (1984) emphasizes the hierarchical nature of any representation of meaning through language, and proposes that different types of communication will emphasize different levels.

> [Monologue] and dialogue pose different problems, for example, they probably operate with differing hierarchical structures. In dialogue, because the audience tends to be small and constraints managed through interactive coordination, personal intentions manifest themselves more easily. Such interaction requires elaboration of the rule structure at the lower levels of the hierarchy, to guide turn-taking, implicature, and management of multiple intentions. In monologue, personal intentions must be accommodated to public exigencies – because the audience is larger, the opportunity for complex statement is greater, and constraints are less easily managed; *more elaborate rule structures at the upper end of the hierarchy, at the level of whole discourse, are therefore necessary for both formulation and interpretation.* [emphasis added] (Miller, 1984, p. 162)

Thus, the discursive skills and knowledge related to the 'formulation and interpretation' of extended written texts, such as those that occur in academic or professional contexts, must involve something other than a day-to-day transactional competence, such as required in informal conversation. Following Miller's ideas, any analytical framework used to examine this type of language use will need to have the capacity to identify 'more elaborate rule structures at the upper end of the hierarchy, at the level of whole discourse' (Miller, 1984, p. 162). Such structures are necessary in order to mediate the meaning to readers who have no possibility of recourse to the types of clarification seeking and interactional feedback available to interlocutors in a conversation. However, to meet this analytical requirement presupposes principled, systematic approaches to describing the hierarchy of knowledge that relates to the enactment of discourse through written text, and within which such upper-level structures may be located. In a previous work, I have proposed that any representation of knowledge through an extended written text, will involve a range of integrated knowledge systems that are influenced by the following:

- the type of language use, such as spoken or written language;
- the conceptual content of the discourse, both empirical and abstract, including knowledge which is explicitly and implicitly referred to;
- abstract organizational or procedural knowledge; and,
- the systems of the language itself (Adapted and summarized from Bruce, 2008a, p. 77).

First, the types of language use on which each of the following chapters focuses include written academic, professional or journalistic genres – each of which is a category of text that is an extended written monologue. Therefore, in examining written monologues, an analytical framework needs to be employed that can account for the knowledge types involved. Such a framework will, of necessity, differ from one required for the analysis of spoken interactions, such as conversations, and may, as Miller suggests, need to allow for a hierarchy of knowledge systems that are drawn upon to mediate meaning between the writer and the reader. It is important, therefore, to identify what the knowledge systems are, and to understand how they interrelate.

The second element of my proposal is that such a framework must also be able to account for the conceptual content of a text, which I suggest will relate closely to the context within which the text occurs. Widdowson (2004) characterizes the elements of context in terms of schematic knowledge that involves both intralinguistic and extralinguistic factors (p. 54). Schemata are pre-learned units of conceptual knowledge or communicative routines that are employed in a particular situation. I suggest that, in relation to academic or professional texts, the relevant extralinguistic factors of context involve the specialist, technical knowledge of the field to which the text belongs, and intralinguistic factors include the forms of communication used in that field. Extralinguistic knowledge schemata tend to be instantiated (activated in the mind of the language user) through the technical lexis of a discipline. For example, for an inorganic chemist, the term 'NMR' (nuclear magnetic resonance) spectroscopy instantiates a schema for an established molecular analytic process using a particular technology, a process that is familiar to members of that particular discourse community. On the other hand, intralinguistic schemata that relate to context involve conscious, contextually related communicative routines that are employed in the staging and reporting of knowledge within a field. Such routines are required to facilitate readers' processing of extended written texts that encode large amounts of subject content. For example, those reading a research-reporting article in an academic journal may be familiar with the macro-organizational schema, such as the conventionalized sections of Introduction, Method, Findings, Discussion and Conclusion. They may be also familiar with lower-level schemata used for structuring the content of the abstract and introduction sections. Oller (1995) refers to these types of consciously applied routine as 'content schemata'. A reader familiar with these schemata processes the content of each section of the article with expectations of what it will include and how it will relate to the other sections of the article. Understanding and acquisition of these intralinguistic schemata involves prior knowledge of texts in a discipline and familiarity with the organizational rules and conventions required for the reporting of research, such as in academic journals.

The third element relating to the representation of knowledge through texts is that of more abstract procedural knowledge used in the organization of segments of text. While the previously mentioned content schemata, such as the sections of an academic journal article, assist a reader to manage the complexity of the ideational content of an extended text, smaller subsections may employ more abstract organizational patterns, for example, chronology, general particular and problem solution, such as described by Hoey (1983). These smaller sections of text often relate to a single, more general rhetorical purpose to communicate one certain type of knowledge. For example, a recount of a series of events will involve chronological structuring; an explanation may employ problem solution (situation response) patterns; and a discursive argument section may employ a generalization-examples structure. Content schemata and these more abstract text-organizing structures (what Carrell, 1987 terms 'formal schemata') tend to operate at different levels in the text and at different levels of consciousness of both writer and reader; however, both form part of what Miller (1984) refers to as elaborated rule structures at the upper level of the representational hierarchy.

The fourth area of knowledge relates to the use of systemic language knowledge, specifically linguistic systems, such as lexis, grammar and syntax. Within an extended text, the operations of, and relationships among, linguistic features are not the same as, and are more complex than, those that operate at sentential level. The variety of interrelationships that hold among linguistic items across sentences and paragraphs is important in communication, and is often described in terms of 'cohesion' and 'coherence'. In an extended text, cohesion results from a writer's use of grammatical and lexical devices to connect ideas together. Linguistic elements of cohesion have been identified as 'reference, substitution, ellipsis, conjunction and lexical cohesion' (Halliday & Hasan, 1976, p. 303). However, it is important to note that the linguistic choices and patterns that create cohesiveness within a text will often be the consequence of relations between propositions, sometimes termed 'coherence relations' (Knott & Sanders, 1998), or what Crombie (1985) terms 'interpropositional relations', such as 'Condition Consequence, Reason Result'. While such relations may be signalled by cohesive devices (syntactically or lexically), they may also be merely the consequence of the juxtaposition of propositional information within a text. Other salient linguistic aspects of cohesion and coherence include the thematization of elements within a text and the collocational patterns relating to lexical choice. Thus, a range of complex, micro-level choices of elements from all of these systems are involved in the creation of a cohesive and coherent piece of text that communicates a comprehensible message.

This brief review of the groups of knowledge elements that together potentially constitute a text and relate to its discursive interpretations serves to underline the complexity of the phenomena that are the object of investigation here. They also highlight the need to develop frameworks that are adequate for the analysis of such complexity. Expressing critical thinking, of itself, may be one of several communicative purposes that is achieved through the types of knowledge that combine to construct the complex discourse that is communicated through a text. Therefore, to approach an examination of how critical thinking is expressed through a text requires an examination that is systematic and principled, and is able to account for different knowledge elements, such as those that fall within the four broad knowledge areas that reviewed here. This requires, as stated previously, analytical frameworks that are sufficiently powerful to achieve this purpose. In Section 2.2, I review previous studies of expressing critical thinking through texts, including how critical thinking was defined and investigated. Following this review, in Section 2.3, I consider genre analysis as a potential framework for this type of investigation.

2.2 Previous analyses of texts for the expression of critical thinking

This section briefly reviews existing studies that have attempted to define and investigate aspects of the expression of critical thinking in different types of text. Under consideration, here are both the approaches employed in defining the construct (of critical thinking) as well as ways in which its textual expression has been operationalized and the particular research methodologies in a range of studies.

In the extant research literature reporting investigations of what is referred to here as critical thinking, there appears to be considerable diversity in both terminology and approaches to defining and operationalizing the underlying construct. This diversity is evident in several edited collections of studies on the subject (see, for example, Del Lungo Camiciotti & Tognini-Bonelli, 2004; Hunston & Thompson, 2000; Hyland & Diani, 2009; Salager-Meyer & Lewin, 2011). In a broad approach that may include expressions of critical thinking, Biber and Finegan (1989) use the term 'stance' to describe 'lexical and grammatical expressions of attitude towards, feelings, judgement or commitment concerning the propositional content of a message' (p. 93). In another approach, the construct has been referred to as 'evaluation' (Hunston & Thompson, 2000), which they suggest involves four parameters: positive/negative; certainty/uncertainty, expected/unexpected and important/unimportant (pp. 22–4). They suggest that evaluations of good/bad and degree of certainty usually have a more real-world orientation, while those communicating levels of importance and expectedness have a more text-oriented function, such as when constructing an argument or case through the medium of an academic text. However, they suggest that the first parameter (good/bad) encompasses others that they identify: 'Evaluation is essentially one phenomenon rather than several, and the most basic parameter, the one to which the others can be seen to relate is the good/bad parameter' (p. 25). In another approach that draws upon systemic functional grammar, the construct is referred to as 'appraisal' (Martin & White, 2005, pp. 42–4), which may involve 'affect' (reacting to behaviour), 'judgement' (evaluating behaviour) or 'appreciation' (evaluation of phenomena). In appraisal theory, it appears that the 'focus is on classifying different elements of aspects of each of these three 'ways of feeling' (p. 42) as aspects of a 'discourse semantic system', and considering how each is realized through a range of grammatical structures. For example, within this discourse semantic structure, 'affect' is subdivided into the three areas of 'a quality, a process or a comment', and these are related to various grammatical resources for their expression. Similarly 'judgement' is subdivided into 'social esteem' and 'social sanction', and 'appreciation' subsumes into 'reaction, composition and valuation', with each of these subcategories related to elements of the lexico-grammatical system. Yet another approach to framing investigations of what is referred to here as critical thinking is Bakhtinian diologism by Dressen (2003), who claims that 'evaluation in academic discourse is a communicative act, which is facilitated and necessitated by *prior speech*. It is the dialogical exchange between … different instances of interaction' (p. 274).

Just as the approaches to defining critical thinking for research purposes are varied, so too are the methods that have been employed in its investigation. For example, studies that are based broadly on Hunston and Thompson's (2000) construct of 'evaluation' have used a variety of methods to operationalize and investigate evaluation. The most frequently used is corpus methods in studies that focus on a specific type of linguistic element, such as evaluative lexis in the Bank of English Corpus (Channell, 2000), adverbial markers in the Longman Spoken and Written English Corpus (Conrad & Biber, 2000), grammatical patterns, such as adjective noun combinations in Cobuild Dictionary definitions (Hunston & Sinclair, 2000) reporting verbs in a sample of book review articles (Diani, 2009) and metadiscourse devices, also in a sample of book review articles (Tse & Hyland, 2009). Using corpus methods, Charles (2006) examined reporting verbs and 'that' clauses in doctoral theses. Other approaches to evaluation have involved manual analysis of smaller samples of texts, such as clause relations in the writing of Noam Chomsky (Hoey, 2000), and narrative structure (Cortazzi & Jin, 2000) using an illustrative text. In another manual textual analysis, Shaw (2003) used Thompson and Hunston's (2000) category of two areas of evaluation (interactive plane and autonomous plane) to compare Introduction sections in economics articles by Danish and English writers. Using the same approach to evaluation, Kwan, Chan and Lam (2012) manually analysed samples of research article introduction systems in terms of moves and submoves, which they termed 'strategies'. Other manual analyses of the textual expression of critical thinking have employed the approach of appraisal theory proposed by Martin (2000b) and Martin and White (2005). For example, Tucker (2003) examined the expression of evaluation in art history articles using systemic functional grammar, focusing mainly on attitudinal verbs. Similarly, Babaii and Ansary (2005) examined a sample of book reviews from three physics journals in terms of their use of the elements of affect, judgement, appreciation and engagement and the particular linguistic exponents of each. Appraisal theory has also been applied to persuasive student essays (Lee, 2015; Mei, 2006).

What previous studies of critical thinking collectively appear to reveal about its expression is the involvement of different elements (lexical, syntactical and text-structuring), operating at different textual levels. Some elements relate to the content of a text (propositional knowledge), while others are involved in communicating more directly the writer's view to the reader (metadiscourse knowledge). However, despite the diversity of knowledge elements identified as expressing critical thinking, most of the studies reviewed here involved investigating a single, textual element, often by the use of corpus methods.

Going beyond this single element approach, each of the studies reported in the following chapters involves examining texts in terms of multiple textual elements and exploring how different textual elements mutually interrelate when employed in the communication of critical thinking. To achieve this type of analysis (and support this integrative principle), the studies use genre analysis. This approach is justified in terms of Bhatia's (2002, 2004) overlapping model of discourse, aiming to account for the three areas of social practice, genre and text. Also, as Hyland (2005a, p. 190) suggests, a genre-based study may be able to provide fine-grained detail about that different ways of communicating criticality, and also indicate how and where they are likely to cluster within a genre's conventionalized rhetorical framework.

Therefore, because the overall goal of this volume is the investigation of the expression of critical thinking through different genres (categories of academic, professional and journalistic texts), and because the previous body of research collectively appears to indicate that this can be achieved through a multiplicity of knowledge elements operating at different textual levels, each study reported in the subsequent chapters of this volume employs a multiple-layer, genre-based approach to the investigation

2.3 Genre as an approach to analysing texts

The concept of a genre as a category of written texts or of spoken language events is found in scholarship and research in a number of fields, such as literature, rhetoric, communication studies, applied linguistics and education. However, a problem with this concept is a lack of agreement on what it is that actually constitutes a genre. This problem is reflected in the multiplicity of ways in which the concept has been operationalized (see, for example, Hyon, 1996; Johns, 2002). For some, the object of genre classification is largely a discursive, socially driven phenomenon. Theorists following this approach see genre as being reflected in the socially recognized functions and conventionalized structures of language events that occur in specific contexts. These events may be shaped by complex contextual elements, participant relationships and communicative and transactional purposes. For other theorists, genre as a classifier of language entities is a more rhetorically motivated, cognitive phenomenon, often described in terms of general rhetorical categories such as argument, explanation, recount and description. Following this approach, genre knowledge is seen in terms of texts or segments of texts and their internal organizational and linguistic characteristics. While this binary characterization does not adequately represent the diversity found in the field of genre studies, the two approaches are discernible tendencies in the wide range approaches to text classification, such as those presented in Table 2.1.

Genre, in effect, is a theoretical tool used to classify existing written texts or spoken language events. The synthesis of knowledge elements that gives rise to these texts or language events forms the underlying construct. In research, the 'construct validity' of a classificatory tool, such as genre, relates to its effectiveness in being able to identify and mirror (or operationalize) all of the characteristics of the underlying construct that it claims to represent. Cohen, Manion and Morrison (2018) say that 'in this type of validity, agreement is sought on the 'operationalized' forms of a construct … is my understanding similar to that which is generally accepted to be the construct?' (p. 256). Thus, construct validity would appear to require agreement by those working in a particular field on how the construct under scrutiny is operationalized for the purpose of research. However, as Table 2.1 suggests, the field of genre studies is characterized by a multiplicity of approaches and competing terminologies. As yet, there appears to be no general agreement among theorists concerning what it is that constitutes genres and how they may be operationalized.

Table 2.1 Approaches to Text Classification

Theorist	Social Focus	Rhetorical Focus
Hasan (1989)	genre	
Swales (1990, 1998, 2004)	genre	
Bhatia (1993)	genre	
Martin (1994, 1995, 1997)	macro-genres	
Schryer (1993)	genre	
Knapp and Watkins (1994, 2005)	text type	genre
Werlich (1976)	text genres	text types
Biber (1989)	genre	text type
Virtanen (1992)	discourse types	text type
Paltridge (2002)	genres	text types
Van Dijk (1980)		macrostructures
Derewianka (1990)		genres
Lackstrom, Selinker & Trimble (1973)		rhetorical modes
Silva (1990)		rhetorical modes
Jordan (1997)		rhetorical modes
Hoey, (1979, 1983, 1991, 1994, 2001)		discourse patterns
Adam, (1985, 1992)		séquences
Bhatia (2002, 2004)		generic values
Council of Europe (2001)		macro-functions
Grabe (2002)		macro-genres

(Adapted from Bruce 2008a, Table 1.1, p. 7).

Given this current state of genre theory, it is appropriate to revisit the issue of what genres are and how they may be operationalized. In this section, three influential theories of genre are briefly reviewed, with consideration given to the types of knowledge that they propose as genre-defining. In Section 2.4, theories of genre and the construct validity problem are discussed. In Section 2.5, in addressing the issue of construct validity, a dual approach to genre discernible in the views of Biber (1989), who works in the field of corpus linguistics and European text linguists (Pilegaard & Frandsen, 1996), is considered as a way of operationalizing genre knowledge more comprehensively in order to account for all of the types of knowledge elements that together constitute a category of text and its related discursive interpretations. Following this discussion, the dual approach to genre knowledge is then used as a basis for presenting my own 'social genre/cognitive' genre model, which is employed in the studies presented in the following five chapters.

Three approaches to genre as a concept for the classification and analysis of texts are briefly reviewed here. They are

- the approach of linguists influenced by Systemic Functional Linguistics (SFL; the Sydney School), (Eggins, 2004; Hasan, 1989; Hood, 2016; Martin, 1986, 1992; 1997, 2000a; Martin & Rose, 2008);
- the English for Specific Purposes approach (Dudley-Evans, 1986, 1989, 1993, 1994; Swales, 1981, 1988, 1990, 1998, 2004; Bhatia, 1993, 1998, 2004; Johns, 1997, 2001); and,
- the North American approach to genre, variously termed New Rhetoric or Rhetorical Genre Studies (see for example, Artemeva, 2008; Bawarshi & Reiff, 2010; Devitt, 2004; Freedman & Medway, 1994; Miller, 1984).

The reason for selecting these three approaches for review is that they represent comprehensive attempts to theorize the classification and construction of written and spoken texts in terms of genre. In the first two approaches, genres as categories of spoken events or written texts are seen as socially constructed, discursive entities that achieve some kind of conventionalized social purpose (or set of purposes) within a particular cultural context or discourse community. Both approaches tend to identify genres in terms of conventionally recognized organizational patterns for the staging of the content of texts, which is then related to specific linguistic features, although their respective terminologies and means of analysis vary considerably. The third approach describes genres in terms of typified social actions, and places less emphasis on the analysis of text than on ethnographic descriptions of the conventionalized uses of language in specific contexts.

The approach to genre influenced by systemic functional linguistics

In SFL, emphasis is placed on the social use of language in the creation of texts and its interpretation as discourse. Language is seen as a 'social-semiotic' – a meaning-making system capable of realizing and expressing the entire range of potential meaning employed by society. It is seen as operating within a functional/structural system. The functional element involves the types of social use to which the language is put (such as a sales request in a shop or placing a bet). The structural element refers to the choices from the lexico-grammatical systems of the language employed in the social situation.

In relating language to the social uses with which it correlates, systemic functional linguists employ the concept of 'register' as a way of analysing the operation of language within types of social situation (context of situation). Martin (1992) explains that 'the socio-semantic organization of context has to be considered from a number of angles if it is to give a comprehensive account of the ways in which meanings configure texts' (p. 494). In his theory of register, Halliday identifies the different 'angles' from which to analyse a social situation as:

> [t]he Field of Discourse [which] refers to what is happening, the nature of the social action that is taking place ...
>
> [t]he Tenor of Discourse [which] refers to who is taking part, to the nature of the participants, their statuses and roles ...
>
> [t]he Mode of the Discourse [which] refers to what part language is playing ... its function in the context, including the channel (is it spoken or written or some combination of the two?) .(Halliday, 1989, in Halliday and Hasan, 1989, p. 12)

According to Halliday, each semiotic variable of a context (field, tenor and mode or FTM) relates to a specific component of the semantic structure of language, which in turn correlates with particular lexico-grammatical (linguistic) features of a text. A register is 'the semantic variety of which a text may be regarded as an instance ... [and which] can be defined as the configuration of semantic resources that the member of a culture typically associates with a situation type' (1978, pp. 110–11).

For some SFL linguists, 'genre' (as distinct from register) involves examination of the larger cultural context (context of culture) within which a text occurs. For example, Hood (2016) describes genre as 'recurring configurations of field, tenor, mode meanings evolving in a culture' (p. 194). In an earlier definition of the concept of genre within the context of SFL, Martin (1984) describes genre as 'a staged, goal oriented, purposeful activity in which speakers engage as members of our culture' (p. 25). The stages or steps that are conventionally followed in the typical organization of the content of a genre are sometimes called the 'schematic' or 'generic structure'. As an example of a generic structure, Hasan (1989, pp. 64–5) describes the essential functional stages of a sales encounter in a shop. Similarly, reflecting this idea of staging within genres, Martin and Rose (2008) identify the core genres for school science as report, explanation and procedural recount and describe their structuring of content in terms of 'stages and phases' (p. 10). However, in another SFL genre study that placed less emphasis on the staging or organization of text, Humphrey and Hao (2011) examined the reading texts encountered by biology students at a Hong Kong university, describing these genres more in terms of the linguistic elements that related to the register variables. Thus, the classificatory concept of genre proposed by some systemic functional linguists relates to socially recognized constructs according to which texts are classified in terms of conventionalized social purposes that they fulfil within a particular 'context of culture'. In their approach to defining genre, systemic functional linguists claim that genres may be identifiable in terms of their staging or functional steps (e.g. Hasan, 1989) and particular recurring configurations of the register variables of field, tenor mode.

The English for Specific Purposes approach to genre

English for Specific Purposes (ESP) is a branch of English language teaching that aims to prepare students for specific occupational or study roles in English-medium contexts. Such courses are often informed by research of the students' future work or study contexts and the types of language that they require. ESP researchers and writers sometimes use genre as a classification device to identify types of text that have a common purpose or goal within a certain field of academic or professional activity. Examples of such genres that have been analysed for ESP purposes are the following: introductions to research articles (Swales, 1981, 1990, 2004); science dissertations (Dudley-Evans, 1986, 1989; Hopkins & Dudley-Evans, 1988); popularized medical texts (Nwogu, 1991); job applications, sales promotion letters and legal case studies (Bhatia, 1993); and grant proposals for European Union research grants (Connor & Mauranen, 1999).

Among ESP researchers and theorists, Swales (1990) proposes a theory of genre, which he describes as 'a class of communicative events, the members of which share the same communicative or rhetorical purpose' (Swales, 1990, p. 58).

Similarly, Bhatia (1993, p. 43) sees communicative purpose as the main criterion for identifying different types of genre: 'Of all of the contextualised factors associated with a conventionalized speech event, communicative purpose is the most privileged criterion for the identification of genres'. According to Swales (1990, pp. 45–57), a genre will have the following defining features:

1. A genre is a class of communicative events.
2. The principal criterial feature that turns a collection of communicative events into a genre is some shared set of communicative purposes.
3. Exemplars or instances of genres vary in their prototypicality.
4. The rationale behind a genre establishes constraints on allowable contributions in terms of their content, position and form.
5. A discourse community's nomenclature for genre is an important source of insight.

While genres are identified in terms of their overall communicative purposes, their internal organization and use of linguistic resources are analysed in relation to (a) 'rhetorical moves and steps'; and (b) linguistic structures that relate to these moves and steps. Swales' construct of rhetorical moves are used to describe conventionalized patterns for the staging of content. Dudley-Evans (1994) suggests that 'decisions about the classification of the moves are made on the basis of linguistic evidence, comprehension of the text and understanding of the expectations that both the general academic community and the particular discourse community have of the text' (p. 226). For example, Swales (1990, p. 141) proposes a three-move structure for the Introduction section of research articles, consisting of

1. establishing a territory;
2. establishing a niche; and
3. occupying the niche.

This organizational pattern is then related to the linguistic elements that may occur within the move framework.

Swales, (1988, pp. 212–13; 1990, pp. 24–7) proposes that genres exist within 'discourse communities'. A discourse community is a group of people that

- has a broadly agreed set of common public goals;
- has mechanisms for communication among its members;
- uses its participatory mechanisms primarily to provide information and feedback;

- utilizes and hence possesses one or more genres in the communicative furtherance of its aims;
- in addition to owning genres, has acquired some specific lexis; and,
- has a threshold level of members with [the knowledge of] a suitable degree of relevant content and discoursal expertise.

Swales describes a discourse community is a 'socio-rhetorical' network that exists to achieve certain goals, and which has commonly used and understood configurations of language. However, Swales' (1990) concept of discourse community has been challenged in a number of areas (see Borg, 2003). Issues that have been raised include how large a discourse community might be; whether spoken language should also be a necessary defining element; the role of purpose as a defining element; and the degree of stability a discourse community ought to have. In clarifying some of these issues relating to definitions of discourse community, Swales (1998, p. 204) distinguishes between the broader concept of a discourse community that may not be physically connected, and which communicates with itself through written communication and 'place discourse communities', which use both written and spoken communication. In analysing genres in a 'place discourse communities', Swales (1998) combines ethnographic interviews or accounts with textual analysis, an analytical approach that he terms 'textography'. This approach has also been used by other researchers working in the field of ESP, who reflect the belief that genre research may need to include more than textual analysis (e.g. Paltridge, 2004; Paltridge, Starfield, Ravelli & Nicholson, 2012). Similar to Swales textographic approach, Bhatia (2004) proposes that genre knowledge needs to be investigated from two perspectives – an ethnographic perspective and a textual perspective (p. 163).

The New Rhetoric/Rhetorical Genre Studies approach

NR or Rhetorical Genre Studies (RGS) (see Artemeva, 2008) is a largely North American approach to genre. In this approach, genre is not defined in terms of the organizational or linguistic characteristics of categories of text, but rather the in terms of social actions that surround the regular creation of such texts (see for example, Bawarshi & Reiff, 2010; Devitt, 2004; Freedman & Medway, 1994; Miller, 1984). Researchers in this tradition tend to investigate the institutional or other social settings in which genres are created and often use ethnographic methods of enquiry. They tend to see more linguistic analyses of genres as categories of texts as 'prescriptivism and [an] implicit[ly] static vision of genre' (Freedman & Medway, 1994, p. 9). The NR/RGS approach emphasizes the changing nature of genres and eschews any view of genres as fixed templates that are regularly reproduced. A term that is frequently applied to this approach is that genres are 'stabilized-for-now' sites of social and ideological action (Schryer, 1993, p. 200). Therefore, researchers in this tradition tend to focus on how users in a particular context creatively exploit genres, and how genres change and evolve. An example of genre research in this tradition that draws principally on interpretative ethnography is Smart's (1998) insider study of the institutional practices of economists at the Bank of Canada. Specifically, Smart is concerned with characterizing the genre of the QPM (the Bank's 'Quarterly Projection Model') in terms of the beliefs of the people who shaped it and the diverse communicative purposes that it fulfils. This study is an example of detailed research where ethnographic methods are applied to gain an in-depth understanding of the discursive and language practices of a large organization and its professional communities.

> What I've gradually come to see is a world in which the economists employ a distinctive discourse combining language, statistics, and mathematics to create specialized knowledge about the Canadian economy, knowledge used by the Bank's executives to make decisions about monetary policy. (Smart, 1998, p. 117)

2.4 Theories of genre and the construct validity problem

Because genres aim to describe and classify language entities that are *operational wholes* (Widdowson, 1983), it is important to consider the nature of the underlying construct, that is, what is being classified, such as a text, its related discursive meanings and all of the constituent knowledge elements, which may potentially be grouped within the four categories that I discussed at the end of Section 2.1:

- the type of language use, such as spoken or written language;
- the conceptual content both empirical and abstract, including knowledge which is explicitly and implicitly referred to;
- organizational (procedural) knowledge; and
- the systems of the language.

Therefore, any theory of genre that aims to address the issue of construct validity in a way that is robust needs to be sufficiently inclusive to be able to account for a range of knowledge elements (such as those listed here) that, taken together, constitute a genre as a complex language entity, such as a conventionalized category of text and its associated discursive interpretations.

In accounting for the type of language use and contextually related elements of a genre, the NR/RGS approach provides a strong focus, with its concern with ethnographic descriptions of language use and the socially situated nature of genres. However, this type of rich, contextual description was not a feature of early genre analyses following the ESP approach with the exception of Bhatia's (1993) analysis of the legal case genre. Similarly context tends to be limited to the identification of register elements of FTM by genre analysts influenced by SFL. However, as mentioned in the previous section, more recent English for Specific Purposes genre studies have combined textual and ethnographic analysis in the previously mentioned approach termed textography as an attempt to widen the approach to what constitutes genre knowledge (see, for example, Swales, 1998; Paltridge, 2004; Starfield, Paltridge & Ravelli, 2014).

In relation to the second area of the conceptual content of genres – empirical and abstract, including knowledge both explicitly and implicitly referred to, none of the three reviewed approaches to genre comprehensively incorporates the theories and research findings from cognitive science relating to human knowledge categorization. This includes research relating to levels of categorization and the types and roles of schematic knowledge in texts (see, for example, Carrell, 1981, 1987; Johnson, 1987; Lakoff, 1987; Oller, 1995; Sanford & Garrod, 1981). Genre theorists influenced by SFL propose that the lexico-grammatical features of language systematically correlate with the socio-semantic features of language identified in relation to the three dimensions of register. However, SFL theory does not acknowledge that human categorization and the cognitive structuring of different types of knowledge relating to rhetorical purpose may also exert an influence on the representation of such knowledge, such as in a text. Van Dijk (2008) observes that SFL generally involves 'anti-mentalism: a lack of interest in cognition' (p. 29), which he sees as one of its theoretical 'defects'. Although, the NR/RGS approach is concerned mainly with ethnographic enquiry, some of its theorists also acknowledge that genres operate as a type of schema or pattern (e.g. Bazerman, 1997; Grabe & Kaplan, 1996), but are generally resistant to the idea of textual analyses of genres as a basis for pedagogy. In contrast to the other two approaches, the ESP approach to genre acknowledges prototype theory (see Rosch, 1978), that is, the idea that texts within a particular genre category may include features that make them both more and less prototypical examples of the genre (Swales, 1990, pp. 49–52).

In relation to organizational procedural knowledge, the role of schemata in the internal organization of texts belonging to a particular genre category is accepted to some extent by ESP theorists. For example, earlier ESP genre analyses involved examining the organizational structure of content of texts in terms of moves and steps, which Carrell (1987) and Oller (1995) term a 'content schema'. However, a central issue with this approach is the adequacy of such 'move and step' analyses to account for all text-organizing structures. For example, the ESP approach of 'moves and steps' does not attempt to account for more general, rhetorical structures also used in the organization of texts (e.g. general/particular and problem/solution), structures that Carrell (1987) terms 'formal schemata'. While acknowledging the roles of two types of schema, 'content' (move and step structure) and 'formal' (more general rhetorical structures), Swales (1990) suggests that it may be difficult to maintain a distinction between the two when examining a genre in that: 'the nature of genres is that they coalesce *what* is sayable with *when* and *how* it is sayable' (p. 88). Thus, ESP genre analyses have not usually allowed for the potential co-occurrence of contextually influenced organizational structures for the staging of content (such as moves and steps) operating in tandem with more general rhetorical structures (such as formal schemata) within texts that operate as procedural knowledge organizing subsections or stretches of text that realize a single, more general, rhetorical purpose. Some SFL-influenced genre analyses include describing textual organization in terms of more content-related staging, such as 'generic structures' (Hasan, 1989, pp. 63–7) and 'schematic structures' (Eggins, 2004, pp. 58–69.), or in terms of more abstract procedural organization, such as 'stages' (Martin & Rose, 2008, p. 345.). Other SFL genre studies confine their focus to register features. NR/RGS genre studies tend to focus less on the organizational staging of texts and more on the social actions that give rise to the texts, asserting that 'genres cannot be defined or taught only through their formal features' (Bawarshi & Reiff, 2010, p. 103).

Approaches to the fourth area of systemic linguistic knowledge also vary considerably among the three genre theories. At the end of Section 2.1, I proposed that relevant language knowledge may include aspects of cohesion, coherence, thematic development and collocation. To this list may be added 'metadiscourse' features (Hyland, 2005b) – linguistic devices used by writers to connect with the reader. A focus on elements of linguistic knowledge is a feature of the ESP- and SFL-influenced approaches to genre, but it is largely eschewed in NR/RGS genre studies. SFL-influenced genre analyses tend to focus on the linguistic features that realize aspects of FTM. For example, in characterizing genres in terms of their FTM elements, Humphrey and Hao (2011) identified the linguistic elements relating to FTM in biology texts. In an SFL-influenced genre analysis that focused on theme and rheme, North (2005) examined thematic development in essays from a particular university course. In ESP genre analyses, there is sometimes a focus on recurring lexical or grammatical features associated with particular moves or steps, such as adversative sentence connectors, negative quantifiers or lexical negation in Move 2 of research article Introductions (Swales, 1990, pp. 154–5), or the use of complex nominal phrases in academic and professional genres (Bhatia, 1993, pp. 148–57). A small number of ESP genre studies have also involved examination of the use of metadiscourse devices, for example, in the CEO's letter part of annual company reports (Hyland, 1998) and in research article abstracts (Gillaerts & Van de Velde, 2010). However, overall, it is fair to say that, with all three approaches, there is variety and eclecticism in the focus on linguistic devices in genre studies. Although analysts seem to believe that they focus on salient linguistic devices that relate to a particular genre, research in this area tends to be undertaken without reference to any kind of overall language knowledge framework (although this may be disputed by some SFL-influenced genre analysts who would argue that register provides the necessary framework).

Thus, in relation to the issue of genre and construct validity, there persists a lack of agreement among theorists and researchers on the issue of a comprehensive operationalization of genre knowledge in terms of the range of knowledge elements that may be potentially genre-characterizing. Furthermore, since the notion of classification or categorization is intrinsic to the concept of genre, I propose that any workable theory of genre also needs to incorporate the insights and findings from categorization theory and research. As stated earlier in this discussion, the construct validity of any theoretical tool used in research relates to its effectiveness in being able to mirror (or operationalize) all of the characteristics of the underlying construct(s) that it claims to represent. While the three existing approaches to genre reviewed here represent serious attempts to address the complexity of the underlying constructs of genres, which should involve all of the knowledge elements integral to the creation and discursive interpretation of categories of texts, two principal problems remain. The first appears to be a lack of comprehensiveness in their operationalization of genre knowledge. For example, no approach has yet proposed a genre-analytical framework that allows for the potential inclusion of elements relating to each of the four areas of knowledge outlined at the opening of this section. The second problem is a lack of systematicity in the range of types of knowledge that may be potentially seen as genre-defining, a problem compounded by an array of terminologies referring to similar and overlapping constructs (see Table 2.1). Also, despite the fact genre is a theoretical concept employed in the categorization of relatively complex language entities, no existing approach draws comprehensively on categorization theory from cognitive science. Thus, in establishing construct validity in relation to the concept of genre as a tool for classifying and analysing texts, it is clear that the research field of genre studies has some way to go. Therefore, in continuing this search for construct validity, as well as the established theories of genre that have been reviewed here, the following section considers the idea of a dual approach to genre knowledge drawing on the fields of corpus linguistics and European text linguistics. This approach then provides the basis for presenting the social genre/cognitive genre model that I use in the genre analyses reported in the next five chapters.

2.5 A dual approach to genre knowledge and the social genre/cognitive genre model

In relation to the role of linguistic knowledge in classifying genres, it is interesting that a corpus-based study by Biber (1989) does not support this approach to operationalizing genre. On the basis of his study, Biber concludes that:

> genres correspond directly to the text distinctions recognized by mature adult speakers, reflecting differences in external format and situations of use ... [g]enres are defined and distinguished on the basis of systematic non-linguistic criteria, and they are valid in those terms. Text types, on the other hand, are defined on the basis of strictly linguistic criteria (similarities in the use of co-occurring features). (Biber, 1989, p. 39)

In his corpus study, by examining linguistic features in relation to a number of dimensions, Biber found systematic clustering of linguistic patterns that related to more general, non genre-specific text types, four of which he found commonly occurred in academic English prose. In a variation of this approach, text types have also been identified in terms of clusters of 'vocabulary-based discourse units' (VBDUs), referring to 'a block of discourse defined by its reliance on a particular set of words' (Biber, Csomay, Jones & Keck, 2007, p. 156).[2] Therefore, Biber's (1989) study and conclusions appear to prefigure a dual classificatory approach that distinguishes the analysis and classification of text types (in terms of linguistic features) from genres, which I suggest involve the analysis and classification of discursive elements that surround the creation and interpretation of texts.

In an approach similar to that of Biber, a number of European text linguists also draw a distinction between 'text types', which tend to relate to segments of text (Pilegaard & Frandsen, 1996; Virtanen, 1992; Werlich, 1976) and 'text genres', (Pilegaard & Frandsen, 1996; Werlich, 1976) or 'discourse types' (Virtanen, 1992), which relate to socially recognized categories of whole texts, categorized in terms of the regularized communicative purpose or function of the text (e.g. novel and editorial). Also, in relation to the teaching of academic writing, Paltridge (2002) argues that courses need a focus on both genre and text-type knowledge. The advantage of the dual approach to genre knowledge is that it allows a theory of genre, in its operationalization to include a wide range of types of knowledge including the four, previously mentioned elements:

- the type of language use, such as spoken or written language, including context-related elements;
- the conceptual content, both empirical and abstract, including knowledge which is explicitly and implicitly referred to;
- abstract organizational or procedural knowledge: and
- the systems of the language itself.

The social genre/cognitive genre model[3]

In further developing this dual approach to genre knowledge, I have attempted to account for these two areas of knowledge by proposing the social genre/cognitive genre model (Bruce, 2008a). This model is based on two important principles from categorization theory in cognitive psychology. The first principle is that complex categories (in this case, genres as complex textual categories) are formed in response to different types of intention or purpose (Barsalou, 1983; Murphy & Medin, 1985). Here different types of purpose relate to the social genre and cognitive genre elements of the model.

> Social genre – refers to socially recognized constructs according to which whole texts (or conventionally recognized sections of texts, such as Methods sections in research articles) are classified in terms of their *overall social purpose*. ... Purpose here is taken to mean the intention to communicate consciously a body of knowledge related to a certain context to a certain target audience
>
> Cognitive genre – refers to the overall cognitive orientation and internal organization of a segment of writing that realizes a single, *more general rhetorical purpose* [such as] to recount sequenced events, to explain a process, to argue a point of view. (Bruce, 2008b, p. 39)

The second principle from categorization theory is that complex categories (such as genres as categories of extended texts) have a top-down, internal organizational structure (Miller, 1984; Rumelhart & Ortony, 1977). Because of the complexity of discourse creation, the model proposes that writers' choices may involve a range of discursive elements that relate to the achievement of different types of social and general rhetorical purpose. Table 2.2 outlines the different elements of the model that may influence or be reflected in textual choices.

I argue that the social genre knowledge elements listed in the table are called 'social' because they involve more text-external, discursive elements while the cognitive genre elements are 'cognitive' because they involve abstract, procedural knowledge and relate to more general rhetorical purposes. Social genres are conventionally recognized categories of whole texts that occur in particular contexts for certain audiences. Cognitive genres, so-called because they describe the use of more abstract, procedural knowledge, are each instantiated by a particular general rhetorical purpose (e.g. argue and explain) that influences the micro-level organization of the text, relationships between propositions and linguistic choices relating to cohesion and coherence. Although a specific example of a particular social genre may exhibit features of a single cognitive genre (e.g. an instruction manual will use Explanation, probably recursively), it is more common for examples of social genres to exhibit features of more than one cognitive genre. For example, a personal letter (a social genre) may draw upon a range of different cognitive genres in relation to the different communicative purposes that may characterize the sections of the overall message as it unfolds (e.g. recounting a series of events, providing an explanation and presenting an argument).

Social genre knowledge

The first element of social genre knowledge in Table 2.2 is that of context. As stated previously, Widdowson (2004) characterizes context in terms of schematic knowledge that involves both 'intralinguistic and extralinguistic factors' (p. 54). It is suggested that, in relation to academic or professional genres, extralinguistic factors involve the specialist, technical knowledge of the field to which the text belongs; and, intralinguistic factors include the forms of communication and technical vocabulary used in the particular field.

The second element of social genre knowledge is epistemology – how experts working in a particular field perceive, validate (prove) and use knowledge. However, to understand how subject experts view knowledge, a necessary co-condition is to understand how they create knowledge. In any particular discipline, the knowledge-creating paradigms used (such as its research

Table 2.2 Genre Knowledge

Social Genre Knowledge
- context
- epistemology
- writer stance (metadiscourse)
- content schemata

Cognitive Genre Knowledge
- gestalt patterns of ideas
- general textual patterns
- relations between propositions

(Adapted from Bruce 2015b, Table 1, p. 47).

methods) strongly influence its knowledge-communicating forms, such as its written and spoken genres.

The third element of social genre knowledge is that of the stance or standpoint of a writer in relation to his/her audience. The Russian formalist, Bakhtin (1986), proposes that writing, like speaking, is 'dialogic' – a dialogue between the writer and the reader, and, as a consequence, writing is constructed with the expectations and knowledge of the reader in mind. In developing Bakhtin's idea of diologism, Hyland (2005b, p. 39) identifies a set of language devices that are used to connect the writer with the reader, language devices which he groups together under the term of metadiscourse and can be used to undertake dialogism through texts.

The fourth element of social genre knowledge of content schemata relates to regularly occurring patterns used in the organization of content within a genre (Carrell, 1987; Oller, 1995). The approach to genre influenced by SFL describes such patterns as 'schematic structures' (Eggins, 2004) or 'functional stages' (Hasan, 1989), and the ESP approach describes them as 'moves and steps' (Swales, 1990). The rhetorical purpose that gives rise to a particular 'stage' or 'move' may relate quite closely to disciplinary content of the text, such as in Bhatia's (1993) analysis of legal cases (e.g. establishing the facts of the case and arguing the case) or may be described in less content-specific terms, such as in Connor and Maurenan's (1999) analysis of grant proposals (e.g. territory, gap, goal and means). However, it is crucial to emphasize that the types of context- and content-related purpose that motivate these 'stages' (or 'moves') differ from the more general types of rhetorical purpose (e.g. argue and explain) that instantiate the cognitive genre elements of the model.

Cognitive genre knowledge

A cognitive genre is a segment of writing that aims to achieve one particular, general rhetorical purpose, such as argue, explain or recount. Cognitive genres are variously described by theorists as text types, rhetorical functions or discourse modes. In relation to academic writing, I have proposed four cognitive genres that occur most frequently in academic texts (see Table 2.3). These are loosely based on the four text types that Biber (1989) found to occur commonly in academic prose and also on a needs-based typology proposed by Quinn (1993). However, in terms of their structure and internal organization, they are conceptualized in terms of cognitive structures rather than linguistic and stylistic features. As I stated previously, the term 'cognitive' is used here because they are textual entities that draw upon aspects of a writer's less consciously applied, procedural knowledge.

The cognitive genre part of the model also reflects the two previously mentioned principles from cognitive science: the role of intentionality in category formation and hierarchy in the organization of complex knowledge. In relation to the first, each category relates to a purpose to communicate a certain type of knowledge – this is the rhetorical purpose in the second column of Table 2.3. The second principle from categorization theory is that complex categories have a top-down, internal organizational structure that relates to the three organizational elements: gestalts (image schemata), discourse patterns and interpropositional relations.

The first element of this structure is gestalt patterns called 'image schemata' by Johnson (1987); these reflect the higher-level organization of ideas. As an example, in a previous study (Bruce, 2003, 2008a), I found that segments of text concerned with the presentation of quantitative data that was non-chronological (termed here Report cognitive genre) typically employed the gestalt pattern termed WHOLE PART for the overall organization of content ideas; the WHOLE was an overview of the data, and the PART was a more detailed presentation of the component elements (of the WHOLE). Furthermore, in the PART section, the component elements were typically organized according to an UP DOWN schema, meaning the presentation of data from larger (or more important) to smaller (less important) components – in descending order of size or importance. The second organizational element of the model is discourse patterns (Hoey, 1979, 1983, 1991, 1994, 2001), which organize the actual written text, for example, patterns such as 'problem solution, general particular'. The third element is 'interpropositional relations' proposed by Crombie (1985), which are

Table 2.3 A Model for Cognitive Genres in Academic Prose

Cognitive Genre	Rhetorical Purpose	Image Schemata (Johnson, 1987)	Discourse Patterns (Hoey, 1983)	Key Interpropositional (Coherence) Relations (Crombie, 1985)
Report	Presentation of information that is essentially non-sequential	WHOLE PART; UP DOWN	General-Particular (Preview-Details)	Amplification Bonding
Explanation	Presentation of information with a focus on the means by which something is achieved	SOURCE-PATH-GOAL; LINK	General-Particular (Preview-Details)	Means Purpose Means Result Reason Result Amplification
Discussion	Focus on the organization of data in relation to possible outcomes, conclusions or choices	CONTAINER; LINK	General-Particular (Generalization-Examples); Problem-Solution Matching Relations	Simple Contrast Contrastive Alternation Bonding Reason Result Grounds Conclusion Concession Contraexpectation
Recount	Presentation of data that is essentially chronological	SOURCE-PATH-GOAL	Problem-Solution	Chronological Sequence

(Adapted from Bruce, 2008a, p. 97).

lower-level, two-part structures that are binary coherence relations between propositions, relations such as Reason Result and Condition Consequence.

It is proposed that cognitive genres as textual patterns are 'prototypes' (Rosch, 1978), which may be realized by writers in ways that conform closely to the characteristics of the model (prototypical instantiations) or in ways that use fewer elements of the model to achieve the same general rhetorical purpose (peripheral instantiations). In relation to the overall social/cognitive genre model, cognitive genres are abstract organizational building blocks that are used in socially driven ways to create texts from which discourses are derived. Evidence for the four cognitive genres of the model as prototypical text-organizing patterns in academic writing was provided by the examination of an interdisciplinary sample of extended academic texts including book chapters and journal articles (Bruce, 2003, 2008a, pp. 99–100). All of the samples contained instances of at least three cognitive genres and 80% of the texts contained all four.

In characterizing a conventionalized category of written texts or spoken language events by the use of any theory of genre, it is acknowledged that the underlying construct is highly complex and multifaceted, and although this model is an attempt at a somewhat more comprehensive operationalization of genre knowledge than has been the case with existing theories of genre, it still cannot claim to be fully comprehensive in relation to all of the elements of the underlying construct. Nevertheless, the model aims to achieve what the Dutch psycholinguists Verhoeven and De Jong (1992) say that 'a model is for, i.e., to explain reality by a simplification' (p. 5).

The overall framework of the social genre/cognitive genre model is employed in the studies of the genres in the following chapters as a basis for identifying those generic elements used to express critical thinking. At this stage, it should be emphasized that the model is a broad, background framework for examining and identifying genre-defining knowledge elements. It is not expected, nor has it been found, that any genre will employ and exhibit all of the features of the model, but rather genres tend to be identifiable in terms of a cluster or subset of its features.

Researching genres using the social genre/cognitive genre model

I have used the social genre/cognitive genre model as the broad background framework for researching a range of genres, including research article methods sections (Bruce, 2008b), research article results sections (Bruce, 2009), undergraduate essays (Bruce, 2010a, 2015a, 2016), online news articles and their related comment threads (Bruce, 2010b), research article literature reviews (Bruce, 2014a), online corporate disclosure documents (Bruce, 2014b), a journalist's commentary writing (Bruce, 2015b) and PhD discussion chapters (Bruce, 2018). In the majority of the studies, I have been aiming at developing an overall description of those particular features of the model that characterize a particular genre. However, in five of these studies (those discussed in detail in the following chapters of this volume), I have also focused on those generic elements used to express critical thinking.

In using the social genre/cognitive genre model as a background framework for investigating genres, the analytical method that I primarily use is manual textual analysis. Doing this type of analysis involves close recursive examination of a sample of texts belonging to a particular genre category, and identifying and marking up its genre-characterizing features in terms of salient elements of genre model summarized in Table 2.2. In relation to the higher-level element of the model of attempting to identify a content schema (move structure) to account for larger organizational structures of the texts (if this element emerges as a salient feature of particular genre), the analysis is inductive. It involves constant comparison and reanalysis of each text in order to settle on the most appropriate descriptive categories for the rhetorically motivated stages (moves) that characterize its organization. However, the analysis of lower-level elements is more deductive. For example, in relation to stance and engagement, this involves the use of Hyland's (2005b, p. 49) metadiscourse model, and in accounting for coherence relations, Crombie's (1985) taxonomy of interpropositional relations is employed.

In a few studies, I have combined manual textual analysis (using the model) with other methods. For example, in one study, I combined the textual analysis of samples of texts with ethnographic interviews (Bruce, 2009). The interviews included open questions that focused on the three areas of social genre knowledge of context, epistemology and writer stance. In addition to the manual textual analysis, in two studies (Bruce, 2009, 2015b), I have also used corpus analysis of the samples of texts to investigate the frequency of use of particular linguistic devices as signallers of key coherence (interpropositional) relations. The purpose of the corpus analysis has been to provide objective linguistic data to support the rater analysis and validate the occurrence of any textual characteristic that I claimed to be genre-defining. However, corpus analysis as part of an overall genre study is only possible in the case of a sufficiently large sample of texts that could arguably constitute a micro-corpus. Most of the genre studies that I have carried out (including the five that I focus on in this volume) use relatively small samples of texts, which, although constituting relatively large data sets for manual analysis, are not sufficiently large for corpus analyses.

2.6 Conclusion

As I established in Chapter 1, the goal of this book is to examine the expression of critical thinking in disciplinary texts by using a genre-based approach. To provide a basis for this research, the key concepts of critical thinking, enacting criticality, text, discourse and genre are further discussed and defined in this chapter for the purposes of this research. Each of the studies that follows is relatively specific in that it examines the expression of critical thinking in one genre from an academic or a professional field. Therefore, to achieve this goal, it is important to establish from the outset the approach taken in these five studies to the rather contested concept of genre. To this end, this chapter provided a brief overview and discussion of three important theories of genre including their key elements, their commonalities, differences and issues that relate to how each approach operationalizes a genre as a category of written and spoken texts. Following this review, the social genre/cognitive genre approach was presented as an attempt to address these issues and to propose a more comprehensive operationalization of the underlying textual and discursive constructs that, taken together, constitute a genre as a conventionalized category of disciplinary texts.

As I suggested earlier in the chapter, construct validity involves a consensus of agreed understandings within a particular research community on the operationalization of the underlying constructs of a concept that is used in research, such as the concept of genre as a classifier of written texts. It is fair to say that, within the field of genre studies, no such consensus currently exists. Therefore, to address this issue of the need for construct validity in genre research, I suggest that in any genre study the rationale for identifying certain types of knowledge deemed to be genre-defining needs to presented, and such explanations should be developed against the background of a comprehensive knowledge framework used in the wider description of different genres. I suggest that such an approach lends robustness to the field and helps to avoid criticisms of eclecticism and a lack of systematicity in genre research. The social genre/cognitive genre model is a step in the direction of providing this type of larger background framework for genre-based research. The model provides an analytical basis for the following chapters, which examine five genres drawn from academic, professional and journalistic writing. The central focus of each of these studies is on those elements used to express critical thinking in a particular genre. Chapter 3 presents the first of these studies, which focuses on the expression of critical thinking in the genre of the university essay.

3

Expressing critical thinking in the university essay

3.0 Introduction

As I stated in Chapter 1, my purpose in this book is to examine how critical thinking is expressed through writing by closely examining five different genres. In this chapter, I consider the first of these, the student assignment genre of the university essay. In Section 3.1, I provide some background information about university essays including how the 'essay' genre has been defined, and then review pedagogic advice about essay writing from textbooks and previous research of the genre, including two descriptive studies that I have undertaken (Bruce, 2010a, 2015a). In Section 3.2, I consider how critical thinking is actually expressed in this genre by presenting the findings of a further study that I undertook. This study was first reported in the journal *English for Specific Purposes, 2016, Vol. 42, (2016, pp. 13–25)* under the title 'Constructing Critical Stance in University Essays in English Literature and Sociology'[1]. In Section 3.3, I suggest how this type of knowledge could be used to inform the teaching of essay writing, and in Section 3.4, I consider the broader implications of this research for understanding how critical thinking is expressed through written text.

3.1 The university essay genre

To provide a basis for considering how critical thinking is expressed through the writing of essays, I first review existing definitions, theory and research that relate to the essay as a university assignment genre. In this review, I begin by outlining the nature and scope of the essay genre and, in particular, consider the commonly expressed requirement that an essay writer should demonstrate critical thinking. Then, in the second part of this section, I consider the types of advice given about essay writing in commonly used writing textbooks and also advice from some landmark research studies. In the third part, I briefly revisit the findings of two previous genre analyses of the same samples of essays employed in the study reported in this chapter (Bruce, 2010a, 2015a). In these earlier, descriptive studies, I examined the organizational and other elements that characterized the essay genre, but not specifically the means used by their writers to express critical thinking. Finally, I outline the purpose and scope of my third study of the same samples, which focused specifically on how critical thinking was expressed through university student essays.

The university essay as an assignment task

University assignment tasks called 'essays' occur across a wide range of subject disciplines. Two large-scale surveys of university assignments, one American and one Australian, found that assignment tasks called essays were most commonly found in the humanities and social sciences (Hale et al., 1995; Moore & Morton, 1999, 2005). Similarly, in the collections of university student texts that constitute the BAWE Corpus, which aims to be representative of university assignment writing in undergraduate (Years 1–3) and postgraduate (Year 4) courses, essays constitute 86% of arts and humanities assignments (602 out of 724) and 56% of social sciences assignments (444 out of 791).

Writers who have attempted to define the essay genre all seem to suggest that a central requirement is to express a critical stance or critical viewpoint through the text. For example, based on research of university essay assignment tasks in two Australian universities, Moore and Morton (2005) suggest that most involve a 'requirement that students argue for a particular position in relation to a given question or proposition' (p. 74). Similarly, Hewings (2010) defines essays as 'relatively short pieces of writing on a single subject, which offer an evaluation of ideas or opinions presented as "claims" or "generalizations"' (p. 253). In the United States, the guidelines for first-year, university composition programmes (WPA Outcomes Statement for First-Year Composition) specify that through their writing (which will include essays), students will display six types of knowledge, the second of which is critical thinking, which the 'Statement' defines as 'the ability to analyze, synthesize, interpret and evaluate ideas, information, situations, and text' (Council of Writing Program Administrators, 2014). Also, in other research of university assignment tasks, Nesi and Gardner (2006) interviewed British university staff from different disciplines, and found that the essay is often employed as an assignment task because of its 'loosely structured ability to display critical thinking and the development of an argument within the context of the curriculum' (p. 108). However, in terms of the length and frequency of essays, they found some variation: 'Some tutors expect short essays every two weeks, others require a 3000-word essay per module per term, and possibly one larger essay of 8,000 to 10,000 words in the final year' (p. 106).

As well as differences in length and frequency, there are also disciplinary differences in the requirements and expectations of essays. For example, Johns (2008, p. 240) suggests that it is difficult to define the essay as a genre as it is a term attached to various types of discipline-specific writing, and its characteristics may vary considerably in terms of structure, register and argumentation across disciplines. Similarly, Paltridge (2002, p. 89) advises students that 'the kind of essay that they write for a particular course is not necessarily ... universal across different disciplines', and that different types of response will be required for essay tasks in different disciplines. Therefore, although there appears to be general agreement that essays are required to develop an overall argument or case in relation to a particular topic, proposition or assignment prompt, it seems that the actual realization of the assignment genre of the essay may vary considerably across subject disciplines in relation to differences in faculty expectations, the nature of the subject content and the types of writing required. Thus, in developing competence in realizing this genre, it is important that student writers understand and distinguish between the different disciplinary requirements and expectations of the genre, and also that they understand how a critical standpoint is expressed through essays. In two previous genre studies of the university essay samples (English literature and sociology), I focused on the disciplinary similarities and differences evident in writing of the genre (Bruce, 2010a, 2015a). In a third study (which is revisited in detail in Section 3.2), the focus is on those elements of the essays that were used to express critical thinking (Bruce, 2016).

Pedagogic advice about essays from textbooks and research

In terms of the pedagogic advice given in relation to essay writing, such as in writing textbooks, it is commonly suggested that essays need an introduction that states the overall argument or thesis, a body section that presents and develops key thesis-supporting points, and an appropriate conclusion that consolidates and restates the writer's position (see, for example, Bailey, 2018; Craswell & Poore, 2011; Creme & Lea, 2008; Murray, 2012; Oshima & Hogue, 2006). In addition to this common textbook advice about essay writing, two streams of theory and research have offered more nuanced guidance concerning the organization of content and structuring of argumentation in essays. In one approach, theorists and researchers, drawing upon SFL, propose different types of internal content structures for essays with different overall communicative purposes (e.g. Coffin et al., 2003; Nesi & Gardner, 2012). In another approach that focuses on argumentation within essays, a number of studies have drawn upon the argument structure proposed by Toulmin (2003). These two approaches will be reviewed briefly here.

In identifying an organizational structure for academic essays as a genre designed to express an extended argument or case, Coffin et al. (2003) propose three ways of structuring essays relating to three types of overall rhetorical purpose: 'exposition, discussion and challenge'. For each type of essay, they propose an internal structure called 'functional stages' (p. 60) involving background information, stance taking (which differs for each type), detailed sub-arguments and some kind of a restatement of the overall position. In extending this approach, Nesi and Gardner (2012), on the basis of extensive corpus research, identify six essay genres, again in terms of the type of overall communicative or rhetorical purpose required; these were: 'exposition, discussion, challenge, factorial, consequential and commentary'. For each essay genre, they propose 'genre stages' for its internal organization, organization in terms of the types of content information that each stage conveys. For example, the essay genre that they term 'exposition' has the proposed genre structure of: 'thesis, evidence, restate thesis'. The essay genre of 'discussion' is proposed to have the structure of 'issue, alternative arguments, final position'. Each proposed set of genre stages is a pattern accounting for the organization of the content of an essay employed to construct an extended argument or case. However, this approach appears to assume one type of rhetorical purpose for a whole essay, such as exposition, but it does not allow for changes of general rhetorical purpose, such as may occur in longer, more extended essays. Evidence for such 'rhetorical shifts' (Selinker, Todd-Trimble & Trimble, 1978), the act of moving from a segment of text that communicates one type of general rhetorical purpose to another (e.g. explain and argue) within an essay, was a key finding of previous studies of the present samples (Bruce, 2010a, 2015a). This issue will be discussed further in the following subsection.

In relation to the investigation of critical thinking through university essays, a number of studies have focused on approaches to the structuring of argumentation using Toulmin's (2003) model for argumentation (involving three fundamental parts – 'grounds, claims, warrants'[2]), such as the studies by

Bacha (2010) and Stapleton and Wu (2015). However, some researchers have questioned the applicability of the Toulmin approach to argumentation in student writing. For example, although students may correctly employ this argument pattern in their writing at a superficial level, they still may not adhere to the communicative requirements of a particular academic community (Sampson & Clark, 2008; Simon, 2008) and the substance of their actual reasoning may still be poor (Stapleton & Wu, 2015, p. 20). In addition, Riddle (2000) found the three fundamental parts of the Toulmin argument pattern (grounds, claim and warrant) are not necessarily fully realized in student writing, as the underlying warrants for reasoning (and even the grounds element itself) may be omitted for the reason that, in many contexts, they are assumed background knowledge. Although some advocates of the Toulmin approach to argumentation, such as Mitchell (2000), suggest that it can provide the basis for constructing extended whole texts, Wingate (2012) points to a lack of evidence to support this claim, and suggest that the pattern relates more easily 'to the analysis and construction of single claims and is less helpful at the macro-level' (p. 147). A further concern about the Toulmin approach is its applicability to different disciplines with differing ontologies and epistemologies. This concern is illustrated by Nesi and Gardner's (2012) corpus examination of 'if ... then ...' claims across disciplines which suggests that 'the nature of the argument from evidence to claim is ... different in each case' (p. 119). In another critique, Andrews (2000) suggests that a misunderstanding and a misapplication of Toulmin's model of argumentation 'has bedevilled composition practice and theory' for the reason that the pattern 'describes a *process*, whereas compositionists have been involved in the reification of [that] process as a product' (p. 8). In relation to writing and the construction of argumentation, Andrews suggests that the key focus should be on the linking of the key propositions (grounds, claim and warrant) and how this is achieved. In addressing these concerns, the types of relation that actually occur between the propositions of critical statements in essays along with how they are signalled is a central focus of the study reported here.

The author's own studies of the university essay genre

In investigating the essay genre, I have carried out a series of three studies (Bruce, 2010a, 2015a, 2016). Each study used two samples of extended essays (of over 2,000 words) from the BAWE Corpus: one sample consisted of English literature essays (as an example of writing in the humanities) and the other sample comprised of sociology essays (as an example of social science writing). The first and the second studies of this series aimed at more holistic analyses of the essays of the two samples to uncover similarities and differences in the disciplinary realizations of the genre. The third (Bruce, 2016), which is presented in detail in Section 3.2, focused on how the essay writers expressed critical thinking – that study is examined closely in the following sections of this chapter.

In the first study (Bruce, 2010a), I analysed two samples of ten essays using the social genre/cognitive genre model in order to gain an overall understanding of the textual resources that they employed. The findings showed that certain elements of the model were salient to characterizing the essay genre as it was realized by the writers of these two samples. In relation to their organization, I found the use of a relatively formulaic two-move structure in introduction sections – 'context' and 'outline'. The context move establishes the topic, such as by describing the historical background of the issue or problem on which the essay focuses. The outline move then provides the reader with a map or guide to the rest of the essay. In the body sections of the essays, I found the use of different 'cognitive genres' (sometimes called 'text types' or 'rhetorical functions') – stretches of text relating to a single general rhetorical purpose, such as explain, recount and argue. As mentioned previously, an important characteristic of the body sections of the essays was that of 'rhetorical shifts' (Selinker, Todd-Trimble & Trimble, 1978) – moving between different cognitive genres. At a lower level, I found differences between the two samples in their use of metadiscourse devices (Hyland, 2005b). Specifically, the English essays made greater use of 'evidentials' (citation and quotation), and the sociology essays used more devices that mapped the arguments and structure of the essay that spoke directly to the reader, such as endophoric markers and frame markers[3].

Disciplinary differences emerged between the two samples of essays in terms of their use of these textual resources. The sociology essays had a more developed move structure in their introductions, and they generally contained more metadiscoursal mapping of the essay at the outset and through the essay. In the body section, the sociology essays used a greater variety of cognitive genres. On the other hand, the English essays appeared to assume greater reader responsibility and used less metadiscourse to explain the shape of the essay; that is, they provided less overt direction of the reader towards the arguments or points being made by the writer. The goal of the writers of the English essays appeared to be development of a shared, received interpretation that relied heavily on direct quotation from the reviewed literary texts as well as from critics and literary theorists, with little or no overt author presence.

In a further investigation (Bruce, 2015a), I extended each sample to fifteen essays, adding an additional five essays to each, the additional essays again being taken from the BAWE Corpus. In this study, I focused particularly on the use of cognitive genres (text types) in the body section of the essay. I again performed a manual analysis of each extended sample, but also created micro-corpora of each. I used these to create a word list and did concordance searching of key linguistic features in order to validate the manual analysis. The findings revealed that, in the sociology essays, the cognitive genre termed 'Explanation' was the predominant textual resource, often employed recursively and in combination with three other cognitive genres (see Chapter 2, Table 2.2). 'Explanation' refers to a segment of text that involves 'the presentation of information with the focus on means' (Bruce, 2008b, p. 43). Compared with the sociology essays, the range of textual resources used in the English essays was smaller. Explanation was still predominant, but the cognitive genre termed 'Recount' is commonly used, which involves organizing text in relation to a chronologically staged mention of salient events or episodes from the literary work under review.

While these two previous studies of the samples uncovered the disciplinary differences in the characteristics of the genre in terms of the organizational and textual features that writers employed to develop an overall case through each essay, they did not focus directly on how the authors expressed critical thinking. For example, they did not examine specific writer statements or textual elements within the essays that expressed a critical/evaluative viewpoint or judgements. Therefore, in the third study (Bruce, 2016), I asked the two following research questions:

- What are the specific statements in each essay that express a critical evaluation?
- What textual resources do these statements employ in order to express a critical evaluation?

3.2 The third essay genre study: Findings (Bruce, 2016)

In this study, the focus of the analysis was on the specific textual resources employed in overt statements expressing critical thinking in the two samples of fifteen essay texts each selected non-purposively from the BAWE Corpus[4]: fifteen essays from sociology with an average length of 2,328 words, and fifteen essays from English literature with an average length of 3,238 words (see Appendices A & B). As stated previously, the samples were enlarged versions of two used in an earlier study (Bruce, 2010a), and each essay of the enlarged samples was previously analysed for its use of cognitive genres as textual norms or prototypes (Bruce, 2015a). The rationale for the choice of the two disciplines was based on two important surveys of undergraduate assignment tasks where essays were found to be the most commonly occurring genre in the humanities and social sciences (Hale et al., 1995; Moore & Morton, 2005). Therefore, at the beginning of this series of three studies, I decided to include one sample of humanities essays (English literature) and one sample from the social sciences (sociology). All of the essays had been assigned the grades of credit or distinction and, therefore, were considered to be examples of competent student writing.

While the previous two studies of part or all of the sample had the purpose of identifying the characteristic features of the university essay genre, this third study aimed to identify those statements within each essay that were an expression of the writer's own critical evaluation in relation to the proposition or issue that constituted the topic of the essay.

The analytical approach

The analysis was carried out manually by the author as the sole researcher. The first step of the analysis was to read each essay repeatedly to get a clear sense of the overall case that the writer was presenting, and to identify those statements that particularly expressed the writer's own critical evaluation in relation to the topic. The sociology and English samples of essays consisted of eighty and eighty-six pages of single-spaced text respectively. Once identified, these statements were extracted from the essays and pasted into a two-column table, which located each statement within the section of the essay (introduction, body and conclusion) and subtopic within which it occurred. These analytical tables for each essay consisted of twenty-five pages of text for the sociology sample and thirty-one pages for the English sample (see Appendix C for an example part of an essay summary). Each critical statement was then scrutinized for the elements of the social genre/cognitive genre model (see Section 2.2) that it employed to construct its evaluation. Summaries of the key elements characteristic of each essay's critical statements are presented and explained in the following Results section.

Results

The overall findings from the analysis of each sample showed that, across the fifteen essays of the English sample, 210 critical statements were made by the essay writers, with an average of fourteen such statements per essay. The smallest number of critical statements in a single English essay was five and the largest number was twenty-five. Across the sample of fifteen sociology essays, there were 121 such statements, with an average of eight such statements per essay. The smallest number of statements in a single sociology essay was three and the largest number was fifteen. In neither sample was there a discernible pattern for the distribution or particular clustering of such statements in certain parts of the essay, such as at the end of subtopics or overall essay conclusions. The only observation that can be made is that the critical statements were distributed throughout each essay.

These statements, once identified, were each analysed for their use of the resources of the social genre/cognitive genre model to communicate a critical stance or viewpoint. Overall, the findings showed that the critical statements employed two elements from the genre model that were integrated. The first is that each statement was framed by a range of coherence relations (operationalized here in terms of Crombie's [1985] 'interpropositional relations'). In particular, the relations that she terms 'Grounds Conclusion', 'Concession Contraexpectation' and 'Reason Result' were most frequently used in both samples. (Together, this group of three relations accounted for 50.5 per cent of the critical statements in the English literature essays and 64.5 per cent of the critical statements in the sociology essays.) Often a critical statement was framed by one, single interpropositional relation; however, in quite a few cases, two or more relations were involved. Also, within these relations, one or more of the devices from Hyland's (2005b) metadiscourse model were often used to help express critical thinking, most commonly hedging and attitude markers. Typically, a critical statement would contain one instance of hedging or one attitude marker; however, a number of statements contained two or more of these metadiscourse devices. The following subsection will define and discuss the use of interpropositional relations and the different ways in which they were encoded. Following this, the next subsection focuses on the use of metadiscourse devices, and specifically the distribution and roles of the particular metadiscourse devices of hedging and attitude markers in the essay samples.

Interpropositional relations

In introducing the social genre/cognitive genre model in Section 2.2, interpropositional relations are proposed as a lower-level element under the cognitive genre part of the model. They are binary relations between two propositions, such as Reason Result and Condition Consequence. These may be signalled grammatically, such as by the use of conjunctions (e.g. 'because' in a Reason Result relation); lexically, such as by the use of nouns or verbs; or merely by the juxtaposition of two propositions without any overt linguistic signalling. This type of structure is sometimes referred to as a 'coherence relation' (Knott & Sanders, 1998). Tables 3.1 and 3.2 are summaries of the occurrences

Table 3.1 Relations Framing Critical Statements: English Literature Essays

Interpropositional Relation	Number of Statements Using the Relation	Percentage Occurrence in the English Sample Statements
Grounds Conclusion	45	20.5
Concession Contraexpectation	39	17.5
Reason Result	28	12.5
Amplification	26	12.0
Means Result	19	8.5
Bonding	17	7.5
Means Purpose	13	6.0
Statement Exemplification	10	4.5
Condition Consequence	7	3.0
Denial Correction	6	3.0
Simple Comparison	6	3.0
Simple Contrast	3	1.0
Supplementary Alternation	1	0.5
Statement Denial	1	0.5

Bruce (2016, Table 2, p. 18).

Table 3.2 Relations Framing Critical Statements: Sociology Essays

Interpropositional Relation	Numbers of Statements Using the Relation	Percentage Occurrence in the Sociology Sample Statements
Reason Result	32	25.4
Concession Contraexpectation	28	22.2
Grounds Conclusion	21	16.9
Amplification	12	9.5
Bonding	8	6.3
Means Result	7	5.5
Condition Consequence	5	4.0
Denial Correction	4	3.0
Statement Exemplification	3	2.3
Means Purpose	2	1.6
Statement Denial	2	1.6
Simple Comparison	1	0.8
Simple Contrast	1	0.8

Bruce (2016, Table 3, p. 18).

of the interpropositional relations employed in each of the critical statements identified in each sample.

What is most noticeable across the two samples is the overall similarity in the types of relation employed, and their frequencies of use when expressing critical statements. The rest of this section focuses on the three most commonly used relations of both of the samples: Grounds Conclusion, Reason Result and Concession Contraexpectation. Each of these relations is defined and then exemplified from the essay samples.

The Grounds Conclusion relation

The Grounds Conclusion relation is the most frequently occurring relation framing critical statements in the English sample and is the third most frequent in the sociology sample. In defining this binary relation between two propositions, Crombie (1985) states that this relation involves 'a deduction is drawn on the basis of some observation' (p. 20). She suggests (1985, p. 81) that some common signallers of this relation are

- given (that), on the basis of, on the grounds that
- basis, conclusion, grounds, deduction, inference,
- deduce, conclude, infer,
- can't/could, might/must, mustn't be + adjective/noun// present participle// have been + present participle.

The following are examples of the Grounds Conclusion relation from the English and sociology samples. The marked analysis shows how other relations may also be embedded within this type of critical statement:

Woolf regarded narrative structures, particularly the meta-narrative of history to be gendered ... *Hence*, it is possible to argue that Mrs Dalloway is in fact an 'anti-narrative ...' (English Text 6)

'Modernist writers continually infer that a unified sense of self is "unnatural" in a civilised person ... *Therefore*, Orwell's vision seems to indicate that, *because of* society's processes reflecting that of the human mind, there must be a conscious and dominating force in society *that* controls the majority of unconscious processes ...' (English Text 7)

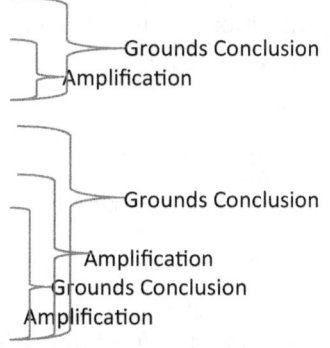

Grounds Conclusion
Amplification

Grounds Conclusion
Amplification
Grounds Conclusion
Amplification

'Ligeia's central thematic preoccupation with interchangeable personalities *could be read as* representation of Poe's possible belief in a fractured and confused American identity.' (English Text 9)

'It could be argued *that* the collapse of the narration is inevitable *as* masculine language is an ineffective medium for the female to use. The text may, *therefore*, be an attempt to demonstrate the difficulty faced by women in trying to articulate their voices within the constraints of masculine language.' (English Text 10)

'The most important *conclusion* that can be drawn from an analysis of sporting practices and masculinity *is* that sporting heroes offer an insight into the way hegemonic masculinity structures the gender order of society ...' (Sociology Text 6)

'That such grotesque experiments could be justified by science and by scientists *seems to justify* Nietzsche's diagnosis of the pathology of modernity ...' (Sociology Text 9)

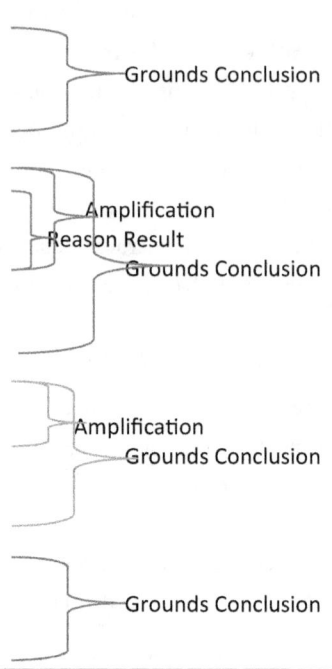

The Reason Result relation

The Reason Result relation is the most frequently used relation to frame critical statements in the sociology sample and the third most frequently used in the English sample. In defining this binary relation between two propositions, Crombie (1985) states: 'The reason member (which very often follows the result member in English) gives a reason *why* a particular effect came or will come about' (p. 20). Signalling of this relation may employ subordinators, prepositions, conjuncts, causative verbs and nouns. The following are examples of Reason Result from both the sociology and English literature samples of texts.

'This implication was significant *as* it was so personal, *and* did not just affect women who wished to enter the medical profession but all female patients.' (Sociology Text 1)

'Overall ... global changes, technological advances and government policies in the 1970s put certain groups of people at risk *and* they were specially vulnerable to unemployment.' (Sociology Text 3)

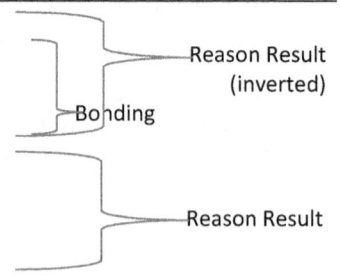

'This group demonstrably made the personal political and engaged many middle class Japanese women with the issue of their subordination, *causing* the government to enforce its termination in 1916.' (Sociology Text 4) — Reason Result (inverted)

'But these are essentially false choices, *as* the goods are only pseudo-individualistic ...' (Sociology Text 8) — Reason Result (inverted)

'*As a result of* this financially selective gateway, independent institutions tend to show a 'remarkable social homogeneity"' (Sociology Text 14) — Reason Result

'Eliot fundamentally misunderstood this, and *as a result*, fundamentally misunderstood God's character.' (English Text 2) — Reason Result (inverted)

'Conrad's narrative is problematic partly *due to* the ambiguity of the story being told.' (English Text 6) — Reason Result (inverted)

'This scene in Emma is deeply significant to the narrative of the novel *as* many truths are revealed in it ...' (English Text 11) — Reason Result (inverted)

The Concession Contraexpectation relation

The Concession Contraexpectation relation is the second most frequently occurring relation framing the critical statements of both samples. Crombie's (1985) definition of this relation states: 'In this relation, the truth of an inference is directly or indirectly denied' (p. 22). She suggests that this relation may be signalled by subordinators, prepositions or conjuncts (p. 88).

The following are examples of critical statements framed by the Concession Contraexpectation from both the English literature and sociology samples of texts.

'This statement *suggests* collective denial, *even though* at this time it would have been shocking to read ...' (English Text 2) — Grounds Conclusion / Concession Contraexpecation

'*Although* the women's suffrage movement is only mentioned in Mrs Dalloway and not in The Good Soldier, it plays an important role in constructing gender and gender roles.' (English Text 3) — Concession Contraexpecation

'Dickinson appears to suggest that speech is a formative part of this 'performance', *but* the polarity established in her opinion is highly problematic *as* it utterly divides men and women, speech and silence.' (English Text 10)

    Concession
    Contraexpactation
    Reason Result (inverted)

'This may be explained in terms of Japan's increasing need to assert itself economically against Western capitalist structures, thus necessitating the mobilization of the female half of the population .... *However*, the extent to which this was truly implemented is questionable.' (Sociology Text 4)

    Reason Result
    Concession
    Contraexpectation

'This seems slightly perplexing [as] 'homemaker' is a non-gendered word, created in fact to be deliberately neutral, *yet* in its meaning it becomes female.' (Sociology Text 11)

    Concession
    Contraexpecation

'*Although* Goffman is sometimes criticized for being 'little more than a cynical observer of white American middle-class mores, it is hard to deny *that* his work has an impact upon how the reader views both the 'self' and society subsequently.' (Sociology Text 15)

    Concession
    Contraexpectation
    Amplification

Metadiscourse devices

In the genre model presented in Section 2.2, metadiscourse devices relate to the element of genre termed stance. Hyland (2005b), whose approach to metadiscourse is employed here, defines the term as 'the self-reflective expressions used to negotiate interactional meanings in a text, assisting the writer (or speaker) to express a viewpoint and engage with readers as members of a particular community' (p. 37).

In the critical statements of the English sample, there were 234 occurrences of four metadiscourse devices: 'hedging, attitude markers, boosters and self mention'. Two were more frequently used: hedges occurred 109 times (46.5 per cent of the 234) and attitude markers occurred ninety-eight times (42 per cent of the 234). Less frequent were self mention and boosters, with fourteen and thirteen occurrences respectively.

In the sociology sample, in the statements that expressed a critical/evaluative judgement, there were 149 occurrences of four metadiscourse devices: hedge, attitude marker, booster and self mention. Attitude markers appeared in the statements of most essays, occurring 110 times (74 per cent of the 149). However, the other three devices were relatively infrequent: hedges twenty-three (15 per cent); self mention nine (6 per cent) and boosters seven (5 per cent).

Hedges and attitude markers are explained and exemplified here.

Hedging

Hyland (2005b) defines hedges as language devices that 'withhold commitment and open dialogue' and gives the examples of words, such as 'might, perhaps, possible, about' (p. 49). Hyland goes on to say that '[h]edges emphasize the subjectivity of a position by allowing information to be presented as an opinion rather than a fact and, therefore, open that position to negotiation' (p. 52).

In the English sample, of the 109 instances of hedging, just over half (fifty-eight) involve modal structures, twenty instances hedging are other verbal structures that involve 'tentative' verbs (e.g. appears, seems, suggests and tends), seventeen involve adjectives (e.g. possible, likely and debatable), nine involve adverbs (perhaps and possible) and there are small other occurrences that use verbs (e.g. 'implied').

In the essays of the sociology sample, the twenty-four instances of hedging were found in only six of the fifteen essays of the sample, of which fourteen instances were found in two essays. Twelve of the instances of hedging are achieved by non-modal verbs (seems and suggests), seven involve adverbs (perhaps) and six use modal auxiliary verbs.

The following extracts from the essays contain examples (underlined) of the four linguistic devices used for hedging in critical statements from the English sample:

> 'Just as Heart of Darkness *could involve* ... so *can* Morpheus's dialogue *be seen to provide* that same sense of discomfort in the viewer ...' (modal auxiliary verb – English Text 8)

> 'Indeed, throughout the play despite her own private statements of authority, her public "self" *appears to have* very little control ...' (non-modal auxiliary verb – English Text 5)

> 'Woolf regarded narrative structures, particularly, the meta-narrative of history, to be gendered ... Hence, it *is possible* to argue that Mrs Dalloway is in fact an "anti-narrative" ...' (adjective – English Text 6)

> 'More wrote Utopia entirely in Latin ... This is *perhaps* why Utopia *appears* a direct and simplistic text with the structure of a compare and contrast technique ...' (adverb – English Text 15)

Attitude markers

In Hyland's (2005b) metadiscourse model, he states that attitude markers 'express the writer's attitude to a proposition' (p. 49). Hyland goes on to say that attitude markers 'indicate the writer's affective, rather than epistemic, attitude to propositions ... [and are] signalled metadiscoursally by attitude verbs (e.g. *agree, prefer*), sentence adverbs (*unfortunately, hopefully*) and adjectives (*appropriate, logical, remarkable*)' (p. 53).

In the English sample, there were ninety-nine instances of attitude markers identified, of which seventy-seven were adjectives and fourteen were adverbs. In addition, there were a small number of nouns and verbs that performed this metadiscoursal function. In the sociology sample, there were 110 instances of attitude markers identified, of which seventy were adjectives, nineteen were adverbs, twelve were nouns and eight were verbs. The following examples from both samples illustrate this use of adjectives and adverbs performing this function.

> 'What is perhaps *more interesting* when observing Woolf's character constructions ...' (adjective – English Text 6)

> 'But the extent to which a man can accurately take on a woman's voice is *questionable* ...' (adjective – English Text 10)

> 'Petrucci's poem "Reflections" *explicitly* demonstrates such breakings of traditional forms using ...' (adverb – English Text 5)

> 'Webster uses the effect of small, intimate spaces *to great effect* in his tragedy The Duchess of Malfi, a play ...' (adverb – English Text 6)

> 'This implication was *significant* as it was personal, and did not just affect women who wished to enter the medical profession but all female patients.' (adjective - Sociology Text 1)

> 'Horkheimer offers us a *useful* outline of the nature of critical theory that should be distrustful of the rules of conduct ...' (adjective – Sociology Text 8)

> 'The link between modernity and the Holocaust is *certainly a strong one*; the creation of Weber's depersonalised "legal rational" society combined with ...' (adverb/ adjective – Sociology Text 9)

> 'It is *evident* that all of the reforms of the late 1950s and 1960s marked a retreat from the social controls imposed in the Victorian era ...' (adjective – Sociology Text 13)

Discussion of the findings

In the university essays examined in this study, I found that each text included a number of critical statements that contributed to the construction of an overall extended argument or case through the essay. In examining these critical statements in terms of the social genre/cognitive genre model, I found that each expressed critical thinking by using two generic elements. First, the statements were framed by a range of coherence relations, operationalized in terms of Crombie's (1985) binary interpropositional relations, most commonly Grounds Conclusion, Concession Contraexpectation and Reason Result. Second, these relations incorporated metadiscourse devices (Hyland, 2005b), in particular attitude markers and hedging. However, it must be pointed out that because of the nature of the intensive manual analysis undertaken, it was only possible to examine a relatively small number of essays in each sample, and that only essays from two disciplines were included. Also because it was not logistically possible to fund and train multiple researchers to provide comparative analyses, the study can only be considered to be an exploratory use of this particular research approach. Nevertheless, while acknowledging their provisional nature, the findings suggest implications that relate to the expression of a critical or evaluative viewpoint in this type of extended essay. These implications include how the findings appear to confirm the statement by Nesi and Gardner (2012) that student writers need to be able to 'comment on' theory and research as part of essay writing; how the statements relate to Toulmin's argument pattern; the types of linking that occurs between the propositions of critical statements (Andrews, 2000); and the important role of metadiscourse devices in the construction of statements that express critical thinking.

The first implication of the findings of the study is that they appear to support the assertion by Nesi and Gardner (2012) who state:

> [i]t is the work of the student writer to become an expert at being able to 'comment on' – *which we interpret here as critically evaluate* – current theory and research as well as to construct arguments and develop a coherent position or thesis throughout an assignment. [emphasis added] (p. 90)

The frequency and distribution of the critical comments in the two samples of essays appear to support this view. It is important, however, to note that commenting by means of these types of critical statement form part of a larger, overall process of constructing and sustaining an extended argument or case through the essay. In the previous studies of the same samples (Bruce, 2010a, 2015a), my finding was that these extended essays contained sequential stretches of text that related to different types of general rhetorical purpose (operationalized as cognitive genres). Writers moved between these types of rhetorical purpose in building a case or extended argument. However, in addition to these 'rhetorical shifts' that occurred in the essays, the critical/evaluative dimension of the writer's perspective was developed through the strategic use of the critical statements that are the focus of the present study. As Nesi and Gardner (2012) state: 'Critiques and Essays build on developing understanding or explanation to include a critical evaluation or the development of an argument' (p. 94).

A second implication of these findings about the elements of critical statements is how they relate to Toulmin's (2003) argument pattern of 'grounds, claim and warrant', an approach that has been used in pedagogy and research related to developing the argumentation skill. Essentially, Toulmin's structure involves a general causal relation between the 'grounds' and the 'claim' and a further causal relation between the binary 'grounds-claim' structure and the 'warrant'; this arrangement of propositions is claimed to be central to the structuring of argumentation. From the findings of the present study using the interpropositional approach, two causal relations (Grounds Conclusion and Reason Result) emerged as frequently used structures in the critical statements examined. However, from the perspective of teaching academic writing and focusing on issues relating to coherence and cohesion, these findings suggest that identifying critical statements in the essays in terms of coherence relations may offer an alternative to the Toulmin argument pattern. First, this approach provides a more nuanced approach to the complex issue of causality, which is described in terms of a range of relations from Crombie's taxonomy (Reason Result, Grounds Conclusion, Means Result, Means Purpose and Condition Consequence), all of which were employed to some extent within the samples of critical statements that were examined (see Tables 3.1 and 3.2). Second, and possibly more importantly, the findings seem to indicate that critical statements, as key anchoring elements of argumentation in the essays examined, *do not always employ a causal relation*, and that concessive contrast (the Concession Contraexpectation relation) was also one of the most frequently used relations in both samples. The importance of concessive contrast (sometime termed *counterclaiming*) as a device in critical argumentation has also been a key finding in other studies (see, for example, Basturkmen & Von Randow, 2014; Bruce, 2014a; Kwan, Chan & Lam, 2012). In addition to this, the findings indicate that a range of other less frequently occurring relations between propositions may also frame critical statements (also see Tables 3.1 and 3.2).

Third, the study also brings into focus the types of cohesive devices used to signal relations between propositions in the statements that expressed critical thinking, responding to the call by Andrews (2000) that the teaching of argumentation needs to focus on the *linking* of the key propositions when teaching argumentation, although it must be acknowledged that Andrews was referring to links between the propositions of the Toulmin argument pattern. However, if one were to take the broader approach, pedagogy that raises awareness of these types of coherence relation and their critical role would also need to focus on how the different ways in which the links between these propositions may be signalled and encoded. The findings suggest that a range of textual devices may be employed as signalling devices within expressions of critical thinking, and their selection would appear to be dependent on their contextual and co-textual location.

Finally, the study also appears to emphasize the importance of the role of metadiscourse devices in expressing critical evaluation. It identifies the two metadiscourse devices of attitude markers and hedging as central to this role, and importantly, it reveals how they operate synergistically in conjunction with the types of interpropositional relation examined to create a critical statement. From a linguistic perspective, it seems that identifying attitude markers is relatively straightforward, with most being adjectives and adverbs; however, hedging proved to be more complex, involving the use of a wider variety of linguistic devices, mainly modal and non-modal verbs but also adjectives and adverbs, awareness of which needs to be developed by novice writers.

3.3 Implications for the teaching of writing

Following the relatively technical consideration of essay writing in this chapter, it is important to consider how these findings (along with previous research concerned with university essays) may be related to the actual teaching of essay writing. In this brief section, I make two points in relation to pedagogy. First I offer comments about the larger organizational structures of essays and how they may be taught. Second, I consider how the textual elements related to expressing critical thinking, as key strategic elements of the larger structures, can be taught.

In relation to the higher-level organization of essays, I suggest that the commonly taught essay schema of Introduction, Body and Conclusion can only be regarded as a very general overall organizational pattern, and it is more salient to consider what should be included in the introduction, body and conclusion, such as when planning a response to the requirements of a particular essay task. As the literature indicates, one size does not fit all. The pedagogic issue, therefore, is to help students to acquire the type of procedural knowledge to analyse essay tasks/prompts to identify the type of essay structure that is most appropriate for their responses. In terms of the overall structures of more compact essay assignment tasks, the structures offered by Coffin et al. (2003) and Nesi and Gardner (2012) appear to offer important starting points. When teaching the organizational structures of different essay types, I suggest that teachers use a top-down, genre-based approach, beginning with a small sample of model texts of a certain essay type as a basis for examining, deconstructing and practising that essay type's organization. A top-down, genre-based approach also provides a proper basis for examining more specific textual features, including key elements of cohesion and coherence. However, in considering more extended university essays (such as more than 2,000 words), it seems that writers may employ a looser, larger-scale structure marked by rhetorical shifts between stretches of text that relate to different types of communicative purpose (e.g. explain, argue and recount). I found this pattern in the first two of my essay studies discussed in this chapter (Bruce 2010a, 2015a); more extended essays tend to involve a concatenation of common cognitive genres (referred to by some as 'text types').

The second pedagogic issue, arising from the study reported in this chapter, is how to address the issue of expressing critical thinking as part of the case-building of essays. The insights afforded by this study suggest that it is only possible to exemplify these types of textual resource (use of key coherence relations in conjunction with metadiscourse devices) within the context of a whole text. Presenting and practising such generic elements in isolation from texts, and then advising students that they will be useful in the future when writing essays would be a relatively meaningless activity. Therefore, following the identification of the organizing textual structure of model texts, the next step would be to identify key critical statements that are employed within the model texts along with their functional roles in the texts. Then once these critical comment structures are identified, it may be helpful to provide students with some decontextualized presentation and practice of the textual resources that they employ, such as commonly used coherence relations and metadiscourse devices. The focus here should be on their meanings and the different ways in which they may be linguistically encoded, for example, practising the different ways of realizing the Concession Contraexpectation relation. The final step is to provide the student with opportunities to create their own examples of the same type of essay and draw upon their knowledge of these devices. A genre-based approach to essay writing instruction, therefore, begins with analysis – identifying, isolating and practising the features of whole texts – and ends with synthesis – providing the student writer with opportunities to incorporate these features into their own examples of texts of the same essay type.

3.4 Implications for conceptualizing the expression of critical thinking in written text

Finally, it is important to consider what this essay study tells us about the expression of critical thinking through written text – the overall goal of this volume. The university essay genre examined in this chapter involves the display of knowledge to promote and demonstrate learning by novice writers, a display that is directed usually towards an audience of one – the academic staff member involved in teaching the writer and grading the essay. The genre appears to have a broad overall shape or organizational structure, but there is some flexibility in its realization according to the discipline within which it occurs. However, it seems to be a near universal expectation among academic faculty, teachers of writing and developers of pedagogic materials that student writers will express critical thinking to support their development of an extended argument or case through the medium of the essay.

In relation to the issue of expressing critical thinking through written text, the overall conclusion that can be drawn from this study of the university essay genre is that its expression involves the interaction of textual resources from different levels. At the most general level, the introduction, body and conclusion schema offered by writing textbooks outlines the broad shape of the text to novice writers. This textbook advice will tend to add that the main idea of the argument (thesis) will be presented in the introduction and somehow developed with supporting evidence through the essay and summarized in the conclusion, although how the introduction will be structured will depend on the essay task and the type of essay required (see Nesi & Gardner, 2012, p. 98). At the next level, it is clear that argumentation or the overall evaluation of the essay involves different types of structuring of the content through its different stages. The two-move structure for essay introductions that I found in the earlier study (Bruce, 2010a) constitutes advice at this level, as do the structures for organizing the content in different types of essay offered by Coffin et al. (2003) and Nesi and Gardner (2012). In the so-called body section of more extended essays, I also found that writers shift between different types of general rhetorical purpose to provide extended development of points through larger sections of text, points that combine to construct the overall case (Bruce, 2010a, 2015a). Finally, at a more specific level, the expression of critical thinking in this genre centrally involves the strategic use of key critical statements by authors that specify and underpin the particular points that they are making. The findings of the study indicate that these statements were framed by particular binary coherence relations, often involving some aspect of causality or concessive contrast, and that they nearly always included metadiscourse elements (attitude markers and hedging) that further signal the particular position of the writer. The distribution of these statements within the broader structure of the essays of the sample was free, and no conventionalized pattern was found. While these critical statements do not, of themselves, constitute the overall argument of the essay, they are crucial elements in its construction, and are the elements that most overtly express the writer's specific evaluative position.

Therefore, what this chapter suggests is the expression of critical thinking through written text, exemplified here in the genre of the university essay, is a complex phenomenon employing elements from different levels within the text that operate integratively. The findings also suggest that its investigation requires an analytical framework that is able to identify these elements and provide insights into how they mutually interact with each other to achieve the expression of critical thinking.

4

Expressing critical thinking in PhD Discussion chapters

4.0 Introduction

In this chapter, I continue to explore how critical thinking is expressed through writing by investigating the PhD Discussion, which is considered by many to be a challenging and relatively unsupported genre. The chapter has four sections. In Section 4.1, I outline the requirements and expectations of the PhD Discussion chapter as articulated in books that give advice about thesis writing and in the findings of surveys of faculty engaged in doctoral supervision/advising. In this first section, I also consider the challenges faced by writers of the genre, referring to the findings of a small number of studies that have identified difficulties faced by novice and second-language writers. In Section 4.2, I review genre research that has examined PhD Discussion chapters and the Discussion sections in academic journal articles. While these studies focus on the organizational and other characteristics of the texts, they have not specifically explored the requirement of the genre to express critical thinking and how this is achieved. In Section 4.3, I then turn to the focal issue of expressing critical thinking through this type of writing. In this section, I present the findings of a study in which I examined PhD Discussion chapters (from Applied Linguistics), again using the social genre/cognitive genre model presented in Chapter 2 to identify the textual means that writers used to express critical thinking in this genre. The study appeared in the journal *ESP Today* (2018, pp. 2–24) under the title of 'The textual expression of critical thinking in PhD Discussions in Applied Linguistics'.[1]

In Section 4.4, I provide some suggestions of how the findings of this study may be used by teachers and students grappling with the writing requirements of this particular genre, and in Section 4.5, I consider the implications of this study in relation to the larger issue of understanding how critical thinking is expressed through academic writing.

4.1 The requirements of PhD Discussion chapters

This section has two parts. In the first, I examine the expectations of PhD Discussion chapters as articulated in published advice books on thesis writing and through surveys of university faculty opinion. In the second, I review research that has identified writer difficulties in developing the Discussion chapter, specifically those difficulties relating to argumentation and the expression of critical thinking.

The importance of expressing critical thinking in the Discussion chapter is emphasized in most books that provide advice about thesis/dissertation writing. For example, Evans, Gruba and Zobel (2011) state that '[t]his is probably the part of the thesis where it is most important to show your ability as a critical thinker' (p. 165). Similarly, Cone and Foster (1993), when providing advice about dissertations in psychology and related fields, state: 'In your discussion section, you will interpret your findings, place them in the context of your hypotheses and the literature that you reviewed, and *examine critically their implications and limitations*.' (p. 237) [emphasis added]. Similar advice is provided by Bitchener (2010), who states that '[t]he key purpose of this chapter is to discuss the meaning and significance of the results or findings of the research you are reporting' (p. 179). Rudestam and Newton (2007) express almost the same idea stating: 'You evaluate the extent to which your study answered the question you posed at the outset, basing your reasoning as much as possible on the data' (p. 196). In these advice books, there seems to be agreement that the Discussion chapter will perform a critically evaluative function in relation to the overall findings of the study that have been reported. Specifically, they discuss the extent to which the findings answer the research question and how they relate to relevant, previously published research and theory in the same field.

Similar to the position taken by the advice books, the findings of studies that have elicited the views of university faculty concerning the functions and characteristics of the Discussion chapter also appear to agree that it should incorporate a strong element of critical evaluation. For example, the faculty in Bitchener and Basturkmen's (2006) case studies saw the Discussion chapter in masters theses as performing an evaluative role in relation to the findings of the study. Lovitts's (2007) focus group study of the views of faculty from ten disciplines about what constituted good PhD dissertations found that many thought that Discussion 'should tie to the Introduction and put the work in a larger perspective' (p. 47).

However, a number of surveys of doctoral students and faculty involved in doctoral supervision/advising suggest that, for those who are relatively new to the requirements of research writing, and especially for second-language (L2) writers of English, developing the Discussion section in RAs and the Discussion chapters in theses or dissertations presents particular problems. For example, Shaw (1991) found that L2 writers of PhD dissertations in English identify the Discussion chapter as the most difficult, as it was the least supported type of writing although they expected examiners to give it most attention. Other studies involving surveys of thesis/dissertation supervisors and students suggest that L2 writers have particular problems with developing and sustaining coherent ideas and arguments in the extended text of the Discussion chapter (Cooley & Lewkowicz, 1995, 1997; Dong 1998; Jenkins, Jordan & Weiland, 1993; Thompson, 1999). A study carried out at the University of Hong Kong, involving surveys of faculty and students, identified four main problem areas in graduate students' writing, one of which appears to relate centrally to the writing of the Discussion chapter. This was 'a failure to substantiate argument with evidence from the literature and a tendency to make claims for [their] own research findings which were too strong or overgeneralized' (Allison, Cooley, Lewkowicz & Nunan, 1998, p. 212). The same perception of writer difficulty with Discussion chapters was found in the case studies of Bitchener and Basturkmen (2006), who emphasize 'the level of difficulty that students experienced in meeting the requirements of this genre' (p. 14). Specifically, they found that the L2 student writers' problems with the Discussion chapter partly related to their incomplete understanding of the particular function of this chapter, and particularly the need to interpret and discuss findings. Some of the faculty in Lovitts's (2007) focus group study felt that the 'discussion/conclusion chapter was a difficult one for graduate students to write, in part, because at this point in their careers most students have an insufficient perspective on the field to really draw things together and address their implications' (p. 47).

Thus, while the advice literature and surveys of university faculty appear to share similar expectations of the Discussion chapter in theses/dissertations, including emphasis on argument construction supported by the expression of critical thinking, research in this area suggests that novice and L2 research writers find this to be a difficult genre to master, and their difficulties often seem to relate to formulating appropriate evaluations of their findings and relating these back to previous research in the field.

4.2 Studies of Discussions

Over several decades, there have been a number of studies in the field of ESP that have investigated Discussion chapters in theses and dissertations, and Discussion sections in RAs. In this stream of research, it appears that the principle focus has been on attempts to establish a 'move' structure for the organization of content, similar to the types of move structure Swales (1981, 1990) proposes for RA Introduction sections.

In attempting to establish a 'move' structure for Discussion chapters, a seminal work frequently referred to is Hopkins and Dudley-Evans' (1988) study that examined discussion chapters in MSc dissertations in the field of biology, and discussion sections in RAs in the field of irrigation and drainage, where they found a 'cycling' or recursive patterns of moves. They found that there was really only 'one obligatory move, *statement of result*, which occurred several times, almost always at the head of a cycle' (p. 117). They proposed a provisional list of ten other optional moves that may form part of a cycle: 'Background information, (un)expected result, reference to previous research (comparison), explanation of unsatisfactory result, exemplification, deduction, hypothesis, reference to previous research (support), recommendation, justification' (p. 188). Their principal conclusion about the arrangement of these cycles or recursive patterns in the Discussion chapter is that they relate centrally to the interpretation of the results by the writer for the reason that 'the discussion sections of articles and dissertations appear to be judged less on the actual results presented than on the way the writer relates them to previous work in the field' (p. 199). In a further study of the evaluation of the results part of a Discussion chapter of a thesis in biology, Dudley-Evans (1994, p. 225) reduced slightly the original eleven-move structure to a nine-move one: 'Information move, statement of result, finding, (un)expected outcome, reference to previous research, explanation, claim, limitation, recommendation'. Drawing upon the key elements from these earlier move structures, Bitchener (2010) proposes a more minimal three-move, recursive structure for Discussion chapters of 1. Provide background information, 2. Present a statement of Results (SOR) and 3. Evaluate/comment on results or findings. However, he includes many of the more specific moves of the earlier proposals as subsidiary steps within a move, such as unexpected results, exemplification and deduction under Move 2. He also suggests that the recursive occurrence of Moves 2 and 3 tends to characterize Discussion chapters.

Also focusing on move structures, a number of studies have been carried out on the smaller related subgenre of the Discussion section of RAs (Berkenkotter and Huckin, 1995; Kanoksilapatham 2003, 2012; Holmes, 1997; Lewin & Fine, 1996; Nwogu, 1991; Parkinson, 2011; Peacock, 2002; Posteguillo, 1999). Yang and Allison (2003), whose study of the Discussion sections of twenty RAs in Applied linguistics reduced Hopkins and Dudley-Evans's (1988) eleven-move structure to a seven-move structure, some of which contain subsidiary steps – the seven moves being: background information, reporting results, summarizing results, commenting on results, summarizing the study, evaluating the study and deducing from the research. Basturkmen (2009), when examining MA dissertation Discussion chapters and RA Discussion sections in the field of language teaching, further condenses Yang and Allison's proposed seven-move structure to one consisting of four moves with three subsidiary steps relating to commenting on results; the moves are background information, summarizing results, reporting a result and commenting on the result by (a) 'explaining' the results, (b)'comparing with results in the literature' and (c) 'evaluating' the result. She found a considerable degree of recursion in the use of the Moves 3 and 4 – reporting results, commenting on results – which she described as 'Result–Comment' sequences.

Overall, it seems that ESP research has tended to focus mostly on establishing patterns for the organization of Discussion chapters in terms of rhetorically motivated moves. Despite some variation in the functions and ordering of moves, 'presenting' and 'commenting on' the research findings are central elements, and moves that perform these functions operate recursively. More recent ESP studies of PhD Theses in the fields of the visual and performing arts, using both textual and ethnographic analysis, have revealed a variety of overall thesis macrostructures, including some theses that still contain 'chapters that describe and/or critique and theorize the author-artists creative work, where the conventional elements "Results" and "Discussion" are intermingled' (Paltridge, Starfield, Ravelli & Tuckwell, 2012, p. 399). Yet beyond a focus on the internal organization of Discussion or its place in the wider thesis, there has been little research that has examined the specific textual elements and devices employed to express critical thinking as it contributes to the construction of argumentation in this genre.

While not discounting the important roles of moves and their related lexical items, in my own study (reported in Section 4.3), I aimed to undertake a more holistic exploration of PhD Discussion chapters/sections to identify the textual expression of critical thinking, again using the social genre/cognitive genre model (see Section 2.2). My reasoning was that the expression of this important element needs to be examined *within the functioning discursive and textual whole* that constitutes the genre of this chapter. As stated previously, employing this genre model as an analytical tool to identify different types of knowledge that shape elements of a particular category of text is justified in terms of Bhatia's (2002, 2004) proposal that discourse includes social practice, genre and text.

4.3 Study of PhD Discussions in applied linguistics (Bruce, 2018)

The previously published study summarized here examines Discussion chapters from five PhD theses in the field of Applied Linguistics. Given the apparent broad agreement in the literature that the Discussion chapter should express a critical/evaluative viewpoint, this study aimed to examine each of the five chapters in order to identify the ways in which critical thinking is expressed within the Discussion chapter.

In this study, the research question explored was the following:

What are the textual means used by writers to express critical thinking in the Discussion chapters of PhD theses in Applied Linguistics?

The sample

The sample for this study comprised the Discussion chapters of five PhD theses produced by graduates of New Zealand universities: three from the University of Auckland, one from Victoria University of Wellington and one from Massey University. Each thesis was an annual winner of a 'Best Thesis Competition' organized by the *Applied Linguistics Association of New Zealand* for the years 2009 to 2013. Theses entered in this competition are judged by a panel from this association, and each year one is selected as best thesis. My principal reason for selecting chapters from theses that were annual winners of this competition for the sample of this study was in order to address the 'variability of quality issues' in PhD theses that Thompson (2012, p. 120) identifies, with the review of each thesis by a panel of applied linguists providing a validating judgement additional to its original examination. As Thompson points out, in countries that follow the British university system, PhD theses tend not to be graded in terms of their comparative quality as they are judged on pass/fail criteria. It would, therefore, be logistically difficult to identify a comparative sample of lower quality PhD theses as the examination system does not disclose this type of information. Although the theses were by both L1 and L2 writers, their selection as competition winners was the sole criterion for their inclusion in the sample. Bibliographic and methodological details about each thesis and about page numbers and word counts of the analysed sections are provided in Appendix D.

Specifically, I identified the sections of each thesis that discussed the findings of the research. In three cases this involved a Discussion chapter, in one case a chapter termed Conclusions and in one case the Discussion sections of five chapters that reported five different research investigations. Altogether the sample consisted of 145 pages of text. In relation to the ethical requirements of the research, the purpose of the study was explained to each of the thesis writers, and their written consent was obtained to quote material from their thesis.

The analysis

The analytical framework that I employed in this study was the social genre/cognitive genre model that I previously outlined in Chapter 2 (see Table 2.2 and the related explanation). The analysis first involved reading the whole of each thesis as preparation for a closer study of the Discussion chapters/chapter sections. The next stage involved intensive examination and marking up of those textual elements within the Discussion chapters that expressed critical thinking. As with the previous study, those elements were analysed in terms of features of the social genre/cognitive genre model following the approach outlined at the end of Section 2.5. As I stated in that section, attempting to identify a schema (move structure) to account for the higher-level organization of the content of the text, the analysis was more inductive, involving constant comparison and reanalysis of each chapter in order to settle on the most appropriate descriptive categories for identifying their content organization. However, the analysis of lower-level elements was more deductive. For example, in relation to stance, this involved the use of Hyland's (2005b, p. 49) metadiscourse model, and in accounting for coherence relations, Crombie's (1985) taxonomy of interpropositional relations was employed.

The findings

The overall findings were that three key elements from both the social and cognitive genre parts of the model emerged as central to the expression of critical thinking as part of the development of the overall argument of the Discussion chapters:

1. In terms of the organization of content within in each of the five theses, a recursive content schema (move structure) emerged as a key evaluation-framing element, described as: 'Point, Support, Evaluation'. 'Point' and 'Support' appear to be fixed or obligatory elements, while 'Evaluation' occurs in 59 per cent of the identified instances of the schema in the sample (see Table 4.1).

Table 4.1 Frequencies of Use of the Schema: 'Point Support Evaluation'

Thesis	Point, Support, Evaluation	Point, Support (no Evaluation)	Schemata Total	Chapter Length, Word Total
Cao (2009)	11	6	17	4,326
Jones (2010)	11	12	23	8,528
Nguyen (2011)	22	17	39	10,788 approx.
Booth (2012)	23	23	46	18,521
Rogers (2013)	26	8	34	15,200 approx.
Total	93	66	159	57,363

(Bruce, 2018, Table 2, p. 14).

2. In the 'Evaluation' part of this schema, key coherence relations were used to make critical statements; these were operationalized in terms of Crombie's (1985) taxonomy of interpropositional relations (see Appendix E). Specifically, a small number of these relations were employed across the five theses to make these key critical statements.
3. At a lower level, within the critical statements, two elements of Hyland's (2005b) metadiscourse model were also employed to help express critical thinking – specifically: hedging and attitude markers.

While other elements of the genre model were employed in these Discussion chapters, such as stretches of text realizing particular cognitive genres or the use of metadiscourse devices other than those identified in the findings, the focus here is solely on those elements of the genre model directly related to the research purpose of the study. Three subsections follow that unpack the findings. The first will explain and exemplify the schematic structure with examples from the Discussion chapters. The next subsection will focus on the critical statements in the Evaluation, and the final subsection will consider and exemplify the use of metadiscourse within these critical statements.

The content schema (move structure): Point, support, evaluation

At a conscious organizational level, I found that each Discussion chapter began with an introductory overview that mapped the content of the chapter for the reader. Following this overview, the chapter was subsequently divided into several larger, numbered sections. In three of the five theses, these larger sections usually began with further metatextual mapping and sometimes concluded with a summary of the key points at the end. Two of the five chapters did not contain this type of metatextual guidance at the beginning and end of the major chapter sections.

However, in relation to the research purpose of the present study, that is, investigating the expression of critical thinking in the Discussion chapters, I found that it was the intra-sectional patterns of content organization in terms of a particular recursive content schema (see Table 4.1) that was the generic element that was most salient to the construction of the overall arguments or discussion of the chapter, and that provided a basis for the expression of critical thinking. This recursive pattern is described as: 'Point, Support, Evaluation'.

Point

'Point' tended to be a brief statement at the beginning of the content schema. The point was the textual element about which the evaluative judgement was subsequently formed in the following 'Support' and 'Evaluation' stages of the schema.

Among the Points in the sample, 52 per cent were a deduction based on a finding, 36 per cent were a statement of an actual empirical finding and 12 per cent were more general claims or statements related to the research. Because the Point stage was realized by writers in these different ways, I did not employ the more general 'Reporting a Result' label as used by Basturkmen (2009) and others for the reason that the majority of the points were not actual empirical findings. The Point usually consisted of one or two sentences and in only a few cases involved a paragraph. The following are three examples of 'Points':

1a. 'The results from Study 2 demonstrate incidental learning of vocabulary does occur through watching television.' (Rogers, 2013, p. 97) – a deduction
2a. 'An important finding was that short turns were frequent and dominant as an exchange pattern across the 10 CMC groups.' (Nguyen, 2011, p. 222) – an empirical finding
3a. 'Methodologically, this study has also contributed to the validation of a classroom observation scheme of WTC behaviour in class.' (Cao, 2009, p. 229) – a more general claim

Support

The 'Support' stage of the content schema immediately follows the 'Point' and is the most extensive stage. The findings showed that the 'Support' develops the point in three possible ways, by

- 'exemplification' – which involved presenting examples from the data of the study to illustrate and provide evidence for the point;

- 'explanation' – which involved interpreting or explaining the point; or
- 'comparison' – which involved comparing the point with the findings or conclusion from other referenced research or theory.

The majority of the 'Support' stages in the five theses use only one of these three realizations. However, in four of the five theses, a minority of the Support stages combine two realizations to support the point. The most common of the combinations were 'exemplification/comparison' followed by 'comparison/explanation'. Combinations of two realizations are found in 34 per cent of Roger's Supports, 18 per cent of those of Nguyen, 14 per cent of those of Booth and 13 per cent of those of Jones.

The following are examples of each of the three possible ways of realizing the Support stage. The first example is part of the Support following Point 1a (earlier), which uses *exemplification*; that is, providing data from the study as evidence for the assertion made in the point.

1b. Participants had mean vocabulary gains of 6.4 words on the Tough Test and 6.8 words on the sensitive test through viewing 10 successive episodes of Chuck. The Experimental Group's gains from the pre- to post-test were significantly greater than those of the control group ... (Rogers, 2013, p. 97)

The second 'Support' example is one that develops its preceding point by explanation. This is the beginning of the Support that follows Point 2a.

2b. There are several explanations for these short turns made by the CMC students. It took most of them, with limited typing skills, so long to type a full idea while at the same time they wanted to maintain the conversation and to get their ideas across, which in turn tempted them to hurriedly enter a turn even though it was not a complete idea. An idea therefore, needed several turns to transfer its complete meaning during which it could be unfortunately interrupted by turns from other members ... (Nguyen, 2011, p. 222)

The third example of a Support involves *comparison*. This type compares the assertion made in the Point in terms of how it is similar to, or differs from, other research. For example, the following Comment, which uses comparison, is that which follows Point 3a above.

3b. Observation was considered more suitable for measuring situational WTC (MacIntyre et al., 2001) and a number of previous studies attempted to operationalise WTC in an L2 classroom in slightly different categories (Cao and Philp, 2006; Pattapong, in press, Peng, 2008). (Cao, 2009, pp. 229)

Evaluation

The Evaluation stage, which occurs in 59 per cent of the instances of the schema, involves writers expressing their own particular viewpoint about the material presented in the 'Point' and 'Comment' stages. Other ESP researchers (Basturkmen, 2009; Yang & Allison, 2003) make evaluation an optional step within the previous move. I propose it to be a separate move because it involves a more personal, critical type of writing. The difference between Support and Evaluation is similar to Sinclair's (1988) distinction between 'attribution' and 'averral'; the Support may provide further detail relevant to, or other writers' views on, the point, whereas the Evaluation is a more direct expression of the writer's own position, and usually employs particular coherence relations (Knott & Sanders, 1998) to make critical statements. These relations are operationalized by Crombie's (1985) taxonomy of binary interpropositional relations. Embedded within these relations were the metadiscourse elements of hedging and attitude markers (Hyland, 2005b). The types of relation and their frequency, and the use of metadiscourse are explained and exemplified in the two following subsections.

The following three Evaluation examples are those that follow the three Supports of the previous subsection. The first Evaluation example relates to Point 1a and Support 1b.

1c. It is difficult to make direct comparisons between the mean gains from the results of Study 2 and previous research because of the differing number of test items and different treatments in the studies. The overarching finding from this research and previous research, however, is that vocabulary can be incidentally learned from viewing videos. (Rogers, 2013, p. 98)

The second Evaluation example is the third part of the content schema relating to Point 2a and Support 2b.

2c. Above all, this text-only method of exchange, in which the priorities were to quickly get ideas across and to smoothly maintain the conversation, also partly explains the reason why the CMC students tended to key in fewer words in each turn. It is concluded in this study that limited computer knowledge and typing skills affected the quantity and quality of the conversation. (Nguyen, 2011, pp. 222–3)

The third Evaluation example relates to Point 3a and Support 3b.

3c. This study modified the scheme of Cao and Philp (2006), contributing to the development of a more refined observational scheme for future classroom WTC studies. (Cao, 2009, p. 229)

Table 4.1 provides the frequencies of occurrence of the full Point, Support, Evaluation schema and those instances that omitted the Evaluation stage.

Use of key coherence relations as critical statements in the Evaluation section

Within the third part of the content schema (the Evaluation), a central and confirmatory element in the expression of critical thinking was the use of key coherence relations to frame critical statements; these emerged as the most overt and direct expression of the writer's own position. Across the five theses, 174 such critical statements were identified. These statements are analysed in terms of Crombie's (1985) taxonomy of binary interpropositional relations. It was found that a small group of these relations was employed to express evaluative judgements in relation to three aspects of the thesis: the research questions or research gap (the overall object or focus of the research), the interpretation of the findings and the comparison of the findings with other research. Table 4.2 shows the actual numbers and percentage frequencies of the relations that frame the critical statements identified in the sample. Some Evaluations contained more than one critical statement.

In the remainder of this subsection, the three most frequent relations used to frame critical statements are defined, and examples of statements using each relation are provided.

Reason Result

Among the relations employed by the critical statements in the Evaluation section, Reason Result was the most frequently used, with forty-two occurrences across the five theses, constituting 24 per cent of the total number of critical statements. In defining this binary relation between two propositions, Crombie (1985) states: 'The reason member (which very often follows the result member in English) gives a reason *why* a particular effect came or will come about' (p. 20). Signalling of this relation may employ subordinators, prepositions,

Table 4.2 Coherence Relations Framing Critical Statements in the Evaluation

Thesis	Evaluation Critical Statements: Totals	Reason Result	Concession Contraexpectation	Grounds Conclusion	Means Result	Amplification	Condition Consequence	Other* Relations
Cao (2009)	27	10	3	3	5	3	0	3
Jones (2010)	24	10	5	1	0	2	3	3
Nguyen (2011)	26	4	3	8	6	1	2	2
Booth (2012)	55	7	14	17	3	4	1	9
Rogers (2013)	42	11	11	5	4	4	6	1
Totals	174	42	36	34	18	14	12	18
Percentages	100%	24%	21%	20%	10%	8%	7%	10%

* This category includes all other relations used across the five theses in the Evaluation part of the schema (Bruce, 2018, Table 3, p. 15).

conjuncts, causative verbs and nouns. The following are examples of Reason Result relations from the five theses.

> <u>Another reason</u> that the results reported in Study 2 might be considered conservative has to do with the nature of the vocabulary testing procedure. (Rogers, 2013, p. 98)
>
> These findings are noteworthy <u>because</u> they indicate that learners tend to believe they incidentally learn vocabulary through watching television. (Rogers, 2013, p. 159)
>
> In summary of the discussion related to Research Question One, the first part of this chapter highlights the high stakes nature of the TOEIC <u>as a result of</u> a complex interplay between the test makers, the test, community stakeholders, and test-takers. (Booth, 2012, p. 270)

Concession Contraexpectation

The Concession Contraexpectation relation is the second most frequently used relation to frame critical statements that occurred in the Evaluation section of the schema, with thirty-six occurrences, constituting 21 per cent of the total number (of critical statements). Crombie's (1985) definition of this relation states: 'In this relation, the truth of an inference is directly or indirectly denied' (p. 22). She suggests that this relation may be signalled by subordinators, prepositions or conjuncts (p. 88). The following are examples of critical/evaluative statements framed by the Concession Contraexpectation from the sample. The underlined words indicate any linguistic signalling of the relation that occurs.

> Results from Study 1 indicate that vocabulary knowledge is a significant factor in the comprehension of television. Vocabulary knowledge, <u>however</u>, does not appear to play as large a role in the comprehension of authentic television programs as it does for short listening passages. (Rogers, 2013, p. 58)
>
> No doubt, more research is needed to confirm the extent to which TOEIC scores are used by companies and for what purposes. <u>Nonetheless</u>, previous research, supported by student perspectives in the present study, appears to confirm the high stakes status of the Standard TOEIC fuelled by perceived demands from the employment sector. (Booth, 2012, pp. 256–7)

Grounds Conclusion

The Grounds Conclusion relation is the third most frequently occurring relation framing critical statements in the Evaluation sections, with thirty-four occurrences, constituting 20 per cent of the total number (of critical statements). In defining this binary relation between two propositions, Crombie (1985), states that in this relation, 'a deduction is drawn on the basis of some observation' (p. 20). The following are examples of Grounds Conclusion relations framing critical statements:

> The results from Study 3 also suggest that lexical coverage may not be as important a factor for incidental vocabulary learning from viewing television as it may be for reading. (Richards, 2013, p. 133)

> For the Captions Group, there were small significant correlations between vocabulary knowledge and comprehension for four of the 10 episodes, and for the no Captions Group, there were small to medium significant correlations for all 10 of the episodes. This indicates that greater vocabulary knowledge may be more important for comprehension of television when captions are not present. (Richards, 2013, p. 258)

> After years of preparing for national standardised tests from middle school to university, individuals continue to prepare for tests for employment, and perhaps later for purposes of promotion. The TOEIC, therefore, provides a powerful mediating tool, for encouraging these cultural norms and conventions. (Booth, 2012, p. 267)

Metadiscourse devices

The third element involved in the expression of critical thinking were metadiscourse devices found in the majority of the critical statements that occurred in the Evaluation section. In the genre model presented in Section 2.2, metadiscourse devices relate to the element of genre termed 'stance'. In the critical statements, two were more frequently used: hedges and attitude markers[2]. Hyland (2005b) defines hedges as language devices that 'emphasize the subjectivity of a position by allowing information to be presented as an opinion rather than a fact and therefore open that position to negotiation' (p. 52), and gives the examples of words, such as 'might, perhaps, possible, about' (p. 49). Hyland (2005b) states that attitude markers 'indicate the writer's affective, rather than epistemic, attitude to propositions ... [and are] signalled metadiscoursally by attitude verbs (e.g. *agree, prefer*), sentence adverbs (*unfortunately, hopefully*) and adjectives (*appropriate, logical, remarkable*)' (p. 53). Table 4.3 presents the frequencies of use of attitude markers and hedges in the critical statements that occurred in the Evaluation move in the five theses.

Table 4.3 Use of Hedges and Attitude Markers in Critical Statements

Thesis	Critical statements in the Evaluation	Containing hedging	Containing attitude markers
Cao (2009)	27	4	10
Jones (2010)	24	5	15
Nguyen (2011)	26	4	12
Booth (2012)	55	33	7
Rogers (2013)	42	42	9

(Bruce, 2018, Table 4, p. 17).

The following are examples of critical statements containing instances of hedging, which are underlined in each example. (It should be noted that some critical statements contained more than one instance of hedging.)

> While the results from Study 3 <u>indicate</u> that knowing more vocabulary leads to better comprehension, an increase of 1.67% <u>appears not to be</u> large enough to consistently make a significant difference in understanding. (Rogers, 2013, p. 129)

> In this way TOEIC scores have <u>perhaps</u> come to provide a measure of the degree by which future workers <u>may be</u> willing to work hard and commit to the interests of the company. (Booth, 2012, p. 256)

> In making this decision, it <u>would be prudent</u> of them to consider research findings that have demonstrated that employing the L2 (English) at an early age as the instructional language <u>will not necessarily</u> lead to academic success ... (Jones, 2010, p. 262)

The following are examples of critical statements (in Evaluations) containing attitude markers, which are underlined in each example.

> This is a <u>promising</u> avenue for future research. (Nguyen, 2011, p. 223)

> Since there is a <u>strong</u> link between active involvement o stakeholders in decision-making and success of implementation ... , it is <u>vital</u> that as many stakeholders as possible are involved in the development of goals. (Jones, 2010, p. 261)

> This study is <u>distinctive</u> in that it investigates WTC through actual classroom interaction data and it has ... (Cao, 2009, p. 228)

Discussion of findings

The PhD Discussion chapter is concerned with constructing an overall argument or case based on the findings of the research carried out. The principal findings of this study of the five PhD Discussion chapters were that three key elements of the genre model (that framed the analysis) combined to construct expressions of critical thinking as part of the writer's extended argument or case. The elements were the recursive organizing schema or move structure (Point, Support, Evaluation); the use of key critical statements in the 'Evaluation' part of this schema; and, within the critical statements, the use of the metadiscourse devices of attitude markers and hedging (Hyland, 2005b). The Point and Support stages of the schema provided the basis or framework for the more overtly critical, third stage of Evaluation, which was found in 59 per cent of the occurrences of the schema. In some cases, its absence from the schematic structure seemed to suggest that writers believed that some points did not need to be confirmed by this critical element, while in other cases, from my perspective as the reader, it seemed that there was scope for adding an Evaluation that reflected the author's viewpoint.

However, as with the study in the previous chapter, it must be acknowledged that, because of the nature of the intensive manual analysis undertaken (157 pages of closely analysed, marked-up text), it was only possible to examine chapters from a small number of PhD theses. Also, because it was not logistically possible to fund and train multiple raters to provide comparative analyses, the study can only be considered to be an exploratory use of this particular research approach. Therefore, this was a small-scale study that ideally would be followed up by further research involving larger samples and texts from different disciplines.

In relation to previous research that has examined content-structuring 'moves' in Discussion chapters (Section 4.1), the findings of this study are broadly similar; they show a recursive pattern of first highlighting some aspect of a finding and then commenting on it in some way. In the PhD Discussion chapters, the communicative purposes of two optional steps of Basturkmen's (2009) 'Comment' move (explaining and comparing) are developed quite extensively in the 'Support' stage, but in most cases the writers used only one of these types of communicative purpose. In addition, in the PhD chapter sample, the Support stage was often realized by a different rhetorical purpose – exemplifying (providing supporting examples from the data) – which was not found in the studies of Yang and Allison (2003) or Basturkmen (2009). Exemplification, however, was a feature in the MSc Discussion studies of Hopkins and Dudley-Evans (1988) and of Dudley-Evans (1994). However, in focusing on the textual expression of critical thinking in this subgenre, I have proposed 'Evaluation' as a third stage (move) in this schema – unlike Yang and Allison (2003) and Basturkmen (2009), who propose 'Evaluation' as a step within their

'Commenting on Results' move. I have identified it as a separate move, differing from the two previous moves because it involves more personal, critical writing compared with that of the 'Point' and 'Comment' stages.

The two other elements that integrate with, and strengthen the 'Evaluation' are critical statements and their embedded metadiscourse devices. The critical statements' frequent use of two causal relations (Reason Result and Grounds Conclusion) is similar to the findings of Parkinson's (2011, p. 164) study of argumentation in Discussions in lab reports and RAs, where she found markers of 'cause', along with 'condition and purpose' to be important elements of arguing and proving knowledge claims. In relation to the use of metadiscourse devices, the use of hedging in research writing has been identified in earlier studies (e.g. Hyland, 1996), and it emerged the most frequently occurring interactional metadiscourse device in a sample of Results and Discussion chapters from engineering masters theses (Lee & Casal, 2014).

4.4 Implications for the teaching of writing

At the beginning of this chapter (in Section 4.1), I reviewed a number of books that offer advice about the Discussion chapter in thesis/dissertation writing. Collectively, they emphasize the need to express critical thinking in Discussions, specifically in evaluating how the findings of the study relate to the research question (or research purpose that motivated the enquiry), and in how they relate to other similar studies in the same field. However, beyond advice at that functional level, these books tend not to offer more detailed guidance about how critical thinking is expressed in this type of writing, such as in terms of the textual means employed.

In offering suggestions about how the findings of this study may be applied to teaching the writing of Discussions in applied linguistics or a related field and expressing critical thinking, I must offer the caveat that this was a small-scale exploratory study, and that there needs to be further research in this area involving other disciplines (and larger samples). However, these provisional findings appear to have implications for teaching the writing of the Discussion chapter of a thesis, which many writers find to be a difficult genre. Specifically, the three generic elements found to express the writers' critical evaluation of their findings may provide a lens through which writers of the genre can be guided to examine samples of texts extracted from Discussion chapters. The schematic structure, for example, could provide a basis for examining recursion in the content organization (moves), such as stating and developing points. It could be used to identify the types of knowledge that the Point stage consists of (an empirical finding or an argument based on a finding). Writers could consider the different ways of realizing the Support, such as by means of exemplification, explanation or comparison. Examples of Evaluations could then be examined for the occurrences of critical statements and the textual means they employ, such as in terms of the key coherence relations used and metadiscourse elements, along with the different ways in which these elements may be linguistically encoded. These 'noticing' activities could provide the basis for a more intense and decontextualized focus on these relations and the different textual means that could be used to express them. Finally, writers' attention could also be drawn to examples where there is no Evaluation in the schema and the effect of this on the overall argument.

While the current thesis-writing advice books focus on the functional role and critique function of this chapter, they tend not to go beyond this in the advice that they offer, such as how these requirements may be realized textually. The findings here, although a work in progress, suggest a framework of procedural and linguistic knowledge that can potentially be employed in the writing of the Discussion chapter and realizing its requirement to express critical thinking.

4.5 Implications for conceptualizing the expression of critical thinking in written text

In considering this second study in relation to the larger purpose of this volume, it is useful to compare its findings with those of the university essay genre study presented in the previous chapter. In terms of their overall communicative purposes, the two genres are broadly similar in that both are expected to construct an overall argument or case. However, the more specific communicative purposes of the PhD discussion chapter, involving its functional relationships with the other chapters of the thesis as well as the audience expectations that relate to this genre, differ somewhat from those of the essay. According to the advice literature on thesis writing and the surveys of academic faculty reviewed earlier in the chapter, the communicative purpose and functional role of the Discussion chapter in the thesis is to evaluate the findings in relation to the original purpose of the research as well as to previous research in the field. These evaluations as expressions of critical thinking contribute to the development of an extended argument or case through the duration of the chapter. The audience for the Discussion is expert members of the academic discourse community of the discipline in which the thesis is written, although the actual immediate audience will be the examiners of the thesis. In many universities, the standard that the thesis must meet often includes the two criteria of making an original contribution to knowledge and being of publishable quality. Thus, in the writing of this genre, there are specific communicative expectations and articulated standards that the writer must meet. Here, as was the case with the study of the essay genre presented in the previous chapter, the focus has been on the specific elements of the genre employed in the textual expression of critical thinking.

When comparing the findings of the two studies (essays and Discussion chapters), there is some overall similarity in how critical thinking is expressed through the texts of the two genres. The key element appears to be the interaction of textual resources operating at different levels. At the upper, organizational level, the PhD Discussion chapter has a more defined content schema than the essay – the highly recursive Point, Support, Evaluation move pattern – the instances of which, taken together, constitute the overall argument at a macro-level. The Point relates to a finding, the Support involves unpacking the finding, sometimes relating it back to previous research, and in the Evaluation move, the writer comments on the finding by making critical statements; these are the generic element that most overtly expresses critical thinking. However, what is striking when comparing the two studies of the essay and the Discussion chapter is the similarity of textual resources used in these critical statements. A comparison of Tables 3.1 and 3.2 of the essay genre chapter and Table 4.2 of the present chapter shows similar use of interpropositional relations to make critical statements, specifically the two causal relations of Grounds Conclusion and Reason Result, and the concessive contrast relation of Concession Contraexpectation. Also, embedded within these relations in the Evaluation move were the same two predominant metadiscourse devices used to construct writer stance, specifically attitude markers and hedging. In comparing the two genres, it would be fair to say that the essay genre, because of its nature, is looser in form and the distribution of the key critical statements is less bound to a higher-level organizational pattern. However, in the case of the Discussion chapter, the integration between the higher and lower-level elements is tighter, and control of this type of argument structure and these expressions of critical thinking is more closely framed by the higher-level schematic structure. Specifically, the critical statements framed by the key interpropositional relations tend to occur in the Evaluation part of the schematic structure, whereas they tend to be more freely distributed through texts of the two essay samples.

What emerges overall from the studies of the two genres (university essays and PhD Discussion chapters) is that the expression of critical thinking, through written text, emerges from the operation of elements working integratively within the texts. The findings also suggest that the analytical framework is able to provide a basis for comparing the similarities and differences in the operation of these elements within the two genres.

5

Expressing critical thinking in research article literature reviews

5.0 Introduction

In Chapter 5, I continue to explore how critical thinking is expressed in academic genres by examining its expression in literature reviews found in the Introduction sections of RAs. Literature reviews occur in all types of academic writing ranging from smaller-scale assignments at undergraduate level through to whole chapters in theses, dissertations and published books. In written genres that report research, such as academic journal articles, the main functions of a literature review are to background and to critique the specialist literature that relates to the entity or issue that is the object of research. This backgrounding and critique then provides a basis for justifying the research that is then reported. In this chapter, I focus on the latter critique function, and specifically examine how critical thinking is expressed through the literature review that occurs in the Introduction sections of research-reporting journal articles in two disciplines – applied linguistics and psychology. While this type of literature review is relatively small, it can be seen as a microcosm of those that occur in larger research-reporting genres, such as whole chapters in theses and dissertations.

In Section 5.1, I consider the requirements of literature reviews as they are articulated in books that offer advice about research writing and in studies that have identified students' difficulties with writing literature reviews, such as in constructing credible critiques. Then, in Section 5.2, I consider the target genre of the Introduction sections of research-reporting, academic journal articles, and briefly review the existing body of research that has examined this subgenre. Following this review, in Section 5.3, I report a study (Bruce, 2014a) in which I aimed to identify the actual generic devices used to express critical thinking in literature reviews in RA Introductions in the disciplines of applied linguistics and psychology. This study was first reported in the journal *English for Specific Purposes*, 2014, Volume 36 (2014, pp. 85–96) under the title of 'Expressing

Criticality in the Literature Review in RA Introductions in Applied Linguistics and Psychology'[1]. In Section 5.4, I discuss the implications of the findings of this study for the teaching of research writing. Then in Section 5.5, I again consider what the study of this particular genre further contributes to the overall goal of the volume of understanding how critical thinking is expressed through written text.

5.1 The literature review in research-reporting texts: Published advice and writer issues

The idea that, through the literature review sections or chapters of research-reporting texts (such as theses, dissertations and academic journal articles), a writer must express critical thinking appears to be a cornerstone value in much of the published 'advice' literature that aims to inform academic and research writing. For example, Bitchener (2010) states that 'the [literature] review is more than a summary ... it includes a critique that ... assesses or weighs up the value of theories, ideas, claims, research designs, methods or conclusions' (p. 61). Similarly, Cone and Foster (1993) state 'you should evaluate the literature critically. Which studies are best and why? Which studies are worst and why?' (p. 112). Also Paltridge and Starfield (2007) assert that '[s]tudents are expected not just to know the literature on their topic, but also to critically evaluate it' (p. 113). However, beyond establishing the need for critique and case-building through the literature review, the 'advice' manuals on research writing are generally silent about how this critique is achieved, such as in terms of the textual features that can be employed.

Among these published manuals that provide 'advice' about literature review writing for novice researchers, there appear to be two detectable tendencies: one which I term the 'study skills' approach and the other, the 'academic writing' approach. Some are a hybrid, combining the 'study skills' and 'academic writing' approaches (e.g. Ridley, 2012). Manuals following the 'study skills' approach (e.g. Cone & Foster, 1993; Rudestam & Newton, 2007) offer advice concerning the collection of texts (to review) and framing the types of questions to apply to the review of literature. They also offer advice about searching databases, referencing and discrete-point aspects of linguistic style. However, this type of manual does not usually address the issue of the actual construction of the text. Beyond emphasizing the need for critique or critical evaluation, they provide little guidance about how it is achieved. On the other hand, advice books following the 'academic writing' approach offer suggestions about the internal organization of the literature review text, such as whether the chapter is thematic, chronological or grouped around research questions or variables and also the organizational 'move structures' of smaller sections within the text. While going further than advice texts in the first category, their focus tends to be on the rhetorical organization of the content within the text in terms of moves and submoves (or steps), such as in terms of claims, evidence for claims and identifying research gaps (e.g. Bitchener, 2010). Manuals of this latter category are valuable in that they provide insights into the various ways that literature review chapters may be organized. They offer approaches to structuring and presenting summaries of literature as well as the need to identify gaps and shortcomings in the extant research. To their credit, most acknowledge that this can be achieved in a multiplicity of ways, but they too, like the 'study skills' manuals, do not usually include a focus on the textual resources, needed to establish this critique function.

In addition to the advice manuals about literature review writing, there are a number of studies that focus on the problems faced by the writers of the literature review, and specifically the difficulty in establishing a critical stance when writing literature review texts. For example, Boote and Beile (2005) identify, among other problems, a failure to synthesize and critique in the literature reviews of doctoral dissertations. Casanave and Hubbard (1992) highlight problems of dissertation writers in analysing and criticizing ideas (p. 43), and an in-depth case study by Zhu and Cheng (2008) examines the difficulties faced by a non-native speaker doctoral dissertation writer in critically evaluating literature. In relation to literature reviews in RAs, Alton-Lee (1998) identified a range of problems from reviewers' comments on submissions to a journal by inexperienced writers, including 'the failure by authors to critically interrogate the material they reviewed' (p. 889).

The RA is an important genre to be mastered by emergent researchers, and the study reported in Section 5.3 examines its literature review and the ways in which critical thinking is enacted in this type of text. However, to provide a research context for this study, the following section begins with a brief review of landmark genre studies that have examined Introduction sections of RAs, focusing on how the conventionalized textual features of the genre are described.

5.2 The subgenre of research article Introductions: Previous research

RAs that appear in academic journals are conventionally divided into the four main sections of Introduction, Method, Results (Findings) and Discussion although these divisions are not fixed, and the naming of these principal sections may vary. For example, the Findings and Discussion sections in some RAs may be conflated, and a Conclusion section may be added after the Discussion. Also the ordering of the sections may vary, for example, the Methods section may be located at the end of some chemistry RAs. A study by Berkenkotter and Huckin (1995) of RAs in physics, biology and general science, published from 1944 to 1989, shows that the genre changed gradually over time to meet the communicative requirements of these disciplines in terms of focusing on new developments in the reported research and easing information-processing for the reader. However, despite some variation in its organization and in the naming and length of its sections, the RA appears to be a relatively conventionalized genre, which, in many disciplines, is the principal vehicle for the reporting of new research.

For academic writers seeking to achieve publication, the Introduction section of the RA is seen as a particularly important, strategic section of the genre. Paltridge and Starfield (2007) state that 'in the fierce academic competition to get papers published in reputable academic journals, the Introduction is extremely important in positioning the writer as having something to say that is worth publishing' (p. 82). Because of its importance, the Introduction has been the most heavily researched section of the RA genre. This research has mostly been carried out by those working in the field of ESP, and has the purpose of informing and supporting the publication efforts of aspirant researchers and, in particular, the growing body of researchers for whom English is a second language. From his research on this subgenre of the RA Introduction section, Swales (1981, 1990, 2004) has proposed a *move* structure or conventionalized pattern for the organization of the content of the Introduction section of RAs (see Table 5.1).

The operationalization of the subgenre of the Introduction section in the ESP stream of genre research has been largely in terms of two main elements: the move structure that relates to the organization of content (see Table 5.1), and recurrent linguistic features that characterize each move. For example, in relation to Move 2, which identifies the niche or research space that a writer is seeking to occupy by his/her research, Swales (1990) states that 'the move opens with an adversative sentence-connector. Across various samples of RA Introductions, about a quarter of Move 2s are initiated with such signals, most commonly *however* but also *nevertheless, yet, unfortunately* and *but*' (p. 154). Within the social genre/cognitive genre model used here to analyse the samples of RA Introductions, Swales's three-move structure is employed to account for the content schema element of the samples of texts (see Table 2.2). It is, therefore,

Table 5.1 Swales' 'Create a Research Space' (CARS) Move Structure

Move 1 Establish a research territory

a. by showing that the general research area is important, central, interesting, problematic or relevant in some way. (optional)

b. by introducing and reviewing items of previous research in the area. (obligatory)

Move 2 Establishing a niche by indicating a gap in the previous research, raising a question about it, or extending previous knowledge in some way. (obligatory)

Move 3 Occupying the niche

a. by indicating a gap in the previous research, raising a question about it, or extending previous knowledge in some way. (obligatory)

b. by listing the research questions or hypotheses (PSIF*)

c. by announcing principal findings. (PSIF)

d. by indicating the structure of the RP. (PSIF)

*PSIF = probably in some fields but rare in others.
(Swales & Feak, 2012, Unit 8, Figure 16, p. 331).
Reprinted with permission from the University of Michigan Press.

incorporated as an important, but not the sole element, of the genre framework used in the analysis of the two samples of texts.

In Swales's CARS (create a research space) pattern for the organization of the content of the Introduction (presented in Table 5.1), the literature review section lies within Move 1(b), which is obligatory and has the function of 'introducing and reviewing items of previous research in the area' (Swales & Feak, 2012, p. 331). However, Samraj (2002), in an interdisciplinary study, found that the literature review may be found in other parts of the Introduction section in addition to Move 1(b). Also the study by Kwan et al. (2012) of Introduction sections from the discipline of information systems focused centrally on literature review elements in Move 2, examining what they termed 'strategies' used by writers to express evaluation, such as 'making inferences, counter-claiming' or 'claiming relevancy' when claiming a niche in their field to justify their research. Therefore, it seems that reviewing the literature may extend beyond the first move of a CARS move analysis.

5.3 Expressing critical thinking in research article literature reviews (Bruce, 2014a)

Building on this previous ESP research of the characteristics of the subgenre of RA Introductions, I undertook a small-scale exploratory study of two samples of fifteen RA Introduction texts from the social science disciplines of applied linguistics and psychology. The purpose of this study was to identify the actual generic features employed by writers to express critical thinking through the literature review in each Introduction section. Using the lens of the social genre/cognitive genre model outlined in Chapter 2 (Section 2.5), I examined different layers of knowledge in the literature review sections to identify those elements specifically used to express critical thinking. As outlined in Chapter 2, the model contains seven potentially genre-characterizing areas of knowledge (see Table 2.2), and it is an attempt at a comprehensive operationalization of genre knowledge. One of the elements of the model is the content schema for describing the organization of the content of the genre. Given the depth of existing ESP research on Introduction sections, I used Swales's three-move CARS structure to examine the content schema dimension of the model as a way of initially identifying the literature review segments within the Introduction sections.

In this section, I first describe the two samples of RA Introduction texts whose literature review sections are the object of the study. I then describe how I used the social genre/cognitive genre model to perform the analysis of the two samples of texts. I then present and discuss the findings of the analysis.

The samples of texts

In designing this exploratory study, I decided to explore literature review writing in two social science disciplines in reports of research that used a positivist approach, which Dornyei (2007) states requires 'substantial initial coverage of the literature' (p. 295). In contrast, reports of interpretative (naturalistic), qualitative studies may employ a different type of initial literature review with a lesser amount of detailed, background knowledge. Therefore, the articles in both samples tended to have the main review of literature integrated within or as a subsection of the Introduction. Applied linguistics was chosen as a newer social science subject that often has an interdisciplinary focus, and psychology was selected as a social science discipline with a somewhat longer history.

To identify a research issue and a potential body of texts from each discipline, I contacted a published researcher in each discipline, each of whom supplied a brief bibliography of approximately twenty published articles reporting research that was closest to their respective areas of interest. From each bibliography, I selected, non-purposively, a sample of fifteen Introduction sections. The size of each sample was based on what I considered feasible for an intensive manual analysis of the texts in this genre-based study. For example, the applied linguistics sample consisted of eighty-six pages of Introduction sections and the psychology sample fifty pages. In most of the texts selected, the literature review was embedded within the Introduction and was not identified as a separate subsection of it. However, four texts had a subtitled literature review section within the Introduction: Texts 3, 10 and 11 in the applied linguistics sample and Text 13 in the psychology sample.

Sample 1, from the field of applied linguistics, included fifteen articles that report research in the area of second-language writing instruction. Specifically, these are studies that examine the learning effectiveness of the written corrective feedback that students receive from writing instructors. In the bibliography provided, at least two of the key researchers in the field appear as the co-author of more than one article, but it was decided to include these in the sample in order to preserve the integrity of the bibliography supplied by the informant – that is, articles that are central to the informant researcher's particular area of research interest. Following the methodological classifications of Cohen, Manion and Morrison (2011), the research approach of the studies of the sample tends to be positivist, the research style experimental and the data collection method involves the use of a task to elicit a sample of writing, which is scored quantitatively, usually to measure the effect of writing instruction that has involved the provision of corrective feedback.

Sample 2 was selected from a bibliography supplied by a researcher from the field of psychology and consists of studies that investigate issues that relate to the acculturation and cultural adjustment of immigrant youth, issues such as stress and identity. Although it was initially envisaged that the RAs in this sample would be less interdisciplinary, this was not the case as the researcher nominated some articles from other, related fields, specifically social work (Text 2), counselling (Text 5), public health (Text 11) and psychiatry (Text 13). Again, using the terminologies of Cohen, Manion and Morrison (2011), the research 'approach' of the studies is positivist, the research 'style' tends to be survey and the data collection is by questionnaire, interview and personal account.

Analysis

I performed the analysis of each sample manually using the social genre/cognitive genre model summarized in Table 2.2 as a heuristic framework. The analysis involved intensive, recursive readings to examine the texts in relation to each knowledge element of the model. At each stage, a paper copy of each text was marked up to identify the particular generic feature under scrutiny. Because I had decided to use Swales' move structure (Table 5.1) to analyse the content schema, the first stage of the analysis involved marking up the whole of each Introduction section in terms of the moves that occurred. Then the specific moves concerned with the review of literature were analysed in terms of their expression of critical thinking. They were examined in terms of other elements of the model – the use of contextual knowledge, epistemological viewpoint relating to the validation of knowledge (such as research methods), writer stance in terms of Hyland's metadiscourse model and cognitive genres, segments of text related to a single, general rhetorical purpose and their particular elements.

The findings

From the analysis of both samples of texts, I found that, when reviewing literature, the writers consistently expressed critical thinking by means of their use of three elements of genre knowledge from the seven listed in Table 2.2:

- recursion in the content schema organization (operationalized in this study in terms of Swales' three-move structure for RA Introductions – see Table 5.1);
- use of the metadiscourse device that Hyland (2005b, p. 49) terms attitude markers; and,
- use of a cognitive genre element – a recurrent concessive contrast relation between propositions, which I identify in terms of Crombie's (1985) Concession Contraexpectation interpropositional relation.

During the analysis of both samples, it became apparent that the second and third elements are often used in combination. For example, attitude markers may be embedded within the Concession Contraexpectation relation, usually in the second, point-making proposition.

Use of content schema (move structure)

The first element of genre knowledge that related to the expression of critical thinking is the conventionalized structuring of content (content schema), which I analysed in terms of Swales' three-move structure for RA Introductions presented in Table 5.1. After doing the initial move analysis, I decided (as mentioned previously) to include Move 2 as part of the literature review because I found that this move employs quotes, paraphrases and citations from other authors to support a writer's argument for their own research space. (Thus the combination of Move 1b and Move 2 constituted the literature reviews examined in the study.) This finding accords with Samraj's (2002) view that the literature review can occur in other moves in the Introduction section, and also with Kwan et al's (2012) focus on literature review elements in Move 2 of their sample. Table 5.2 outlines my analysis of the move structure of the whole of each Introduction section from the applied linguistics articles and Table 5.3 shows the move structures of the psychology article Introductions.

What emerges from the move analysis of both samples is not a linear but a *recursive* use of Swales' move structure, often beginning with an abbreviated statement of the three moves, and a return to expanded versions of Move 1b (review of prior literature) and Move 2 (the research space). Also, when the literature reviews dealt with different streams of research or theory or separately, there also tended to be the same recursive Move1b/Move 2 sequence, with one sequence for each stream of research or theory. This recursive use of the CARS move structure was also found by Kwan (2006, p. 50) in her study of PhD literature review chapters.

In relation to the expression of critical thinking in literature reviews, the recursive presentation of Move 1b and Move 2 appears to have an evaluative, highlighting function at two levels. First it is a way of emphasizing the importance of the literature review and niche-claiming moves of each Introduction section by first announcing them in abbreviated forms and then returning to a more

Table 5.2 Move Structure in the Introductions of the Applied Linguistics Texts

Text	Move Structure
1	1a, 2, 1b, 2, 3a
2	1a, 2, 3a, 1b, 2, 3a, 3b
3	1a, 2, 3a, 1b, 2, 3b
4	1a, 1b, 2, 3a, 2, 3b
5	1a, 1b, 2, 3b
6	1a, 2, 3a, 1b, 2, 1b, 2, 3b
7	1a, 1b, 2, 1b, 2, 3a, 3b
8	1a, 1b, 1b, 2, 3b, 3a
9	1a, 3a, 1b, 2, 1b, 2, 3b
10	1a, 3a, 1b, 2, 3a, 3b
11	1a, 1b, 2, 1b, 2, 1b, 2, 3a, 3b
12	1a, 1b, 2, 1b, 3b
13	1a, 1b, 2, 3b, 1b, 2, 1b, 2, 1b, 2
14	1a, 1b, 2, 1b, 3a, 3b
15	1a, 1b, 2, 3a

(Bruce, 2014a, Table 2, p. 89).

Table 5.3 Move Structure in the Introductions of the Psychology-related Texts

Text	Move Structure
1	1a, 1b, 2, 3b, 1b, 3a
2	1a, 1b, 2, 3a, 1b, 2, 3a, 1b, 2, 3a
3	1a, 2, 1b, 3a, 1b, 3a
4	1a, 1b, 2, 1b, 2, 1b, 3a
5	1a, 1b, 2, 1a, 1b, 3a
6	1a, 3a, 1b, 2, 3a, 1b, 3a
7	1a, 1b, 2, 1b, 2, 3a, 3b
8	1a, 1b, 2, 3a
9	1a, 1b, 2, 1b, 2, 1b, 2, 3a
10	1a, 1b, 2, 3a
11	1a, 1b, 3a
12	1a, 1b, 2, 1b, 2, 1b, 3a
13	1a, 1b, 2, 3a
14	1a, 1b, 2, 1b, 3b
15	1a, 1b, 2, 3a

(Bruce, 2014a, Table 3, p. 90).

in-depth treatment of both moves. At a more detailed level, the Move 1b and Move 2 pattern operates as a type of recursive 'topic comment' relation as a way of developing the points of the argument or case of the literature review. For example, Move 1b introduces and reviews previous research studies in a descriptive way; Move 2 then comments evaluatively by indicating a gap in this previous research, such as the lacks or shortcomings of the previous studies. The following summary of moves from Applied Linguistics Text 6 shows the first occurrence as the overview of the literature review followed by more detailed 'topic comment' occurrences. (This text will be also used to exemplify the other two generic elements used to express critical thinking).

- Move 1a outlines the issue of corrective feedback and L2 language development, and includes six illustrative references.
- Move 2 introduces the research issue by questioning the generalizability of previous studies, and it raises the issue of the influence of the learning environment on the provision of corrective feedback.
- Move 3a states the three purposes of the study.
- Move 1b follows with an extended review of previous research on corrective feedback.
- Move 2 recurs briefly, highlighting the conflicting findings reported in the preceding Move 1b and pointing to these findings as further evidence for considering the variable of instructional setting.

- Move 1b recurs reviewing a smaller number of studies that have examined the link between context and corrective feedback.
- Move 2 then recurs briefly by pointing to the lack of inter-contextual studies.
- Move 3b states the three research questions.

Thus recursion in the literature review-presenting moves (1b and 2) is employed to introduce, highlight and subsequently develop in detail the case that the literature review is presenting, that is, the need to consider the variable of the learning environment in investigating the learning effectiveness of corrective feedback. This use of the functional staging of a text to achieve an evaluative purpose was also identified in the study by Cortazzi and Jin (2000) in terms of the related roles of 'complication, resolution and coda' stages of narrative structures, with the latter two stages commenting evaluatively on the former.

Writer stance – use of attitude markers

The second element of the social genre/cognitive genre model found to express critical thinking in the samples of texts were linguistic devices used to establish writer stance, devices termed attitude markers. In Hyland's (2005b) metadiscourse model, he states that attitude markers 'express the writer's attitude to a proposition' (p. 49). Hyland goes on to say that attitude markers 'indicate the writer's affective, rather than epistemic, attitude to propositions ... [and are] signalled metadiscoursally by attitude verbs (e.g. agree, prefer), sentence adverbs (unfortunately, hopefully) and adjectives (appropriate, logical, remarkable)' (p. 53). When identifying this device in the sample, along with single lexical items, it seemed salient to include word groups (usually noun or verb phrases) in order to provide a complete sense of the use of a particular evaluative item by including its co-occurring words.

While all of the attitude markers of each text of the two samples were recorded in the analysis, it is not possible to list them here. Instead, Table 5.4 provides a summary of those found in the longest occurrence of Move 1b in the applied linguistics texts, and Table 5.5 presents those used in the main occurrence of Move 1b from the psychology texts. Care was taken to include only attitude markers that reflect the writer's own viewpoint and not the reported viewpoints of others. While not exhaustive, these tables provide illustrative examples of the type and nature of this metadiscourse device.

The total number of attitude markers over the whole of each sample was 133 in the literature reviews of the fifteen applied linguistics texts, compared with sixty-six in

Table 5.4 Sample of Attitude Markers in one Move 1b Occurrence: Applied Linguistics Texts

Text	Move 1b
1	'no statistically significant differences; makes comparison difficult; highly inferential nature of coding; mixed results[from multiple studies]'
2	'may affect its effectiveness; the important role of; relationship has to be demonstrated',
3	'very few have included; post-test only required; not compared with a control; limited research base; conflicting findings [from multiple studies]'
4	'ineffective or harmful; perplexed; elusive; inadequate',
5	'cannot be used to claim; suffer from other problems; contentious; other design flaws; less than satisfactory'*
6	'provision of CF is often arbitrary; ambiguous; unsystematic; little empirical evidence; limited to; needs to be interpreted cautiously; conflicting results'
7	'sufficient evidence; further research is required; research evidence to suggest; it is possible; it may well be the case'
8	'such a view is not unproblematic; difficult to argue that; some doubts; also lend support; constitute a perfect environment' *
9	'this view .. has minimized if not dismissed; relatively few studies; even less research; a number of methodological limitations; (research findings) have failed to provide'
10	'seems to be some doubt; so far been limited to; has yet to be explored; limited research; is effectively helping; limitations in the design and execution; raises questions about'
11	'conclusion ... should be treated with caution; neither study found statistically significant differences; growing but far from conclusive body of research'
12	'need to be examined closely; but students were not required to do anything; no significant differences between them; improvement was not statistically significant'
13	'only a few studies have; conflicting results; evidence ... supports further investigation'
14	'statements ... require further discussion; have certain limitations; it would be foolhardy to assume; no certain way of knowing; given so few published studies'
15	'the revision research is not relevant; the question ... is quite important; this discussion can be taken as an implicit rejection; important consequences for the debate'

* For reasons of space, not all the attitude markers from this Move 1b section were included. (Bruce, 2014a, Table 4, p. 91).

the fifteen psychology texts. Therefore, these critical attitude markers are relatively sparse in each text, with an average of 8.8 occurrences in the literature review of the applied linguistics texts and an average number of 4.4 in the psychology texts. Each attitude marker tends to occur in conjunction with a considerable amount of detailed description of the research or theory under review.

The mapping of attitude markers within the move structure in the example text (Applied Linguistics Text 6) is provided in Table 5.6. In each occurrence, the attitude marker is italicized, bolded and presented with some co-text.

Table 5.5 Sample of Attitude Markers in one Move 1b Occurrence: Psychology Texts

Text	Move 1b
1	
2	'varied and inconclusive results; failed to demonstrate'
3	'may help in some aspects; may not be totally beneficial; it is important to differentiate; reflect the complexity of'
4	'relatively few studies; limited research … warrant additional scrutiny'
5	'limited research on Asian immigrants; did not present a true picture; understanding … is of particular interest'
6	'the implications … are ambiguous'
7	'findings … neither consistent nor conclusive; a major limitation; calls into question; no substantial evidence; highlight the importance of; one of the most interesting and robust pieces of research'
8	'it remains unclear'
9	'considerable disagreement; no real consensus … lack of consensus'
10	'found the opposite; findings are mixed'
11	'limited evidence'
12	'common assumption has not been consistently affirmed; association … is insignificant'
13	'only a few studies examine … fewer empirical studies investigate; inconsistencies probably indicate'
14	
15	

(Bruce, 2014a, Table 5, p. 91).

Even with little contextual information, it can be seen that the attitude markers were used to deficitize aspects of the research that is being reviewed, often by identifying a methodological or conceptual weakness. As Swales (1990, p. 155) notes, this often involves some kind of negation, usually lexical, but also through the use of negative quantifiers. The use of a lexical resources to perform this evaluative function accords with previous corpus studies that have noted evaluation through the use of verbs (Charles 2006; Diani, 2009; Tucker, 2003), adverbials (Conrad & Biber, 2000; Dressen, 2003) and a combination of lexical resources (Channell, 2000; Shaw, 2003; Stotesbury, 2003). I also found that attitude markers occurred often (but not always) within a Concession Contraexpectation interpropositional relation; this relation is explained and exemplified in the next subsection.

Use of the Concession Contraexpectation interpropositional relation

The third element used to express critical thinking in the samples is a particular concessive contrast relation between two propositions, a relation that Crombie (1985) terms 'Concession Contraexpectation'. Her definition states 'In this

Table 5.6 Attitude Markers in Applied Linguistics Text 6

Move 1a	
Move 2	'however … it is **not clear** to what extent
Move 3	
Move 1b	'teachers' provision of CF is often **arbitrary, ambiguous and unsystematic**'
	'argue **convincingly** … but **little empirical evidence**'
	'the repair rate needs to be interpreted **cautiously**'
Move 2	'Given these **conflicting** findings, it seems **worthwhile** to examine … '
Move 1b	'there have been **few studies*** of the contextual factors'
	'evidence for a **clear** role of pedagogical context'
	'produced **significantly** more modified output'
Move 2	'there have been **no studies*** **specifically** comparing'
Move 3	

* 'few studies' and 'no studies' fall somewhat outside of the definition of attitude markers, but are included here because of the critique role that they play (Bruce, 2014a, Table 6, p. 92).

relation, the truth of an inference is directly or indirectly denied' (Crombie, 1985, p. 23). Crombie explains that this relation may be signalled linguistically by subordinators, prepositions, conjuncts and adjuncts (p. 88). The order of the propositions appears to be significant in relation to the expression of critical thinking. When the order of the propositions is affirmative/negative, the writer tends to be cautiously criticizing someone else's work. For example:

> While the findings from this research are interesting and may well be indicative of the effectiveness of corrective feedback, they were not compared with the accuracy scores of a control group so cannot be read as evidence. (Applied Linguistics Sample, Text 3, p. 105)

> Truscott (1996) … built his first argument against the value of WCF around the belief that a simple transfer of information (in the form of WCF) cannot be expected to work. However, this stance does not take into account the fact that learners who notice the difference between target-like input and their non target-like output are able to modify it as target like output. (Applied Linguistics Sample, Text 7, p. 194)

> Despite wide-ranging research on acculturation, there is limited research specifically on Asian immigrants due to the 'model minority' stereotype. (Psychology Sample, Text 5, p. 172)

However, when the order of the propositions was reversed, negative/affirmative, they tended to be positively evaluating the writer's own research agenda:

> Given the substantial differences in the purposes and designs of these studies, care needs to be taken in any attempt to generalize the findings. However, overall,

the results point to an advantage for explicit over implicit corrected feedback in studies in which the treatment involved production. (Applied Linguistics Sample, Text 8, p. 349)

In short, this research base, limited as it is in terms of its target forms/structures, demonstrates, nevertheless, that written CF is effective in helping L2 writers improve the accuracy of their writing. (Applied Linguistics Sample, Text 10, p. 209)

The Concession Contraexpectation relation often had the role of making an important critical point, sometimes at the end of a paragraph or as the key part of a concluding argument.

Tables 5.7 and 5.8 provide aggregate summaries of all of the occurrences of this relation from the different occurrences of Move 1b and Move 2 in each text of the two samples. The relations are shown in terms of the order of the propositions: negative/affirmative or affirmative/negative.

In terms of its role in literature review texts, I found that the Concession Contraexpectation relation was often used to make an important point, often at the end of a paragraph or as the key part of a concluding argument. This role appears to fulfil the important rhetorical strategy of *counterclaiming* identified by Kwan et al. (2012, p. 197). The examples that they provide appear to mirror this relation, especially those from behavioural science research texts.

Table 5.7 Numbers of Occurrences of the Concession Contraexpectation Relation in the Applied Linguistics Texts

Text	Move 1b	Move 2
1	negative/affirmative (3) affirmative/negative (3)	affirmative/negative (3)
2	negative/affirmative (2)	
3	affirmative/negative (7) negative/affirmative (1)	
4	negative/affirmative (1)	affirmative/negative (6) negative/affirmative (3)*
5	negative/affirmative (5)	
6	negative/affirmative (2)	negative/affirmative (1)*
7	negative/affirmative (3) affirmative/negative (3)	affirmative/negative (1)
8	negative/affirmative (2)*	
9	affirmative/negative (2)	
10	affirmative/negative (6)	
11	affirmative/negative (4)*	negative/affirmative (1)
12	affirmative/negative (4)	
13		affirmative/negative (1)
14	affirmative/negative (4) negative/affirmative (2)*	
15		

* The occurrences of the relation in more than one occurrence of the move are combined here (Bruce, 2014a, Table 7, p. 93).

Table 5.8 Numbers of Occurrences of the Concession Contraexpectation Relation in the Psychology Texts

Text	Move 1b	Move 2
1	affirmative/negative (1)	
2	negative/affirmative (1) affirmative/negative (1)*	affirmative/negative (1)
3	negative/affirmative (1) affirmative/negative (1)	
4	affirmative/negative (1)*	affirmative/negative (1) negative/affirmative (1)
5	affirmative/negative (2)	affirmative/negative (1)
6	affirmative/negative (3)*	
7	affirmative/negative (1)	
8	affirmative/negative (1)	affirmative/negative (1)
9	negative/affirmative (2)*	
10	affirmative/negative (1)	
11	affirmative/negative (1)	
12	affirmative/negative (3)*	
13		
14		
15		affirmative/negative (1)

* The occurrences of the relation in more than one instance of the move are combined here (Bruce, 2014a, Table 8, p. 93).

Discussion

The findings from this study show that, in expressing critical thinking in the review of literature in the Introduction sections from the two samples of RAs, writers use three generic features: recursion in the organization of the moves, attitude markers and the Concession Contraexpectation relation. However, because the study used small exploratory samples, no claims are made here concerning disciplinary difference in the expression of critical thinking through this type of literature review. Also because it was not logistically possible to fund and train multiple researchers to provide comparative analyses of the texts, the results from this exploratory study can only be considered to be indicative. Nevertheless, from the study, issues that can be considered include: how its findings relate to previous research; the possible need for a more integrated approach to researching the textual expression of critical thinking (such as using a genre-based approach); and the actual teaching the writing of the literature review in the RA Introduction, which is discussed in Section 5.4.

Several of the elements identified in the present study as communicating critical thinking appear to confirm earlier studies in this area, such as the use of rhetorical structuring (Cortazzi & Jin, 2000); the use of lexical resources to evaluate (e.g. Channell, 2000; Conrad & Biber, 2000; Tucker, 2003); and especially the issue of 'counter-claiming' as an important strategy of literature reviews (Kwan et al., 2012). However, what identifies this study as different from some of the earlier corpus-based research is the use of the genre-based approach and manual analysis in order to identify different types of devices used to communicate critical thinking and to examine how they mutually interact in its communication. The co-occurrence and interrelatedness of these elements again appear to suggest that approaches to researching the expression of critical thinking need to move beyond studies that focus on a single rhetorical or linguistic element (identified by corpus searching), and to consider ways of theorizing and researching a text and its related discourse as an integrative whole. This study aimed to examine different knowledge elements at different levels, broadly framed by Bhatia's (2004, p. 19) proposal that discourse involves the knowledge areas of social practice, genre and text. As with the other studies reported in this volume, the social genre/cognitive genre model employed here attempts to operationalize the underlying constructs of genre and text in terms of a number of knowledge areas in order to provide a lens through which to search for those elements specifically involved in the communication of critical thinking. This approach builds to some extent on previous ESP genre analyses that have focused on the conventionally recognized purposes and content structuring of texts (in terms of moves), sometimes linked to linguistic elements (Swales, 1990, 2004). However, the focus here on textual elements identifies them through potentially more inclusive non-linguistic categories, such as attitude markers (from Hyland's metadiscourse theory) and the Concession Contraexpectation relation (from Crombie's taxonomy of interpropositional relations) – categories that allow for a range of different types of linguistic encoding of these devices.

5.4 Implications for the teaching of writing

In Section 5.1, I reported that published manuals that offer advice on research writing generally agree that the literature review should perform a critically evaluative function in relation to the existing literature in the field, as part of building a justification for the research that is to be reported (e.g. Bitchener, 2010; Cone & Foster, 1993; Paltridge & Starfield, 2007). Also in that section, I pointed out that a range of studies have found that novice research writers have difficulties in achieving this critique role in literature review writing (Alton-Lee, 1998; Boote & Beile, 2005; Casanave & Hubbard, 1992; Zhu & Cheng, 2008). Therefore, for those involved in teaching research writing, and in particular teaching the writing of the literature review, addressing this issue of how to express critical thinking – how to build a critique of literature – would seem to be important.

Although exploratory and indicative, the findings of this study suggest that the three identified elements of the genre used to express critical thinking could usefully be considered in pedagogy that focuses on research literature review writing. First, in relation to the move structure, this could involve a top-down analysis of small number of literature review texts from different disciplines, identifying the moves that specifically relate to the literature review. In particular, Introduction sections could be examined for instances of the Move 1b–Move 2 ('topic, comment') pattern as a way of expressing evaluation at a macro level. A second area for a pedagogic focus could involve consciousness-raising about attitude markers, what they are and the types of linguistic features that can be used to perform this function. Once student writers are familiar with this device, then the location and role of attitude markers in their sample of literature review texts could be considered. Finally, there would seem to be value in introducing students to the Concession Contraexpectation relation, including the various ways in which this is encoded (see Crombie, 1985, pp. 22, 88–91). When students are familiar with the function and the range of possible linguistic forms for expressing this relation, they could then examine its occurrences and roles in the previously examined literature review texts, roles such as in critique, point-making and boundary marking. However, also when considering the study, it is important to emphasize that the findings here indicate that these devices are used sparingly to express critical thinking. This suggests that any pedagogic focus on these should caution against future overuse of these devices by novice writers in their own outputs.

5.5 Implications for conceptualizing the expression of critical thinking in written text

This concluding section of the chapter reflects again on what this third study contributes to the overall goal of this volume, that is, of investigating how critical thinking is expressed through written text. The research study reported in this chapter examined the RA literature review, which, compared to the relatively loosely structured genre of the academic essay (Chapter 3) and the more extended genre of the PhD Discussion (Chapter 4), is a highly conventionalized, carefully crafted piece of 'high-stakes' published writing, which aims to report research to an expert, discipline-specific audience. This genre differs from the essay and Discussion chapter in two respects. First, rather than displaying knowledge to promote and demonstrate learning by novice writers (as is the case of the academic essay), or achieving a 'rite-of-passage' presentation of an extended, evidence-based, academic argument, such as in the PhD Discussion chapter, the RA is intended to reflect a maturity of knowledge and written expression characteristic of a fully fledged member of an academic community. The mature writer uses the genre as a way of demonstrating their expertise by introducing and, importantly, *justifying* the need for their research to uncover further knowledge in the field beyond what is currently known. Second, while the essay genre had a broad overall shape and some flexibility in its realization and the Discussion chapter had a fairly regular recursive content schema, RA Introduction sections have a highly conventionalized move structure to which published writers appear to conform closely. This move structure has been described in many studies in terms of Swales' (1990) CARS move structure, each move identifying a key communicative purpose that has to be achieved within this relatively dense, compact type of writing.

In the Introduction section of the RA, a key function of the literature review appears to be the presentation of the overall justificatory argument or case for the research being reported in the subsequent sections of the article (method, results and discussion). In terms of how critical thinking is expressed in the literature reviews of the two samples of texts, the findings from the study reveal the involvement of three generic elements operating at different levels. First, at the level of the organization of the content of the text (the content schema), the move structure emerged as a case-presenting, evaluative element in terms of the 'background-critique' relationship of the recursive Move 1b – Move 2 textual relation. Secondly, at a more specific level, evaluative statements framed by Crombie's Concession Contraexpectation relation, emerged as an important element in the expression of critical thinking. These statements had the roles of both critiquing the research and theory of others and positively evaluating the research approach of the study; their critiquing or affirming roles depended on the order of the propositions (affirmative/negative or negative/affirmative). The third element was use of the metadiscourse device of attitude markers, which reinforced the critical view of the writer. In RA literature reviews, like the studies reported in the two previous chapters, this study also shows that the expression of critical thinking through text is complex, involving knowledge of the discipline and genre knowledge relating to the conventionalized texts used for communication within the discipline.

Overall, in the three academic genres examined in Chapters 3 to 5, the core principle that emerges is the *integration* of higher and lower-level elements to achieve the expression of critical thinking and of building the overall case of the writer. The higher-level elements relate to the structuring of content through sections or moves. A range of similar coherence relations are used to frame critical statements at a propositional level. At a lower level, key metadiscourse devices that help to construct the writer's stance can be found embedded within these statements and sometimes distributed elsewhere within the text.

6

Expressing critical thinking in corporate disclosure communication

6.0 Introduction

In Chapters 3, 4 and 5, I considered studies that examined the textual expression of critical thinking through three academic genres – essays, PhD Discussion chapters and RA literature reviews. In this chapter, I move away from academic writing and consider a business genre from the area of corporate disclosure communication, specifically the genre of the 'Fund Manager Commentary' (hereafter the FMC). This category of text is a monthly or quarterly voluntary disclosure document in which managers of investment funds provide a regular report on the state of their funds to investors and the wider public. The FMC is usually a relatively brief document of about two pages in length, and it is either posted on the company's website or sent to investors as an email newsletter. It usually includes the current earnings of the fund, its immediate past performance during the reporting period, the state of the markets in which the fund invests (including salient external events and trends) and the investment strategies that will be pursued in the immediate future. The FMC genre is the product of the internet era, reflecting the electronic medium through which it is produced, which means that it is often a multimodal document containing text, graphics that display quantitative data and banners, and it may include hypertext links.

The study reported in this chapter first appeared in the *International Journal of Business Communication*(2014, pp. 315–36) under the title 'Enacting Criticality in Corporate Disclosure Communication: The Genre of the Fund Manager Commentary'(Bruce, 2014b).[1] In researching this genre, I first attempted to identify and understand its key characteristic features and its communicative purposes as a basis for then identifying those generic features specifically used to express critical thinking. This is similar to my approach to the university essay genre, where descriptive work on the genre was first carried out (and reported as separate studies) before examining the expression of critical thinking in that genre.

I begin the chapter by defining the term 'corporate disclosure' and by considering the various purposes for publishing disclosure documents. I then review the approaches that have been used to research such documents. Following this, I present the study of the FMC genre, its sample, methodology and some discussion of the findings. As with the three previous chapters, I then discuss the implications of the study for the teaching of writing – in this case, professional writing. I again conclude the chapter by considering the implications of this study for the wider purpose of this volume – how critical thinking is expressed through disciplinary writing, including how its expression in the FMC genre is similar to, and differs from, its expression in the academic genres of the previous three chapters.

6.1 Corporate disclosure and it purposes

Corporate disclosure has been traditionally understood to be the publication of financial results, annually or quarterly, by publicly listed companies in order to fulfil what is a legal requirement in many countries. Gibbins, Richardson and Waterhouse (1990) define disclosure as 'any deliberate release of financial information, whether numerical or qualitative, required or voluntary, or via formal or informal channels' (p. 122). However, Clark Williams (2008) extends this definition to include the disclosure of non-financial information. She states that corporate disclosure is

> any purposeful public release of information – *financial, social or environmental*, required or voluntary, qualitative or quantitative – that is likely to have an impact on the company's competitive performance and on the strategic decision making of its internal and external audiences. [emphasis added] (p. 237)

The principal genre of corporate disclosure is the 'annual report', the publication of which is a legal requirement in many jurisdictions. The annual report is essentially a public document that summarizes the current financial position of a company, and it reports any changes that may have taken place during the previous year. In the United Kingdom, publicly listed companies are required to produce an annual report called the 'Operating and Financial Review', which is published according to guidelines established by the British Accounting Standards Board. In the United States, similar annual financial statements must be prepared by publicly listed companies and submitted to the Securities and Exchange Commission. The regulatory requirements for annual reporting are different in the two countries, with the UK approach being principles-based, while the US approach is more rule-based (Beattie, Dhanani & Jones, 2008, p. 191). Publicly listed companies in most other developed countries are obliged to meet similar corporate disclosure requirements. In the past, annual reports contained mostly quantitative data outlining the financial position of a company; however, according to Beattie et al. (2008), the annual report genre has 'changed beyond all recognition in the past generation' (p. 219) in terms of growing in length and changing in its focus, which was previously on financial data, while more recently voluntary data and promotional aspects receive a greater emphasis.

Because of the centrality of the mandatory annual report, much of the research on the communication of corporate disclosure has tended to focus on this genre (see, for example: Day, 1986; Lee & Tweedie, 1977; Rutherford, 2005). Two sections of the annual report genre that have been actively investigated by researchers are the non-compulsory section of the President's letter (Abrahamson & Park, 1994; Bhatia, 2008; Hyland 1998, Judd & Tims, 1991; Salancik & Meindl, 1984) and the mandatory core section outlining a company's financial state, which in American annual reports is called the 'Management's Discussion and Analysis' (M. D. & A.). This section must '[d]iscuss the registrant's financial condition, changes in financial condition and results of operations ... [and] such other information that the registrant believes to be necessary to an understanding of its financial condition, changes in financial condition and results of operations (Securities Act, 1933, §229.303a). A number of studies have examined the M. D. & A. section of annual reports in terms of the nature and usefulness of the information reported (Barron, Kile & O'Keefe, 1999; Bryan, 1997; Clarkson, Kao & Richardson, 1999; Schroeder & Gibson, 1990).

Apart from the annual report, there are a number of other communications of disclosure, some of which are voluntary rather than legally mandated. Types of voluntary corporate disclosure identified by Gibbins et al. (1990, p. 125) include the following: press releases, newspaper articles, trade journal articles and securities commission filings. Other voluntary disclosures include earnings releases, reports posted on websites and html newsletters disseminated by email. In relation to changes in the informational focus of disclosure reporting, Clark Williams (2008) notes that companies are increasingly engaging in voluntary disclosure communications in order to address the social and environmental impacts of their activities either as defensive public relations or promotional tools. Clark Williams' view accords with the previous studies by Yuthas, Rogers and Dillard (2002) and by Clark, Thrift and Tickell (2004), who suggest that in corporate communications, promotional purposes or impression management (partly related the role of the media in influencing financial markets) have led to increasing levels of voluntary corporate disclosure.

Laskin (2009) also suggests that, because investor relations were damaged during the first decade of the twenty-first century by major corporate collapses and the by 2008 banking crisis (and its aftermath), there is an increasing need for companies to convey the impression of transparency and openness in order to retain the custom and support of investors. Therefore, it appears that within a climate of economic uncertainty, businesses feel the need to communicate more regularly with their clients or investors. This drive to promote the perception of more accessible and transparent communication has led to an increasing use of electronic disclosure communication via the internet, such as through e-newsletters and the posting of reports and announcements on company websites. Electronic media have also facilitated the wider dissemination of corporate disclosure documents, including both mandatory and voluntary disclosures. This medium has not only led to changes in the form and presentation of existing disclosure documents, but has also facilitated the emergence of new electronic genres, such as the FMC genre, which is the object of the present study.

6.2 Previous approaches to corporate disclosure research

In corporate disclosure research, the object of research in studies of the genre of the annual report has varied widely to include linguistic elements, including word frequencies (Rutherford, 2005); discourse connectives (Crawford Camiciottoli, 2009); the use of metadiscourse (Hyland, 1998); readability (Schroeder & Gibson, 1990); and the use of narrative in reporting (Jameson, 2000). The genre has also been researched in terms of contextual elements, such as strategies in disclosure management (Gibbins et al. 1990), ethical characteristics of the discourse (Yuthas, Rogers & Dillard, 2002), interdiscursivity (Bhatia, 2008, 2010) and diachronic changes (over time) in its form and structure (Beattie et al., 2008). This wide range of different elements of the genre that have been the object of previous disclosure research has meant that these studies have also employed a similarly wide range of research methodologies, such as analytic induction and grounded theory (Gibbins et al., 1990); narrative analysis (Jameson, 2000); manual analyses of discursive or linguistic elements (Bhatia, 2008, 2010; Hyland, 1998; Schroeder & Gibson, 1990); Habermasian ethics (Yuthas, Rogers & Dillard, 2002); and corpus methods (Crawford Camiciottoli, 2009; Rutherford, 2005). In an earlier review of approaches to researching the annual report during the 1990s, Stanton and Stanton (2002) examined seventy studies, and identified at least five main research purposes including the following: image management, marketing, organizational legitimacy, political economy and accountability. Therefore, it is reasonable to say that research that has examined the annual report (the most heavily researched corporate disclosure genre) has been characterized by variety and eclecticism in terms of both research purpose and research methodology, and that most studies have tended to focus on one or a limited number of elements of the genre as they are employed in disclosure communication.

Although previous reports of corporate disclosure research often employ the term 'genre' to refer to a category of text, such as the annual report genre, it seems that few research studies of communications of corporate disclosure have actually employed an approach that attempts to operationalize a category of disclosure communication texts more holistically in terms of a range of the textual and discursive elements integrated within a single genre. Therefore, to address this methodological lacuna in disclosure research, the study reported in this chapter (Bruce, 2014b) used the social genre/cognitive genre framework presented in Section 2.2. This study had two aims: first, to characterize the FMC genre in terms of its principal conventionalized elements; and second, to examine the textual expression of critical thinking in the types of evaluative judgements and advice-giving communicated by fund managers to their readership. The following sections first review the methodology of the study and then present a summary of the findings that relate to the first research aim. Following the presentation of those elements that characterize the genre, there is a focus on those that relate to the second research aim, that is, how the investment managers enact criticality through the FMC genre.

6.3 Study of the fund manager commentary genre (Bruce, 2014b)

In the study reported here, I used the social genre/cognitive genre model and its component elements, as outlined in Section 2.2, as a framework for analysing the textual realization of the FMC genre. I acknowledge that creating and interpreting a written genre involves discursive, communicative processes that involve not only the text but also the social and cognitive operations of the interlocutors who create and interpret the text. However, in this study, as in those presented in the previous three chapters, I focus specifically on an examination of the texts themselves as the central 'artefact' or 'fixed object' of this larger discursive process following the archaeological metaphor of Rogers, Gunesekera and Yang (2011, pp. 260–1)

The sample of texts

The focus of the research is on voluntary disclosure in FMC texts that are publicly available, web-based documents. A non-purposive sample of thirty fund manager commentaries from investment funds was identified from internet sources and was downloaded for the purpose of analysis (see Appendix F). All thirty commentaries were posted during 2011. The source countries and their respective numbers of texts were the following: North America (the USA and Canada), twelve texts; the United Kingdom, eight texts; Australasia (Australia and New Zealand), eight texts; and South Africa, four texts. The sample includes commentaries on managed funds that invest in property, equities (stocks), bonds (central government, local authority, municipalities and utilities), convertible securities, and metals and metal equities (such as mining stocks). From the information available, thirteen funds reported positive or better than benchmark returns, sixteen posted negative or below benchmark returns and one was a newly inaugurated fund that had no historic performance data. Appendix F provides details about each FMC text, including the company name, the source fund and the nature of the fund's investments.

The analysis

I performed the analysis of the sample of the FMC texts as the sole rater using the knowledge categories of the social genre/cognitive genre model as the analytical framework (see Table 2.2). As I acknowledged in relation to the previous three studies using this model, in characterizing a particular genre, certain elements of the model may be more salient than others, depending on the context, modality and communicative purpose of the genre. The analysis, therefore, was carried out in two stages: a preliminary and then a detailed analysis. The preliminary analysis involved examining the sample of texts to determine which of the seven elements of the genre model were salient to a characterization of the target genre. The detailed analysis then involved re-examining the texts to investigate, in greater depth, those model elements previously identified as salient and genre-defining. At this stage, a paper copy of each text was marked up to identify its genre-defining elements. Then, having developed a detailed characterization of the genre, those elements more specifically relating to the expression of critical thinking were identified.

Findings from the preliminary analysis

A preliminary reading and analysis of the sample of thirty texts was carried out in order to identify the salient elements of the social genre/cognitive genre model that were recurrent features of the target genre. As a result, it was found that the four social genre elements were salient to a description of the FMC genre – context, epistemology, content schemata and writer stance. However, because the texts were mostly relatively concise reports of one or two pages, crafted to be read on-screen, there was little extended, general rhetorical development of the sections of the commentaries. Therefore, identifying and analysing embedded stretches of text in terms of cognitive genres was not considered relevant to an investigation of the FMC genre.

In relation to the social genre element of writer stance, I found that two of Hyland's (2005b, p. 49) interactional metadiscourse devices were commonly used: 'attitude markers' (express the writer's attitude to a proposition) and 'self mention' (use of the first person). Also, as a result of the preliminary analysis, I decided to extend the scope of the metadiscourse device of attitude marker somewhat beyond Hyland's definition to include 'semantic prosodies'. These are chains of non-adjacent words that writers used to express their attitude or viewpoint by establishing positive or negative evaluative themes across the sentences of a text. For example, a negative evaluative theme regarding world economic data for the second quarter of 2011 in Text 3 included the words '(economic data) disappoint, uncertainty (about growth in the US), soft patch (in the global economy), (Greece) defaulting, slow down (in China)'. An example of a positive evaluative theme in Text 13 relating to UK economic data in the third quarter of 2011 included the words 'enjoyed (a significant rally), improved (investor sentiment), healthier state (macro data), improved (retail sales)'.

Findings from the detailed analysis: Overall characteristics of the genre

The following are summaries of the findings of the detailed analysis of the sample of texts in terms of the four areas of social genre knowledge of context, epistemology, content schema and writer stance.

Context

This involves schematic knowledge (extralinguistic and intralinguistic). A schema is a pre-learned unit of conceptual knowledge or a communicative routine. Extralinguistic schemata tend be part of the knowledge of a specialist field, in this case the field of the investment fund manager. A schema is usually instantiated (triggered) by the use of a specialized vocabulary item. For example, a potentially declining stock market scenario and its negative consequences for investments can be summarized by the single term 'downside risk', which triggers this particular (pre-learned) schema including all its related elements in the mind of a reader who has this specialist knowledge. In the FMC genre, the schema-triggering terms can be generally grouped into three areas of field-specific knowledge relating to:

- General economic conditions and government policies, such as fiscal policy, fiscal management, fiscal deficit, fiscal discipline, monetary policy, quantitative easing, macroeconomic concerns, sovereign debt (crisis), (bondholder) haircut, US debt ceiling, safe haven, sovereign debt (rating), contagion, emerging/developed markets, duration/ position, yield curve, retracement and soft/hard landing;
- Different types of market and their operation, such as the markets for bonds, equities, fixed interest securities, commodities, upside potential/downside risk, exposure to, large-cap/small-cap stocks, secular demand/decline and leverage performance/risk; and,
- Fund operation and performance, such as portfolio (allocation), (investment) strategy, liquidity, benchmark index, contributors/detractors, asset value, underperform/outperform (a market/ benchmark), earnings multiples, underweight/overweight (position/exposure), volatility (in performance) and market volatility.

Although the FMC genre is a communication to a wider audience of investors, most of the texts made frequent use of these technical, schema-triggering terms. However, there were instances of texts (e.g. Texts 4 and 5) that made somewhat less frequent use of technical terminology in an obvious attempt to address the investor audience in more non-specialist language. In the FMC genre, intra-linguistic schematic knowledge relates to the text-organizing content schema (move structure) and the particular use of interactional metadiscourse, which are both described later in this section.

Epistemology

From the study of the FMC sample, the epistemology of the funds management profession that emerges is the view that fund (and fund manager) performance is a quantifiably measurable activity, compared with and validated in relation to established market benchmarks and indices. Statements outlining a fund's performance, sometimes at the beginning of the text, reflect this view, for example:

Text 4 'For the quarter ended June 30, The Oakmark Fund increased just over 1% compared to a near zero return for the S&P 500.'

Text 8 'The PIMCO Municipal Bond Fund returned 0.79 at NAV and outperformed the Barclays Capital Municipal Bond 1-10 Year Blend (1-12) index by 1.24%.'

Text 12 'For the quarter ended 9/30/2011, Janus Overseas Fund, as reflected by the Fund's Class T shares, underperformed its primary benchmark, the MSCI All Country World ex-US Index, returning –27.83% vs. –19.85% for the index.'

Content schema

A content schema is a conventionalized pattern for organizing the content in a particular genre or category of texts in terms of communicatively motivated stages termed 'moves', based on Swales (1981, 1990) approach to genre. Each move is identified in terms of the type of content that it aims to present, and not in terms of some more general rhetorical purpose. The analysis of the sample of FMC texts showed them to have a four-move structure presented in Table 6.1.

The move structure reflects the 'work-in-progress' character of this particular genre, with moves relating to the past, present and future of the fund. The ordering of the moves is variable, but thirteen of the texts have the order of Moves 1, 2, 3 or Moves 1, 3, 2. In twenty-four texts, Move 4 comes after Moves 2 and 3. In six texts there is some recursion – more than one instance of a move. (For example Text 24 has the structure of Moves, 1 3, 2, 4, 3. The repeated moves are usually Moves 2 or 3.)

Table 6.1 Move Structure of the Fund Manager Commentary Genre

Move	Function	Role	Frequency of occurrence
Move 1*	The fund's overall yield for the reporting period	Optional	In 23 texts
Move 2	The fund's immediate past performance during the reporting period	Optional but common	In 28 texts
Move 3	The past performance of the economy and/or markets during the reporting period and predictions about their future direction	Obligatory	In 30 texts
Move 4	The investment strategies that would be followed in the immediate future	Optional	In 24 texts

* In some cases, the yield information of Move 1 was presented in a table or some other type of graph instead of a prose statement. (Bruce, 2014b, Table 1, p. 324).

Identification of the moves in the texts was partly based on my own subjective judgements as the rater, but it was also facilitated by the fact that, in many of the texts, the moves were also announced by subheadings. For example, Move 1 was identified by subheadings in eleven texts, such as 'Fund Performance' (Text 3) and 'Performance Summary' (Texts 8 & 12). Move 2 was introduced by headings in thirteen texts, such as 'Portfolio Performance' (Text 6) and 'Portfolio Review' (Texts 7 & 16). Move 3 was signalled by a heading in seventeen texts, such as 'Market Summary' (Text 3), and subheadings announcing Move 4 occur in fifteen texts, such as 'Strategy Notes' (Text 3) and 'Outlook' (Texts 13, 14, 16 & 21). (Appendix G contains a complete summary of the move-announcing subheadings in the sample.)

Writer stance

Writer stance involves the use of 'interactional metadiscoursal' devices to establish the writer's evaluative position in relation to market conditions and fund performance. The two principal devices of 'attitude markers' and 'self mention' are discussed here in terms of their occurrences and roles within the move structure.

Move 1: This brief move, usually a statement or a table, contained little metadiscourse that established the critical or evaluative position of the writer.

Move 2: In this longer move, establishing writer stance through the use of metadiscourse devices occurred within twenty-three of the twenty-eight texts.

The devices were principally attitude markers and instances of author self-mention. A common presentational sequence in Move 2 (that occurred in twelve texts) involves a description of the investments that were positive 'contributors' to the investment fund followed by those that had a negative effect on the fund performance, termed 'detractors'. Attitude markers are used to establish semantic prosodies (evaluative themes) that support this positive/negative sequencing of the news about the past company performance. Typically in this sequence, the positive section and its positive chain of attitude markers are longer than the negative section. For example, in Text 6 the opening, 'good news' positive section contains the extended chain of 'strong, positive, strongest, contributor, (prices to) soar, spike, increase, top (performers), perform well (four occurrences), benefit from'. The negative aspects of the immediate past performance of the fund are then described in a shorter section with the negative prosodic chain that included the words 'detractors, concerns, down a bit'. Commentaries from other funds that had achieved negative results during the reporting period did not use this positive/negative sequence, but they still made use of metadiscourse to establish the writer's stance. For example, Text 21 begins with the negative news with the setting up a negative semantic prosody of 'underperformed, detractors', followed by the highlighting of some positive investment outcomes 'contributors, better than expected'.

Move 3: In this obligatory, extended move concerned with reporting and evaluating market conditions, writers again make extensive use of the two metadiscourse devices to establish their stance. Attitude markers, usually within extended semantic prosodies, occur in all thirty texts and self mention was a feature of twelve texts. An example of a positive prosody from Text 16 is 'better-than-expected (earnings), improving (economic data), an impressive (average rise in profits, positive (impact)'. Another feature of Move 3 was the use of simile and metaphor in some texts when setting up an evaluative theme. For example, Text 26 in discussing recurrent market concerns about the Greek debt crisis and its effects on markets describes it as 'a bad horror-movie monster', and the theme continues with the words 'resurrected, uncertainty, cause of fear'. Similarly, in Text 28, the market turmoil is described as 'a perfect storm of concern'; this text also uses 'contagion, cascaded, wither'.

Move 4: In the final move outlining the future investment strategy of the fund, writer stance shifts to the personal position of the fund manager. Therefore, there is greater use of self-mention (often in combination with attitude markers), with both devices strongly evident in twenty-three of the twenty-four texts that contain Move 4. For example, in Text 20, this combination of self-mention and attitude marking is a recurrent feature, for example 'we still believe, our central expectation, our stronger view'. Other examples of this type of writer position in Text 7 include 'we continue to believe, we remain confident' and in Text 30 'we believe (multiple instances), we focus on, in our view'. Such personal mention of attitude or position tends to lead to personal statements of actions, for example, 'we are intentionally maintaining, we anticipate increasing' (Text 7), 'we will continue to focus on' (Text 13) and 'we plan to take advantage of' (Text 23). In addition to self-mention in relation to perceptions and intended actions, positive self appraisal of strategies through prosodies is also a feature of this move. Examples of positive prosodies are found in Move 4 of Text 25 is 'improving (capital management), strong (support), improving (returns)' and in Move 4 of Text 21 'good (growth), good shape (companies), growing well'.

Findings relating to the textual expression of critical thinking

As a disclosure genre, the FMC appears to have the overall ostensive aim of informing a mixed audience of expert and non-expert readers, including investors and the general public, about the management of their fund and its performance in ways that appear as transparent and informative as possible within the scope of a relatively brief text that has to achieve a range of functions (summarized by the four moves). However, an adjunct, subliminal aim appears to be the need for managers to display professional astuteness and competence when discussing the management of their funds, especially given the difficult market conditions of 2011. The element of astuteness is reflected in writers' efforts to appear well-informed and critically evaluative when analysing market trends, and when developing, applying and justifying investment strategies. Two elements of the FMC genre are employed in this communication of the critical judgements of the writers. First, it is conveyed structurally through the organization of the move structure, and second, it is communicated more overtly through the use of interactional metadiscourse devices, in particular, attitude markers.

The move structure appears to have a prototypical order reflected in the numbering in Table 4.1. However, as noted previously, this order is sometimes altered to meet the communicative goals of individual fund managers, goals relating to the particular context and the performance of their funds. For example, Move 1, highlighting the fund's yield, is the opening move in about half the sample of texts (fourteen texts). However, funds with negative or below benchmark yields tend not to open with Move 1 (eight texts), and four texts with negative yields omit Move 1 completely. Ten texts, six with negative yields, begin with Move 3 (market conditions) as a justificatory move, which is then followed by Move 2 in seven of these texts. Five texts (two with positive yields and three with negative yields) place Move 1 at the end of the text, usually in a table.

The second element of metadiscourse is used in the more direct expression of critical thinking in the genre. For example, attitude markers are used extensively in Moves 2, 3 and 4, usually in chains (semantic prosodies) that emphasize a positive or negative theme. As mentioned, in the event of good news reports in Move 2, attitude markers are used to emphasize the positive elements of fund performance. In the majority of texts, Move 2 is an impersonal report, but in twelve of the twenty-eight texts, self-mention (the first person) is employed. Attitude markers are most extensive in Move 3 in the analysis of macroeconomic conditions, the state of markets and the potential effects of their trends on the manager's fund and his/her future strategy. In Move 3, attitude markers are more colourful and extravagant (e.g. Text 14, 'worried, hits, fled, defensive') and there is use of metaphor (e.g. Text 9 'drifting sideways, grinding out'; Text 23 'to weather turbulence'). Evaluation in this move tends to be less cautious as it relates to external factors and influences beyond the fund manager's control. However, in Move 4, ownership of investment strategies is reflected in the use of self-mention (e.g. Text 13 'in our opinion'; and Text 21 'our central expectation, our stronger view) and the more cautious, measured use of attitude markers (Text 30 'benefit, well managed, strong, above-average').

Discussion

The findings from this study suggest that the corporate disclosure genre of the FMC is a relatively formulaic category of texts with a discernible organizational structure that aims to achieve multiple communicative purposes. These purposes relate to communicating directly with investors about the fund, its returns and its management, and indirectly by conveying the impression of critically evaluative, professional expertise in relation to fund manager decision-making. The direct communicative purposes of the genre are realized through the move structure and the types of information conveyed, including current yield, immediate past performance and the related management decisions taken, evaluation of market conditions and future investment strategies. The indirect effect of conveying an impression of critical expertise in the fund's management is achieved by each writer's use of the textual and discursive resources of the genre, specifically the staging of information through the move structure and the use of metadiscourse devices in establishing their stance. The focus of this study has been on the textual resources employed to achieve these purposes. However, because of the smallness of the sample employed (thirty texts) and the lack of multiple raters (whose analyses could be compared), the findings may be considered to be indicative rather than generalizable. Nevertheless, two possible implications arise from this study for the future research of corporate disclosure communication and the future application of genre theory to investigate this type of communication. The first relates to the need for holism in researching examples of business communication, such as corporate disclosure, and the second implication concerns the applications of the findings by business communication practitioners concerned with interpreting and communicating disclosure.

While prior research of disclosure genres, as mentioned previously, has tended to focus on either a contextual issue or a single linguistic element, in this study, I attempted a somewhat more multifaceted analysis. This involved examining the textual realization of the target genre in terms of the four social genre elements of context, epistemology, writer stance and content schema. In support of this principle of holism, when investigating professional discourses, Bhatia (2008) suggests 'one may need to adopt a multi-perspective and multidimensional framework' (p. 170). In corporate disclosure research, this study is a step in that direction. However, it must be acknowledged that although several elements of the textual realization of the genre were examined, the study (like the others reported in this volume) is essentially an analysis of texts as the 'linguistic trace of a discourse process' (Widdowson, 2004, p. 169). The next step in this type of research would be to examine the discursive contexts within which the texts of this genre are created and processed, 'bringing together the rhetor and the receiver and the text and the context' (Rogers, 2000, p. 466). Thus, in addition to analysis of the text, this would involve investigating the fund managers as the creators of the texts and the investors as the reader audience. Operationalizing the discursive enactment of the genre by the two principal interlocutor groups would involve triangulation of the type of textual analysis undertaken here, with further data collection that would include obtaining the communicative practices and perspectives of commentary writers, along with the discursive interpretations of the readers – the fund investors. However, since the text is the central artefact and product of this genre-creating, discourse process, it is my view that a multifaceted analysis of this artefact still remains a core element of genre research.

6.4 Implications for teaching professional writing

On the basis of the findings of this small-scale, exploratory study, it would be unwise to make strong claims about its implications for the teaching of business communication writing, or the writing of the FMC genre. However, taking a wider view and relating the findings of the study to the others examined in this volume as well as to genre-based pedagogy (see Hyland, 2004), I will make some more general suggestions relating to the teaching of professional writing. As I proposed in the previous chapters, writing pedagogy that focuses on a complex genre and aims to include a focus on how critical thinking is expressed should follow the two phases of analysis and synthesis.

The findings of this study suggest that, when approaching the teaching of a business or professional genre, the principle of holism is important, meaning that pedagogy should account for all of the layers of knowledge integrated within the whole of the text. As I suggested with the academic genres, this can involve gathering a small sample of texts (of the particular target genre), and helping students to notice, deconstruct and practise their key features (the analysis phase) before they are then encouraged to create their own examples of the target genre (the synthesis phase).

In the analysis phase, an early step could be to identify the technical lexis and the related professional knowledge commonly employed within the category of texts under investigation. In the FMC genre examined in this chapter, this involved a range of business- and investment-related terms. Closely related to the specialist knowledge and lexis is identifying the epistemology of the field within which the text occurs. This involves understanding the type of knowledge of the field, and how it is discovered and validated (proven) within the field from which the texts are taken. In the FMC genre, this involved understanding that investment fund performance is conceptualized as a metric that is able to be compared with other fund indices.

When analysing the organization of the texts of the genre category, such as in terms of moves or the conventionalized sections of the genre that communicate different types of information, something to consider here is the length of these sections. Are they relatively brief or do they involve more general, rhetorical development, such as could be described in terms of cognitive genres? In the case of the FMC genre, the four moves were relatively brief and were largely identifiable through the subheadings used. Finally, the issue of writer stance and engagement is important (Hyland, 2005b). This involves examining the devices that the writer uses to convey their particular viewpoint to the reader, including expressions of critical thinking. In identifying this type of knowledge, the metadiscourse model can provide a useful starting point. However, in the case of the FMC genre, the analysis extended beyond this to identifying semantic prosodies (positive and negative themes developed through chains of attitude markers) and also the use of metaphorical language and imperatives in stance-building, neither of which was a feature of the academic genres.

When considering the generic elements of a category of text that are used to express critical thinking, it is important to consider how lower level, stance-building devices (such as attitude markers and metaphors) combine with other elements of the genre (such as its organizational pattern) to express a critical or evaluative viewpoint. The lesson of the studies of this volume is that, when considering how critical thinking is expressed, these devices should not be considered in isolation, but as part of the textual whole of which they form a part.

Having identified the key elements of the target genre during the analysis phase, student writers could then move to the synthesis phase where they are given tasks where they create partly completed examples of the same genre. These tasks could be implemented as joint group activities where there are opportunities to discuss and consider the appropriate use of the types of knowledge identified in the analysis phase. The final step of the synthesis stage is for the student writers to create their own examples of the genre, using the knowledge that they have accrued, with less or no pedagogic support.

6.5 Implications for conceptualizing the expression of critical thinking in written text

In relation to the larger purpose of this book, the findings of this study, like the studies of the academic genres in Chapters 3 to 5, demonstrate that the generic devices used to express critical thinking (through the texts of the FMC genre) are both organizational at a higher level in the text (in terms of the move structure) and linguistic in the form of attitude markers and metaphor. However, unlike in the previous academic genres where the use of attitude markers was sparing and often hedged within a Concession Contraexpectation relation, such as in the literature reviews in Chapter 5, in this genre they are used more frequently and are chained to establish positive or negative themes – called 'semantic prosodies' here. This difference seems to relate back to differences between the overall communicative purposes of the FMC genre and those of the academic genres reviewed in the previous three chapters. While the academic genres of the essay, the PhD Discussion chapter and the literature review in RA Introductions are concerned in some way with an ostensibly rigorous evaluation of theory and/or research, the FMC genre (like its parent genre of the company annual report) has an underlying communicative purpose of impression management. Unlike the discipline-specific, specialist audiences likely to read the academic genres, the audience for the FMC genre is potentially much larger and less specialist. It may include fund investors and investment advisers with a personal or professional stake in the management of a fund as well as the wider public who may be potential future investors in the fund. Therefore, while the devices used to express critical thinking in the academic genres and the FMC genre share some common characteristics, the different context and different communicative purposes that unfold in the move structure result in some differences, such as the more extensive use of the device of attitude markers combined with the use of metaphorical language.

7

Expressing critical thinking in journalistic commentary

7.0 Introduction

In this chapter, which reports the last of the five studies, I examine the textual expression of critical thinking in a journalistic genre, the genre of the newspaper commentary column, focusing on commentaries by a journalist who takes a particular ideological perspective. Specifically, the chapter presents a study that examines the discursive resistance to neoliberal ideology through the writing of the British journalist Polly Toynbee in her regular commentary column in *The Guardian*.[1] Toynbee's column critiques neoliberal ideology as it manifests in public attitudes and government policies in the areas of politics, health, education, the economy and foreign affairs. Using the social genre/cognitive genre model presented in Chapter 2, this study involved the analysis of a sample of thirty examples of Toynbee's column in terms of the knowledge elements of the model including: context, epistemology, writer stance, content structuring and cognitive genres. As was the case in the studies reported in the previous chapters, the findings indicate that the writer constructs her resistance by using a complex range of macro- and micro-level textual devices, described in terms of elements of the genre model.

To frame the political and discursive context of this set of texts, I begin the chapter by defining the key terms of 'hegemony, ideology and neoliberalism'. I then present the ideological position of Polly Toynbee, whose texts are examined in this study. The sample and methodology of the study are then explained, followed by the results and some discussion. Because this study focuses on the complex, idiosyncratic argument structure and expressions of critical thinking of one writer, I have not attempted to draw implications from it relating to the teaching of critical thinking in writing. However, in the final section of the chapter, I again consider the implications of this study for the wider purpose of this volume, that of exploring how critical thinking is expressed in different types of disciplinary writing, considering how the textual resources used are similar to, and differ from, the genres of the four previous chapters.

7.1 Key terms and concepts: Hegemony, ideology and neoliberalism

Hegemony

The concept of 'hegemony', as originally proposed by Gramsci (1971), suggests the capture and exercise of power by means other than direct domination, such as by the development and promotion within a society of a set of dominant ideas that override and dismiss opposing voices. Key elements of the exercise of hegemony are, therefore, discursive and semiotic. An example of discursively enacted hegemony can be seen in the set of neoliberal ideas used to frame the discussion of social, economic, educational and political issues within contemporary British society, beginning with Thatcher's Government in the 1980s and persisting into the present era (Levitas, 2005). So pervasive has been this particular hegemony that politicians from both the left and right continue to subscribe to, and enact its ideas (Bennett, 2013), while resistance has largely been left to intellectuals, trade unionists and certain journalists, such as *The Guardian* columnist Polly Toynbee, whose writing is the object of the present study.

Discourse and ideology

Here the definitions of the terms 'text' and 'discourse', first presented in Chapters 1 and 2 are revisited as a basis for defining the term 'ideology', and for establishing how it differs from 'discourse'. In Chapter 2, I used Widdowson's (2004) definition of text as 'the linguistic trace of a discourse process' (p. 59). For the purpose of the studies in this volume, text is taken to mean the words on the page, which may be a written document or the written transcription of a spoken monologue or dialogue. Also using a definition of Widdowson (2007, p. 7), 'discourse is taken here to refer both to what a text producer means by a text and what a text means to the receiver'. Discourse, therefore, encompasses the social and cognitive operations that surround and give meaning to text. However, as I also pointed out in Chapter 2, Van Dijk (2008) cautions that the term discourse does not itself equate to an institutionalized mode of thinking or an ideology: 'We do not *understand* by "discourse" a philosophy, ideology, social movement or social system, as in the phrases "the discourse of liberalism" or "the discourse of modernity," unless we actually refer to collections of talk and text' (p. 104). Therefore, following this approach in referring to the set of ideas that characterize neoliberalism (defined later), the term 'ideology' will be used here rather than discourse. Ideology here refers to a set of related, value-laden ideas used by a certain group to achieve certain political and social purposes, although it must be emphasized that ideology is discursively enacted through written and spoken texts. This definition largely accords with that of Thompson (1990) who defines ideology as 'the ways in which meaning is mobilized in the service of dominant individuals or groups' (p. 73).

In examining the enactment of ideology through a written genre, the challenge that faces the discourse analyst is to ensure that any study is based on an adequate and comprehensive operationalization of all of the aspects of the particular discursive and textual knowledge and practices involved. For example, in analysing the elements of discourse that relate to the artefact of a written text, as undertaken in the studies reported in this volume, I have previously emphasized that this operationalization needs to acknowledge that the text writer and reader draw upon personalized knowledge and strategies than may potentially include the following: content knowledge related to the larger societal context and domain of the text; knowledge of the immediate communicative context including the social or interactional setting (such as the positioning of a writer in relation to his/her audience); abstract procedural or organizational knowledge (often relating to more general rhetorical purpose); and systemic linguistic knowledge. I acknowledged in Chapter 2 that texts as a type of semiotic, of themselves, do not constitute discourse, but I take the position that they are stable, analysable, material artefacts of the discourse in which they play a central communicative role. In this genre-based study, a collection of thirty journalistic commentary texts and the discourse that relates to the texts (involving an ideological struggle) constitute the object of analysis. As with the other studies presented in this volume, this operationalization is attempted through use of the social genre/cognitive genre model presented in Chapter 2. The genre-based approach was also considered appropriate here since the sample of thirty texts all perform the same overall function of political commentary, are created under the same constraints and appear within issues of the same newspaper.

The ideology of neoliberalism

In examining the use of the term neoliberalism in a wide range of scholarly and RAs, Boas and Gans-Morse (2009) note three broad tendencies in its definition, each of which focuses in some way on the centrality of the free market as proposed by economic theorists such as Hayek (1978) and Friedman and Friedman (1962). The core idea of neoliberalism is the economic freedom and autonomy of the individual. According to Harvey (2005), the neoliberal view is that 'individual freedoms are guaranteed by freedom of the market and of trade' (p. 25), and that 'human well-being can best be advanced by liberating individual entrepreneurial freedoms and skills within an institutional framework characterized by strong private property rights, free markets and free trade' (p. 2). In order to advance the economic freedom of individuals, neoliberalism tends to oppose forms of social solidarity that constrain its exercise, such as trade unions, professional associations, social housing and socialized medicine – in fact any type of institution or regulation seen as somehow impinging on the right the individual to exercise their individual economic freedom and autonomy.

Because social solidarity can involve forms of centralized planning and government regulation, these too can be seen as opposing individual freedom, therefore, small government and minimal regulation and planning are seen as essential to the existence of this type of individual freedom. As Polanyi states, 'planning and control are ... attacked as a denial of freedom' (1957, p. 256). In Britain, an example of a significant reduction in government control was the so-called 'big bang' involving the deregulation of financial markets in 1986. Another significant reduction of the controls of government in the financial area was the deregulation of the banking sector by the incoming Labour government in 1997.

A consequence of the neoliberal economic view of individual freedom, as Harvey (2005, p. 33) notes, is 'the financialization of everything ... a deepened the hold of finance overall on other areas of the economy, as well as over the state apparatus'. Epstein (2005, p. 3) defines financialization as 'the increasing role of financial motives, financial markets, financial actors and financial institutions in the operation of the domestic and international economies'. Examples of financialization include the sale of social housing, the privatization of socialized medicine and the performance of regulatory functions by private companies on behalf of the state, such as prisons being operated by private security companies and the enforcement of government regulations by private providers, such as private companies inspecting and approving new building construction. As well as the complete privatization of state-owned enterprises, such as banks, airlines and utility companies, financialization also involves so-called 'public-private partnerships' (PPPs) where, for example, private companies construct and/or operate state infrastructure, such as private companies being paid by the state to operate prisons. As Clarke (2004, p. 35) expresses it:

> the economic calculus of neo-liberalism expels that which cannot be counted – but it seeks to bring more and more of human activity within the economic calculus. Most things – even those previously decommodified or uncommodified – can be brought to market.

Neoliberal ideology and especially its central characteristic of financialization were strongly evident in the policy responses by the UK Government to the global financial crisis that began with the banking crisis of 2007/2008, with the Government taking over and funding the Northern Rock after a run on this bank in 2007. Then, after the collapse of the FTSE100 on 8 October 2008, the UK Government made available £500 billion in loans and guarantees to banks and other financial institutions, which was followed by another £50 billion the following January. However, in contrast to this support given to major financial institutions during this period of increasing unemployment and social hardship, there were continued reductions in welfare expenditure. An example of this was the 'benefit cap' implemented in July 2013 under which a person's state benefits and their housing benefit were limited to a maximum of £500 per week for families, regardless of the number of dependent children, and benefits for single people were capped at £350.

While it is usual to see neoliberalism largely as an imposed, top-down political ideology centred on issues relating to economic control and the role of markets, the social geographer Barnett (2005) cautions that the era of neoliberal economics has also coincided with other bottom-up, socio-cultural processes that, as populist tendencies, have been instrumental 'in provoking changes in modes of governance, policy and regulation' (p. 8). Barnett suggests that these processes include changing expectations in relation to entitlements, decline in deference in relation to access and expertise, and anti-paternalistic attitudes, such as in women's health movements and resistance to discrimination on the basis of gender, race and disability. However, while this era has seen the emergence of these influential, bottom-up social trends that have potentially supported the expansion of neoliberal hegemony in the United Kingdom, it is argued here that the top-down imposition of ideas by governments, think-tanks, business, universities, the press and other institutions has still played a greater role in creating a current dominance of neoliberal thinking that has persisted into the twenty-first century.

The writer's own ideological position

The journalist who is the author of the texts under investigation here, Polly Toynbee, is an advocate of social democracy, having been active in the British Social Democratic party formed in 1981, and currently the British Labour Party. She is also a member of the Fabian Society, whose aims include the achievement of greater equality of power, wealth and opportunity within society and the acknowledgement of the value of collective action and public service, aims that reflect an ideological position contrary to the central ideas of neoliberalism. In her book publications (Toynbee, 2003; Toynbee & Walker, 2008), she is concerned with exposing the conditions of the poor and the rising economic inequality in the United Kingdom. These concerns are also the central focus of her newspaper journalism, including the sample of her commentary texts from *The Guardian* which are the object of this study. The context of their publication, *The Guardian* newspaper, has a history of championing liberal, anti-establishment causes, and it is owned by an independent trust (not a major commercial news organization). The readership of *The Guardian* is generally considered to be on the mainstream left of British political opinion. Past polls have suggested that approximately half of its readership are Labour voters.

7.2 Methodology

The sample (see Appendix H) consists of thirty examples of Polly Toynbee's column published in *The Guardian* from 15 March to 12 June 2013 during the austerity period immediately following the global, financial crisis. As with the other studies reported in this volume, I performed the analysis of the sample as the sole rater, using the social genre/cognitive genre model presented in Section 2.2 as a heuristic framework for examining each text. The analysis involved a process of repeated, intensive readings of each text (each reading focusing on one particular knowledge element of the model) and of building-up a multi-dimensional descriptive summary of each text by first entering the details of the context and epistemological elements into an overall table, then marking up a paper copy of each text for the other five areas, and finally transferring these notes into the overall summary table.

7.3 Results

What emerged from the multiple analyses of the sample of thirty texts was that the four social genre elements were most salient to a description of the target genre: context, epistemology, content schemata and writer stance (see Section 2.2, Table 2.2). In relation to the cognitive genre dimension of the model, there was consistent use of two cognitive genres (text types), termed Recount and Discussion, although they tended to be peripheral rather than prototypical realizations of each type. The following are summaries of the findings of the detailed analysis of the sample of texts in terms of the four areas of social genre knowledge of context, epistemology, content schema and writer stance. Following this, the use of cognitive genres will be reported

Context

Each commentary addresses a current issue (at the time of writing) related to social services, economics, health, education and politics in the United Kingdom. Examples include cuts to the funding of the National Health Service, the housing crisis, performance pay for teachers, immigration, welfare cuts, the Government's austerity policies and a referendum on Europe (see Appendix H for a full list of the texts). While the discussion in each commentary text tends to focus closely on the topic of the day, two overarching themes central to Toynbee's critique emerge across a number of commentaries. One is the shrinking of the state and the public services that it provides, explicitly mentioned in Texts 3, 10, 12, 21 and 27. The second is the rising inequality and the upward redistribution of wealth, which receives explicit mention in conjunction with the topics of Texts 3, 4, 8, 23, 25 and 27.

The types of schematic knowledge drawn upon in each commentary relate to detailed knowledge of the particular issue being raised in the text and knowledge invoked by the wide range of supporting metaphorical imagery that Toynbee draws upon in constructing and lending weight to her arguments. In relation to the issues that are the focus of each article, the types of knowledge invoked include awareness of current British political issues, including the current legislative agenda, twentieth-century political history (such as the Atlee and the Thatcher eras), the careers of current and past British politicians, and the occasional non-British issue, such as the case of Edward Snowden. In relation to the types of knowledge activated by metaphorical references in the column, there are specific text-external references, such as to British social history, as in 'Jarrow marching' (Text 9); to literature, as in 'want children Gradgrinded' (Text 8); to world affairs, as in 'to be Belarus' (Text 5); or to world events, as in 'the Berlin Wall moment' (Text 9). However, the vast majority of metaphors involve original imagery constructed by the writer herself. Examples of this type of original device are 'George Osborne's palanquin was born aloft' (Text 9) and, referring to Thatcher's funeral, 'her apotheosis with full military honours' (Text 11). The latter type of metaphor is heavily dependent on the reader's awareness of the literary, poetic, historical or cultural knowledge that Toynbee refers to, for example, the types of schematic knowledge instantiated by words like 'apotheosis, palanquin' and 'tumbril'. The use of metaphorical knowledge appears to be a central element in constructing writer stance, which is addressed in that part of the findings.

Epistemology

In relation to epistemology – views about the nature of knowledge and its validation – the writer appears to take a 'nominalist' view; that is, concepts and events as objects of thought are largely created by the human mind that perceives them. She constructs this epistemological position through a 'multiple perspective' approach, involving the use of different rhetorical angles employed in the staging of the texts. Typically, the different rhetorical 'angles' of the column involve the following: a brief attention-grabbing section that highlights the particular issue of concern, then a critical recount of the highlighted event, followed by a discussion or evaluation framed by the writer's own perspective, within which an alternative position is often proposed. (This multiple-angle approach is explicated in further detail when describing two other genre elements: the three-move structure in the content schema section and the related realization of two of these moves by use of cognitive genres.)

In taking this epistemological approach, Toynbee challenges neoliberal 'recontextualizations' of social practice (Van Leeuwen, 2008), that is, the discursive portrayal of events or issues by politicians or the conservative press, framed in terms of the dominant neoliberal ideology for the purpose of advancing justifications for policies and specific actions taken. For example, in a column that challenges the rationale for, and stories around, benefit cuts (Text 8, 4 April 2013), she strongly resists justifications for welfare cuts based on the highly publicized case of one Mick Philpott, portrayed in the media as a serious abuser of welfare, and used by the Government as a case to support welfare cuts. She recontextualizes the same cuts in terms of their effects on the deserving poor, supported by the example of the case of Martine White, a thalidomide victim, previously active in the workforce, who had suffered a brain tumour and was waiting for spinal surgery. In the same column, she emphasizes the social injustice of the welfare cuts by contrasting benefit cuts for the very poor with tax cuts for the very richest in British society, both of which were occurring at the same time.

Writer stance

In the social genre/cognitive genre model, writer stance is defined as the stance or standpoint of a writer in relation to his/her audience. In previous studies that have used the same genre model to examine academic texts, stance was analysed in terms of the set of language devices that Hyland claims are used to connect the writer with the reader, and which he terms metadiscourse (2005b, p. 49). However, in the present study it was found that, while Toynbee makes extensive use of the metadiscourse device of attitude markers, she also employs a range of other devices to appeal to the reader, including metaphor, rhetorical questions and imperatives. Of these, metaphor is the most commonly used.

Metaphor is used extensively in the portrayal of politicians and policies as well as in more direct resistance to such policies. In performing these two often overlapping evaluative functions – portrayal and resistance – two forms of metaphor are used. The first involves brief, pithy instances that are singular occurrences inserted into the general flow of the text. The second involves longer, more extended metaphorical imagery that aims to create more detailed scenarios in the mind of the reader.

Examples of brief metaphors used both to intensify and add an evaluative quality to descriptions include the following: 'an avalanche of benefit cuts' (Text 5); 'wasteful turf-war competition' [among NHS contractors] (Text 6); 'the poisoned anonymity of the internet' (Text 6); 'the indignation tipping point' (Text 12) and 'the last glue holding together this organisational chaos' [of NHS reorganization] (Text 20). Larger, more extended metaphors are used to create a more developed scenario in the readers' mind of how Toynbee characterizes and criticizes particular situations. For example, in describing George Osborne's 2013 budget, a health metaphor is used: 'Their remedy has failed so far, but more of the same medicine'. The health metaphor continues in the same text with criticism of Government policies leading to increasing house prices: 'But take a heady sniff from Osborne's best propellant – a feelgood house price bonanza for the 65% lucky enough to own their own homes' (Text 3, 21 March 2013).

The second most frequently used element to establish writer stance is the metadiscourse device that Hyland (2005b) terms 'attitude markers'. In his metadiscourse model, Hyland states that attitude markers 'express the writer's attitude to a proposition' (p. 49), but specifically indicate 'the writer's affective, rather than epistemic, attitude to propositions … [and are] signalled metadiscursively by attitude verbs (e.g. agree, prefer), sentence adverbs (unfortunately, hopefully) and adjectives (appropriate, logical, remarkable):' (p. 53). While Toynbee uses attitude markers less frequently than metaphor, the device is still present in all thirty texts of the sample. Examples include 'this *ideological and vengeful* upheaval of often vulnerable lives' (Text 1); 'the final *wicked* twist' (Text 5), 'she [Thatcher] certainly was *divisive*' (Text 9), 'its [the Government's] *relentless* course' (Text 14), '*frighteningly high* [mortgages]' (Text 19) and '*wildly unrealistic* [to get people out of hospital and into the community' (Text 20).

Two other devices that Toynbee uses to connect directly with her reader audience are rhetorical questions and imperatives. Compared with the previous two devices, instances of these are less frequent, with rhetorical questions occurring in twenty-nine, and imperatives occurring in nine of the thirty texts. Examples of rhetorical questions are: 'Don't we already know what happens when we pump money into sub-prime loans to people that banks don't care to lend to?' (Text 3); and, 'How can you build up a brilliant community service when all the money is sucked into hospitals with near 100% full beds?' (Text 6). Imperatives, although arguably the most direct appeal to the readers, are the least-used of the writer stance devices, occurring in only nine of the thirty texts. Examples of imperatives are 'Don't imagine that it's over: the press has a long and vengeful memory' (Text 2); and, 'Go shopping with a mother on a low income to watch the skill and discipline it takes.' (Text 7).

Content schema

The fourth element of social genre knowledge relates to regularly occurring, conventionalized patterns used in the organization of content within a genre, described here as 'moves' (Swales, 1990). The staging of content within the sample of texts of Toynbee's column is identifiable in a regular three-move schema found in all thirty texts. They are:

Move 1   Attention-grabber
Move 2   Contextualization
Move 3   Evaluation

Move 1, the 'attention-grabber', is a brief section that attracts the reader's attention to the issue that is topicalized to introduce the particular commentary text through a series of forceful statements that may make use of metaphor to set the scene, evoke imagery and establish schemata and references in the mind of the reader.

Move 2, termed the 'contextualization', is a section that has the purpose of providing further detailed information about the topic. This move is often in the form of a loose recount with embedded evaluative comment, ostensibly so that the reader can better understand the issue in terms of its history, the reasons for its occurrence or its significance or implications.

Move 3, termed 'Evaluation', presents the writer's viewpoint often in the form of a discursive argument with recommendations for future actions or policies. In most texts, this is an extended, rhetorically developed section; however, in a small number of texts, it is a briefer comment (e.g. Texts 3, 24, 25 and 28).

The three-move content schema underpins the multiple-angle view employed by the writer in constructing her commentary, as discussed in relation to epistemology.

Cognitive genres

The cognitive genres that are employed in each article relate to the general rhetorical aims that the texts draw upon. The cognitive genres, segments of text relating to a single rhetorical purpose, usually coincide with the articles' content moves. Move 2 (Contextualization) tends to be realized by Recount cognitive genre, as this Move is usually concerned with presenting information that is sequential or chronological. Longer instances of Move 3 (Evaluation) often employ Discussion cognitive genre, the presentation of a contrastive argument, which offers an evaluation of the event or issue (reported in Moves 1 and 2) and argues for a particular solution. However, because of the dialectical nature of the commentary texts, these Moves employ fairly loose realizations of the cognitive genres, interspersed with digressions, justifications and comments.

Critical thinking in Toynbee's commentaries: Themes, textual resources and an example

Through her columns, Toynbee's challenge to neoliberalism is two-pronged. She uses all of the identified generic elements (as illustrated here by the worked example of Text 15) to communicate themes for the purpose of both critique and advocacy. The first and most extensive critique theme is the shrinking of the state, that is, the deliberate reduction of the activities and services provided by the state and the effect of this reduction on society, such as on the poor (Text 7), children and the disabled (Text 8), the vulnerable migrant (Text 17), the unemployed (Texts 12, 25 and 26) and the aged (Text 30). The second critique theme is rising inequality resulting from the upward redistribution of wealth, which receives explicit mention in conjunction with the topics of Texts 3, 4, 8, 23, 25 and 27. In conjunction with critique, Toynbee's resistance also involves advocacy of an alternative ideological position in which she aims to re-establish and strengthen social democracy, and to articulate policy alternatives – such as increasing taxation on the richest in society to fund welfare spending and ways of improving the housing situation and the care of the aged.

The critique and advocacy elements of Toynbee's resistance also operate at a more micro-level within the move structure of many of the texts. For example, in the first two moves of a text, she is often engaged in an oppositional critique of the policies of the present government, and then in the third move she shifts into advocacy, such as of alternative policy recommendations, often directed towards the Labour opposition. This balance of critique and advocacy within one text is exemplified in the following close analysis of Text 15.

Text 15: 'Amid Tory disarray, Labour's critical moment looms'

Text 15 from the sample exemplifies the features of the genre and their use in communicating the writer's position. This text appeared on Friday 17 May 2013, the week of the opening of Parliament and the Queen's speech outlining the British Government's legislative agenda for the current year. After the speech, about 100 Conservative backbench MPs, upset about the lack of any plan for a referendum on British EU membership, proposed an amendment to introduce such legislation. As a result, there was considerable debate and controversy about EU membership in Parliament during that particular week, the debate deflecting public attention away from some of the more controversial aspects of the announced legislative agenda and the serious social issues emerging at the same time. Through her column, Toynbee challenges what she sees as the discursive diversion of the debate on EU membership, and places the focus back on what she sees as the more pressing social issues, including how Labour should address them. In this text, Toynbee uses the full range of the devices of the genre to develop her arguments.

In Move 1, the Attention-Grabber, quoted here, she attacks the use of the Euro-scepticism debate as a distraction from what she sees as more important issues:

> The madness of the Tory party defies belief. Forget banging on, these out-of-control crazies are in the grip of a brain fever, crushing themselves to death in a stampede for the Euro-exit. Top dogs fight over the bone of the leadership, but who in their right mind wants to lead this rabble? Is it catching, does this frenzy infect the voters? No, Europe remains remarkably low – and falling – on their list of concerns.

In Move 2 – the Contextualization – she immediately shifts the focus back onto the problems facing the coalition government. She begins with the sentence 'Out here, a cascade of bad news this week was ignored by the unhinged government benches. Report after report revealed ...', and she then specifies the problems of the following: rising unemployment; a house price bubble (caused by the Governments' 'help to buy' scheme); and deteriorating health statistics caused by commercial outsourcing by the NHS. In Move 2, she also challenges propaganda that supports the neoliberal discourse through which welfare recipients are portrayed as *shirkers and skivers* in comparison with *strivers*, citizens in employment and business and, thereby, seen as contributing to society. The stance devices used in Move 2 to signal the writer's position are the following:

Metaphor	*Stuck in* part-time or zero-hours contracts zero-hours contracts, *thrown off* disability benefits, to the *glee* of estate agents, the Chancellor's scheme *bubbles up* prices, *stoking the furnace of demand, illusory growth on the booming never-never,* NHS showed *symptoms of imminent trouble,* David Cameron's *great Achilles heel,* A&E is the *pressure point,* a *near melt down, twisting the language,* the public is *harder-hearted,* people would *stand on their own feet*
Attitude Markers	An *unhinged* government, *mismanagement* of just about everything, (house) building was *shockingly low,* his *great* commercial outsourcing, deploying *bogus* figures, Tory MPs *obsess over* Europe

In Move 3, the Evaluation, she shifts into advocacy of ways in which these critical issues can be addressed. For example, she proposes reducing benefit costs and the house price bubble by controlling the housing benefit to private landlords and by building more social housing; means-testing the benefits that the rich receive; funding childcare so that mothers who are welfare beneficiaries can enter the workforce; and addressing rising child poverty. The stance devices used in Move 3 to signal the writer's position are the following:

Metaphor	Expects Labour *to stumble and fail*; *cap on spending*; *the parameters of the debate are framed by Osborne*; housing benefit *poured into private landlord's pockets*; an *iron box* for current spending, the first *totemic one* [policy], the *government's assault on the most vulnerable*; *set a current spending budget in concrete*; *to strap them into this straitjacket*, *to finance his failures*
Attitude Markers	Labour's own *critical moment*; a *tough challenge*; the *exorbitant waste* on housing benefit; a *better chance* of cutting poverty

7.4 Discussion

The examination of the texts of Toynbee's column and their related discourses in this study reveals that her regular commentary on current political and social issues is integral to her wider, ideological resistance to the hegemony of neoliberal ideology in British society, a hegemony that began with 'reforms' initiated by the Thatcher government in the 1980s and that was still being perpetuated by the policies of the conservative-led government in 2013 when these commentaries were written. While each of Toynbee's columns addresses a specific current issue, two central aspects of neoliberal policies are underlie her critique. The first is the deliberate reduction of the activities and services provided by the state and the effect of this reduction on society, such as on the poor (Text 7), children and the disabled (Text 8), the vulnerable migrant (Text 17), the unemployed (Texts 25 & 26) and the aged (Text 30). The second is the upward redistribution of wealth, which is a consequence of neoliberal economic policies.

The genre model used in this study reveals that Toynbee's critical viewpoint is constructed through a complex interweaving of contextual knowledge, epistemology, information-structuring (through the three moves) and devices to establish writer stance. The textual realizations of these moves in terms of Recounts interspersed with evaluative comments (for Move 2) and Discussion (Move 3) underpins these complex communicative purposes. In terms of establishing the strength of her critique and engagement with her readership, a central element is that of writer stance achieved through the use of metaphor, attitude markers, rhetorical questions and imperatives.

The discursive complexity of Toynbee's column is reflected by the fact that, in many of the commentary texts, the writer is engaged both in an oppositional critique of the policies of the government of the day, which tends to be the main focus of Moves 1 and 2, and an evaluative critique and recommendations that are often directed at the stance and policies of the Labour opposition in Move 3.

In this move, the critique has to be consistent with Move 2, that is, she must maintain a consistent stance of resistance to the neoliberal ideas realized by the policies of the coalition government (and some of the past, neoliberal policies of New Labour), while at the same time positively evaluating, encouraging and recommending policy directions that move away from this ideology by the current Labour opposition. Thus, while she cannot ignore aspects of the immediate, more neoliberal past of the British Labour Party, she also endeavours to emphasize the policy differences that exist between the present government and opposition, and to show evidence of the present Labour opposition, having learned the lessons of history. In relation to this aspect, a number of her columns urge Labour to continue to chart a new course, which she states will involve 'cauterising the past' (Text 21) and exhibit greater boldness in articulating alternative policies. However, while Toynbee is willing to criticize the neoliberal elements of New Labour's policies, she is equally willing to praise the social programmes that they undertook, but criticizes the fact that these programmes were not publicized and were sublimated in deference to the prevailing neoliberal orthodoxy in British public and political life. A telling comment to this effect emerges in Text 27 (2 July 2013), where she states

> the government gets away with demolishing what Labour did because the social democratic idea behind it was never embedded in the national psyche. … Blair and Brown were defeatists, convinced that Britain was essentially conservative, individualist, imbued with Thatcherism. Confronted with the Mail, Sun, Times and Telegraph, the culture looked immutable, a force to be appeased.

It is this embedded nature of neoliberalism in the national psyche that is the object of Toynbee's critique, and while it seems that elements of the centre-left political establishment are now adopting a cautious, gradualist approach in their opposition to neoliberalism, Toynbee's commentary articles constitute a more forceful, vigorous challenge to this prevailing ideology, a challenge that involves a complex, discourse-constructing task through her commentary columns.

7.5 Implications for conceptualizing the expression of critical thinking in written text

Of the five genres examined in this volume for the expression of critical thinking, Polly Toynbee's column, in many ways, emerges as perhaps the most complex. It is complex in terms of the range of subject matter that she tackles, which includes a wide range of political, social and human rights issues. It is also complex in terms of the generic devices that she harnesses in the expression of her critique. The corollary of this discursive and textual complexity is the range of different types of reader knowledge required in order to be able to interpret and understand her critique. Although the audience for her column is potentially the general public, or those members of the general public who read *The Guardian*, clearly the discursive complexity of the column assumes a literate and informed readership. This assumption is illustrated in the findings of the analysis relating to the genre elements of context and stance, and especially in her use of metaphor in the latter area.

In terms of the larger aims of this project, this final genre analysis in many ways summarizes and confirms the findings of those that precede it. Expressing critical thinking through genres as categories of written text is a multilayered phenomenon involving higher- and lower-level generic elements operating synergistically in texts. What emerges again in this study appears to be the fact that it is the proceduralized framework of the genre that provides the scaffolding and resources necessary for the expression of critical thinking through this integration of textual elements. In the case of Toynbee's column, as in the case of other genres examined in this volume, this involves organizational patterns for the higher-level structuring of content, operationalized here in terms of the move structure and also the cognitive genres in the textual realizations of two of the moves. It also involves lower-level elements in stance-building, which in the present genre draws upon the four elements of metaphor, attitude markers, rhetorical questions and imperatives. However, the communicative effect of the genre involves more than the analysis of the elements of the linguistic trace of the discourse process; it is the discourse process itself, involving a clash of ideologies, and requiring access to all of the types of knowledge that lend that meaning to the linguistic elements used by the writer, types of knowledge that are essential to the ratification of the ideas of the texts by the readers.

8

Expressing critical thinking through writing

8.0 Introduction

In the opening chapter of this book, I undertook an overview discussion of the concept of critical thinking, acknowledging its provenance in Western philosophy and science as well as the emphasis placed on developing and exercising this skill by present-day educational institutions. In the opening chapter, I also considered the diverse ways in which critical thinking has been defined and taught in the academy, aligning my own approach with those who see critical thinking and its expression as evaluative judgements situated within specific contexts and disciplines rather than as general skills in logic, argumentation and problem-solving. Through the subsequent chapters, I narrowed my focus to how critical thinking is expressed through different types of disciplinary writing, including the types of discursive and textual means employed through the studies of five different genres. My rationale for taking this approach is that expertise in writing and the ability to express critical thinking through writing are essential for entry into, and participation within any academic or professional discourse community. As Paul Prior (1998) states, '[i]n disciplinarity, much of the work on alignment is centring around texts, around the literate activities of reading and writing' (p. 27). I think that it would be uncontroversial to add to Prior's statement that exercising critical thinking through literacy skills is a core element of this alignment, attested to by the fact that this attribute occupies a central position in the graduate skills profiles of most Western universities.

In this concluding chapter, I attempt a summation of the overall findings of the studies and case-building that I have undertaken through the previous chapters. In Section 8.1, I revisit the principal finding of the five studies, specifically that writers' expression of critical thinking involves the integrative use of generic elements operating at different levels within texts. I consider the differences between the textual elements used to express critical thinking in academic and non-academic writing, acknowledging that any observations made here can only be considered provisional because of the small range of genres examined and the type of solitary manual analysis undertaken. In Section 8.2, I engage in a wider discussion of how the findings of the studies reported in this volume relate to other research that has explored this issue, referring in particular to four key edited works that have each presented a series of studies on this subject. In Section 8.3, I will summarize my comments about the implications of these studies for the teaching of writing. Finally, in Section 8.4, I conclude by considering ways of further developing the genre-based approach of these five studies in future research that examines the textual expression of critical thinking.

8.1 What do the findings tell us about how critical thinking is expressed in texts?

Effectively, the overall findings of the five studies can be summarized by three points, each of which I will develop in this section.

- Generic elements operating at different textual levels are used to express critical thinking;
- Higher- and lower-level elements are integrated; and
- Academic and non-academic genres differ somewhat in their use of these generic elements.

Generic elements operating at different textual levels are used to express critical thinking

The first key finding from the five studies is that the expression of critical thinking utilizes elements that function at different levels within the texts examined. These include the following: higher level, content-organizing structures, intermediate-level coherence relations (between propositions) and lower-level linguistic devices.

At a higher level, critical thinking is expressed through structures that organize the overall content of the text; these are structures that present a macro-level, overall statement. Higher- or macro-level statements were observable to some extent in all of the five genres examined. In relation to the essay genre study reported in Chapter 3, my two antecedent studies of the same samples (Bruce, 2010a, 2015a) showed the higher level features to involve the two moves for the introduction section (background and outline) and for the recursive and changing use of cognitive genre (text-type) structures to develop key points being made by the writer, points that engaged different types of general rhetorical purpose and led to a conclusion. In the PhD Discussion chapters examined in Chapter 4, evaluation or critical thinking emerges at this higher level in the texts through the use of the recursive content schema: 'Point, Support, Evaluation'. In the literature reviews in RA Introductions (reported in Chapter 5), a recursive 'Background Critique' pattern emerged as the higher-level organizational structure expressing evaluation. This pattern was realized by means of the use of Moves 1b and 2 of Swales' CARS move structure.

Similarly, this type of macro-level statement that framed the generic structure in the academic genres was also evident in the studies of the two non-academic genres included in this volume. These were the business genre of the FMC in Chapter 6 and the journalistic genre of the newspaper political commentary in Chapter 7. In the FMC genre, the four-move structure of (a) fund yield, (b) fund performance, (c) market conditions and (d) future investment strategy constituted the macro-level statement. Similarly the three-move structure of Toynbee's political and social commentary column of (a) attention-grabber, highlighting an issue; (b) contextualization; and (c) evaluation, together combine to create an overarching statement structure in the writer's realization of this journalistic genre.

At the next level within the texts, evaluative statements employing binary coherence relations between propositions emerged as an important way of expressing critical thinking in the three academic genres. In the essay genre (see Tables 3.1 and 3.2) and in the PhD Discussions (see Table 4.1), there is a similar use of causal and concessive contrast coherence relations to frame the key critical statement or points being made in both genres. In terms of Crombie's (1985) taxonomy, the writers of these two genres used her Concession Contraexpectation relation and the causal relations of Reason Result and Grounds Conclusion. In the literature reviews in RA Introductions, the Concession Contraexpectation relation emerged as most salient to the expression of critical thinking. However, it is interesting to note that the use of these binary coherence relations did not emerge as such an important device for expressing critical thinking in the two non-academic genres of the FMC and the newspaper commentary column. Rather, in these genres, a range of devices used at a lower level in the texts emerged as key elements in the expression of critical thinking.

At a lower level (in the five genres), key linguistic elements that were identified in terms of Hyland's (2005b) taxonomy of metadiscourse devices played an important role in expressing critical evaluations in the three academic genres–and especially the devices that Hyland terms attitude markers and hedging. In the essays, attitude markers (lexical expressions of the writer's affective attitude towards a proposition) were an important element within the critical statements in both samples. The device of hedging (adding cautiousness or tentativeness to claims) was used more frequently in the English literature essays and less so in the sociology essays. Attitude markers and hedging were evident in some of the critical statements in the five PhD Discussions examined; however, their frequencies of use varied considerably across the Discussion chapters of the five theses. Attitude markers also occurred in expressions of critical thinking in the RA literature review texts (Chapter 5), where I found a higher frequency of use (approximately twice as many) in the applied linguistics texts compared with the psychology texts. In the two non-academic genres, the metadiscourse device of attitude markers was used to express evaluation along with the literary device of metaphor. In the case of the political commentary column of Polly Toynbee, rhetorical questions and imperatives were also employed. In the FMC business genre, attitude markers were used in chains (semantic prosodies) to establish positive and negative evaluative themes.

Integration of higher- and lower-level elements in the expression of critical thinking

The second key finding that emerges from the five studies is that the expression of critical thinking involves the integrative use of the higher- and lower-level devices discussed in the previous section. In the study of the university essay genre reported in Chapter 3, this was particularly evident in the close integration of the coherence relations used to express critical statements, embedded within which were the metadiscourse device of attitude markers and hedging. (Examples of this integrative expression were provided in Section 3.3.) In the genre of the PhD Discussion chapter, examined in Chapter 4, there was also a particularly close integration of the three levels. This integration involved the content schema (Point, Support, Evaluation), in the latter section, of which (Evaluation) key interpropositional relations were used to make critical statements. In addition, embedded within these critical statements were the two key metadiscourse devices of attitude markers and hedging. In the study of the literature reviews (that occur in RA Introductions) reported in Chapter 5, a similar integration of higher-level moves, a particular coherence relation (concessive contrast) and metadiscourse devices (attitude markers) was found. In the case of the two non-academic genres of the FMC and the newspaper commentary column, the integration involved the higher-level move structure and the lower-level lexical and rhetorical devices in order to express critical thinking. In the FMC genre, the move structure was integrated with chains of attitude markers (semantic prosodies) and metaphors to establish positive and negative evaluative themes. In Toynbee's commentary column, the three-move structure was also integrated with lower-level devices (including attitude markers, metaphors, rhetorical questions and imperatives) to construct the writer's extended critiques.

Differences between expressing critical thinking in academic and non-academic genres

A key difference emerged in the expression of critical thinking between the three academic genres (examined in Chapters 3 to 5) and the two non-academic genres (Chapters 6 and 7). This difference was the relative lack of use in the non-academic genres of the intermediate-level device of particular coherence relations (usually some type of causal or concessive contrast relation) to frame key critical statements.

In the academic genres, this type of statement appeared to play a pivotal role in expressing critical thinking by presenting particular points that helped to construct the overall argument of the text. The surrounding co-text provided contextual information and evidence for the point expressed in the critical statement. In addition, metadiscourse devices, specifically Hyland's (2005b) attitude markers and hedging, tended to be located within these critical statements reinforcing their evaluative character. The following two sentences are examples of the use of these types of generic element in academic texts.

> 'Conrad's narrative is <u>problematic</u> partly *due to* the ambiguity of the story being told.' (Chapter 3, English Essay Text 3)
>
> [Reason Result relation (inverted) containing the attitude marker 'problematic']
>
> '*While* the findings from this research are <u>interesting</u> and <u>may well be</u> indicative of the effectiveness of corrective feedback, they were not compared with the accuracy scores of a control group so cannot be read as evidence.' (Chapter 5, Applied Linguistics Text 3)
>
> [Concession Contraexpectation relation containing the attitude marker 'interesting' and the hedge 'may … be']

In contrast, the non-academic genres appear to make less use of this type of strategic critical statement framed by these types of coherence relation, but more extensive use of evaluative lexical devices (including attitude markers), which were distributed throughout the text. The focus of the two non-academic genres tended to be on declarative statement and information-giving, within which there was liberal use of the lower-level devices, especially attitude markers and metaphor, rather than the type of more carefully staged point development by the use of causal and concessive contrast relations in the academic texts. The following two examples show the greater emphasis on lexical (and other lower-level) resources in the non-academic texts to express critical thinking.

> We remain <u>less sanguine</u> about the opportunities in fixed-income investments, where it <u>appears</u> that the continued <u>suppression</u> of interest rates by a number of central banks has enabled many <u>unhealthy</u> businesses to stay afloat. (Fund Manager Commentary, Text 5)

> [*attitude markers*: less sanguine, suppression, unhealthy; *hedging*: appears]

> Don't imagine you will wake up tomorrow to some <u>new press landscape</u>. <u>Worst excesses</u> of <u>grubbing for dirt</u> may be slightly checked – though <u>cut-throat</u> competition for dwindling sales will still, warns Roy Greenslade, mean doing whatever it takes to get <u>highly intrusive material</u>: wait for the next <u>frenzy</u> over a McCann-type case to see if this works. (Toynbee's Guardian Commentary, Text 2)

> [*imperatives*: 'Don't imagine ...', 'wait for the next ...'; *attitude markers*: 'worst (excesses)', 'highly intrusive (material)'; *metaphors*: 'new press landscape, grubbing for dirt, cut-throat competition, frenzy']

8.2 Similarities and differences between these studies and previous research

In this section, I return to some discussion of previous landmark research and theories that have focused on how critical thinking is expressed through written text, and I consider how they relate to the findings of the five studies reported in this volume. As I noted in Chapter 2, previous research studies in this area show a high level of diversity in their definitional approaches and the object of the research, although, in terms of methodology many use corpus analysis. My discussion in this section considers both commonalities and differences between the findings of the series of studies of this volume and those from the existing literature of the field. I will also suggest that some of the studies of this volume take and extend certain findings and ideas from these previous studies.

The expression of critical thinking through written text, sometimes termed evaluation or appraisal, has been the object of research studies over at least the last three decades, and specifically those reported within four collections of studies in edited volumes (Del Lungo Camiciotti & Tognini-Bonelli, 2004; Hunston & Thompson, 2000; Hyland & Diani, 2009; Salager-Meyer & Lewin, 2011). As I observed in Chapter 4, the pattern that emerges from these edited collections is that most of the studies that they report focus on a single linguistic feature investigated using corpus methods, but some include one or more studies using a different analytical method, such as studies that use appraisal theory, clause relations or narrative structure, and involve some human analysis of text by a rater.

In the first of these edited volumes, Hunston and Thompson (2000) begin by attempting to outline the scope of research in this area in terms of a range of elements. In their introductory chapter, they suggest that evaluation in text has three purposes: expressing opinions, maintaining relations and organizing the discourse. They suggest that evaluation can occur at the level of the organization of the text (citing Hoey's Problem Solution Evaluation as an example of a textual structure at this level) through the grammatical structure of the text and through lexical features. They also suggest that there are different parameters of evaluation, such as good/bad, important (relevant)/unimportant (irrelevant), certain/uncertain, but that the overarching parameter, which subsumes the others, is the good/bad parameter. These elements of the scope of evaluation are then related to the different studies of contributors to their volume.

In the studies reported in Hunston and Thompson's (2000) edited work, there is no suggestion that critical thinking or evaluation that manifests through texts may be a particular property of genres as categories of text. Rather the data sources of several of the studies reported in the contributing chapters are general corpora, and the research focus is on the evaluative functions of single linguistic elements as they occur in these corpora, such as evaluative lexis, adverbial markers of stance and adjective noun combinations. However, two chapters raise issues that relate in some way to some of the findings of the present studies. These tend to be in chapters that explore ideas and frameworks rather than report empirical studies. For example, the chapter by Cortazzi and Jin (2000) discusses evaluation as a property of narratives using an illustrative text. While much of their chapter considers how narratives are used to perform evaluations, such as a research tool in ethnography, they also review Labov and Waletsky's (1967) six-part narrative structure, which suggests that the higher-level organizational structure of narratives may also have an evaluative function. The structure is: 'abstract, orientation, complication, resolution, coda, evaluation'. According to Cortazzi and Jin, the evaluation 'underlines the point of the narrative, revealing the speaker's attitude to what has been recounted and how the teller thinks it should be interpreted' (2000, p. 105). Also in the chapter by Thomson and Zhou (2000), which considers that evaluative role of cohesion and coherence, the authors argue that coherence and cohesion within a text involves both the propositional as well as the evaluative coherence of the text. They focus particularly on sentence-initial adjuncts (adverbials) and the types of evaluative relation that they signal, specifically concession, expectancy and hypothetical/real patterns. Although prefiguring the role of the particular coherence relations in forming critical statements in the academic genres studied in this volume, the approach of Thompson and Zhou differs from the present studies by beginning with specific linguistic forms (sentence-initial disjuncts, usually adverbs) rather than with categories of discursive meaning that may be signalled by these linguistic devices. Proposing the latter approach, in her theory of interpropositional relations, Crombie (1985) identifies discursive meanings through her taxonomy of binary coherence relations, the signalling of each of which may be achieved grammatically, lexically or merely by the juxtaposition of propositions. Nevertheless, Thompson and Zhou's work points to the importance of these types of meaning relation for the expression of evaluation or critical thinking within text, something that emerged particularly in the findings of the three academic genres in the present volume.

In the edited volume by Del Lungo Camiciotti and Tognini-Bonelli (2004), the majority of the studies are also corpus-based, using corpora such as MICASE, and focus on one particular linguistic feature. However, three studies involved manual analysis of smaller samples using a particular theory of discourse. Two of these use APPRAISAL theory as a basis for a manual analysis of samples of certain categories of text, but again the focus was on the use of a linguistic device to express a single evaluative function. In one, Tucker (2004), examined evaluation in art history discourse, examining seven texts (comprising 4,000 words) taken from art history journals, focusing on ATTRIBUTE (an element of appraisal theory) in the form of predicative adjectives. In the other, Webber (2004) examined syntactic negation as a form of ENGAGEMENT (as proposed by appraisal theory) in eight applied linguistics articles. However, in this volume, the one study that took a more multivariable approach was that of Shaw (2004), who manually analysed book reviews from the *Economics Journal* between 1913 and 1993, looking in terms of a range of features used to express evaluation, including clause relations, Gricean implicature, co-text, wording (lexis), irony and extra-textual information. Shaw appears to argue that the evaluative value of single lexical items depends less upon the linguistic category to which they belong than on the discursive settings in which they occur. This may involve the preceding and following sentences, such as in evaluative statements that he accounted for in terms of Hoey's clause relations. Discourse knowledge may also involve extra-textual information, such as in the use of irony to critique. He also points to the role of reader knowledge of economic theories to understand certain evaluative points made in the texts. Overall, the comments in the chapter by Shaw prefigure the need for a more multivariable and holistic approach to exploring the expression of critical thinking through texts, one that involves both discursive meanings and textual features.

However, in relation to the investigation of the expression of critical thinking through written text, probably the most important and insightful chapter in the edited work by Del Lungo Camiciotti and Tognini-Bonelli is the final chapter by Drew, who raises a key concern about reliance on corpus-based analysis for this type of research, arguing that by using corpus methods:

> linguistic phenomena – again words, clauses, grammatical constructions etc. – are abstracted from their textual or other contexts, and quantified: their comparative distributional frequencies are then the (inductive) basis for assessing the pragmatic or rhetorical role played by that particular word or construction. But the matters outlined above would be addressed and I think largely resolved by investigating, before codifying and quantifying a given linguistic feature, how that feature *works* in discourse more generally, as well as in their particular textual and interactional contexts. (2004, p. 221)

Essentially Drew argues that any investigation of how critical thinking is expressed through written text should involve both qualitative and quantitative analytical methods, and that *the qualitative should precede, and be validated by, the quantitative*. He goes on to recommend that 'the aim should be to ground quantification on a more secure understanding of the *pragmatic and rhetorical meanings* of linguistic selections and constructions, *through qualitative analysis of discourse*' (p. 221) [emphases added]. Drew's concern effectively echoes the same issue raised by Widdowson (2000) about the use of corpus methods in linguistic analysis, which he states 'cannot account for the complex interplay between linguistic and contextual factors whereby discourse is enacted. It cannot produce ethnographic descriptions of language use' (p. 7). Thus the comments of Shaw and Drew in this volume point to the need for a more holistic, discourse-focused approach when examining texts for the means that they employ to express critical thinking. Such an approach does not necessarily preclude the use of quantification, such as through the use of corpus methods, but it does suggest that elements that are examined through this type of quantification need to be understood first in terms of their discursive, evaluative role before quantifying their frequency and distribution in the texts under investigation.

The volume by Hyland and Diani (2009) differs somewhat from the two previously reviewed edited books. In this work, the studies examine the expression of evaluation in samples of texts drawn from specific genres that fall within the broader grouping of 'review genres', which they define as 'texts and part-texts that are written with the explicit purpose of evaluating the research, the texts and the contributions of fellow academics' (p. 1). Included are eight chapters that examined book reviews, two that deal with publisher blurbs, and two that deal with science review articles and literature reviews, respectively. In the Introduction, the editors undertake a discussion of evaluation, reviewing key approaches to how it has been defined and theorized.

However, of the eight studies that examined book reviews, six used corpus methods. Two focus on a particular linguistic form, such as reporting verbs and 'that clause' complements, while other studies use corpus methods to search for devices that are classified non-linguistically, including metadiscourse devices, positive and evaluative statements or evaluative acts (praise and criticism). Two studies of book reviews did not use corpus methods and examined more than one type of textual element. One was a diachronic study, again by Shaw (2009), of eleven academic book reviews in the *Economic Journal* from 1913 to 1993 by means of manual analysis and by using Hunston and Sinclair's (2000) model of aspects of evaluative acts. However, the study that is somewhat closer in approach to the multilevel, multivariable approach of the present volume was the study by Moreno and Suárez (2009) that compared book reviews in English and Spanish academic journals in terms of moves, critical comments within the moves, and other elements, such as metadiscourse devices within the critical comments. This study involved close manual analysis of the texts, and involves quantification in understanding the distribution of the critical comments within the moves in order to compare their occurrences in the Spanish and English texts, and also for comparing the balance of positive and negative evaluative comments. Like the studies of Thompson and Zhou (2000) and Shaw (2004), the study by Moreno and Suárez (2009) acknowledges that understanding the expression of critical thinking in written text involves different textual elements operating at different levels. Like Drew (2004), their approach seems to suggest that understanding these elements and their integrated operation in texts should involve some manual, qualitative analysis.

Finally, the collection of studies edited by Salager-Meyer and Lewin (2011) consists of an eclectic series of eleven studies focusing on a variety of text categories. The studies are grouped into five sections, one of which was entitled 'Genre Research', which contained five of the studies. Although four focused on samples of texts relating to a single genre, as in much of the previously reviewed research, the analytical focus of each was on a single element used to express critique. Examples were: the analysis of negative comments in physics book reviews using appraisal theory (Babaii, 2011); impolite expressions in medical journal editorials (Giannoni, 2011); personal reference and mitigation (by hedging) in grant proposal reviews (Koutsantoni, 2011) and move analysis to examine the Introduction sections of articles in the field of literary criticism (Lewin & Perpignan, 2011). However, an interesting study in this volume is that of Navarro (2011), who develops the previously proposed notion of 'critical acts' as a pragmatic construct, suggesting that these have to be first identified qualitatively and then scrutinized for their use of lexico-grammatical resources. As a result of his study (critical acts in a series of Spanish academic book reviews), Navarro identified these resources to the categories of field, role, reviewer, reviewee and co-text, the latter including a range of subcategories (rhetorical structure, metadiscourse, connectives, lexis, modality, comparison and quantification). While Navarro's approach doesn't quite meet Drew's recommendation of 'investigating ... [how] a given linguistic feature works in discourse more generally, as well as in their particular textual and interactional contexts' (2004, p. 221), it represents an effort to move beyond the approach that focuses on a single feature of a sample of texts, and attempts to account for the discursive complexity of this concept of critical acts.

8.3 Implications for the teaching of writing.

In this section, I return to the possible implications of the studies of this book for the teaching of writing. However, rather than rehearsing again the specific suggestions appended to four of the studies about how they may inform the teaching of writing of a particular genre, I will summarize here my suggestions for pedagogy that may help learner writers to acquire the resources to express critical thinking through their texts. Writing instruction that has this aim, I propose, requires a genre-based pedagogy that promotes a deep level of engagement with texts and their discursive meanings; such a pedagogy involves two major phases, which I have previously termed analysis and synthesis.

The analysis phase

Analysis involves introducing students to, and practising the key textual resources employed in, realizing a genre, including those used to express critical thinking. In particular, this phase requires that the writing teacher's knowledge goes beyond understandings of sentence-level grammar and the types of relatively superficial advice found in many writing textbooks that enjoin students to: structure their writing (e.g., with an introduction, a body and a conclusion) and, to express a 'critical' or 'evaluative' voice, without actually explaining how this is achieved. I suggest that the pedagogic knowledge required for an effective analysis phase involves having the means to undertake *an adequate contextualization of the genre and its purposes*, and *a comprehensive and systematic operationalization of the constituent genre knowledge*. In approaching the types of complex genre studied here, acquiring knowledge that can be used in the pedagogic analysis phase requires teachers to carry out a deep examination of texts of the target genre category and identify the multilayered resources that they employ.

As I proposed in previous chapters, when implementing pedagogy, the analysis phase undertaken with students may be carried out using a small sample of model texts of the target genre category. It begins with a thorough contextualization that involves understanding the writer's purpose (such as case-building through the text) and their overall positioning in relation to their audience (readership). This aspect of contextualization may also involve clarification of the wider functional role of the genre within a particular disciplinary discourse community, especially in cases where knowledge of this role is occluded to the novice writer. The contextualization may also involve some understanding of the specialist knowledge of the field and discipline within which it occurs. I proposed in Chapter 2 that this will include the epistemology of the particular subject area and its specialist lexis (technical terms).

After the context has been established, student-guided analysis (of its actual texts) requires a systematic approach that considers, and introduces, student writers to the different layers of knowledge that combine to create the texts of a target genre. A framework for this type of analysis may employ the social genre/cognitive genre model (used in the previously reported studies) as a possible concatenation of the different types of knowledge that can occur at different levels within texts. However, whatever framework is used, the key principle is holism, which requires an adequate operationalization of the salient areas of discursive and textual knowledge employed within the particular genre under scrutiny. When examining the actual texts, I suggest that the analysis phase follow a top-down approach beginning with the organization of the text. In formulaic, conventionalized genres, this may involve examining texts in terms of a particular move structure. In other genres, moves may not be a salient, genre-defining element, but it may be useful to identify the use of sections of text relating to a more general, rhetorical purpose – text types, or what I term cognitive genres. At the next level, inter- and intra-sentential elements that promote cohesion and coherence across the text can be examined. At this level, the roles of salient discourse-marking features need to be identified. To achieve this, it may be useful to look for the occurrence of particular, recurring coherence relations using a relevant theory, such as Crombie's (1985) interpropositional relations. Finally, at a lower level, writer stance and engagement devices may be examined using Hyland's (2005b) model of metadiscourse devices. However, as the two studies of the non-academic genre indicated, other elements, such as metaphor, rhetorical questions and imperatives may also be used in the stance-building role. The lessons of the five studies of this volume are that, to uncover the textual expression of critical thinking, one must look beyond a single linguistic element and treat the text as a multifaceted, discursive whole, a whole in which writers integrate a number of elements. Once a thorough and detailed analysis has been undertaken and student writers have become familiar with the salient constituent, generic elements, the pedagogy can pass to the synthesis phase.

The synthesis phase

Synthesis involves helping novice writers to use the types of procedural and linguistic knowledge identified in the analysis phase to create their own examples of the genre. As part of this second phase, I have suggested in previous chapters that once particular generic features related to critical thinking have been established (extracted from a model text, presented and practised), students can proceed to creating texts that employ the generic features. This can begin with scaffolded joint activities involving discussions around the meanings and functions of the identified generic features. An early stage of this may involve jigsaw reading activities, such as assembling a cut-up version of a model text, requiring discussions around what goes where and why. This phase could also involve presenting an existing text with sentences or a paragraph sections gapped and requiring to complete the gap-fill parts of the text with particular textual elements that meet the requirements of the genre. Following this type of fairly controlled, synthesis task, students can move to joint constructions of texts where the composing process and selection of elements can still be a transparent, interactive process among student writers, but they require more original text-creation on the part of the student writers. The final part of the synthesis stage, is where students are provided with tasks that require them to create their own examples of a text of the same genre category without pedagogic support or guidance during the composing phrase. However, an early draft could be submitted to the writing instructor for feedback followed by conferencing before the final draft and author editing (based on feedback received) is completed.

8.4 Implications for future research

As I acknowledged at the beginning of this volume, attempting to uncover the means used to express critical thinking through written text is a challenging endeavour, and it is one on which there has been little agreement among theorists and researchers who have addressed the issue. Although most of the studies in the four edited collections reviewed in Section 8.2 adopt a single variable approach to examining the textual means used to express critical thinking, it is also evident that these edited collections contain other studies and a thread of commentary that points to the complex and multifaceted nature of the phenomenon under investigation (e.g., Drew, 2004; Moreno & Suárez, 2009; Navarro, 2011). Consonant with these ideas, the studies reported in this volume use a genre-based approach in attempting to account for this complexity, and to identify the multiple elements that combine to express critical thinking. However, it must be stated that, because of the complexity of the undertaking, the studies of the previous five chapters are an exploratory use of this genre-based approach; the exploratory nature of this research was the result of logistical limitations, specifically the lack of means to hire and train multiple analysts to perform the genre analysis. I would suggest, therefore, that further development of this approach would address and go beyond the methodological constraints of these exploratory studies. Specifically, future research extending the genre-based approach of the present studies may involve:

- The use of larger samples and multiple analysts to perform the genre analysis;
- The use of corpus tools to support the manual genre analysis; and,
- The inclusion of ethnographic investigations of the contexts exploring the human enactment of criticality that relates to a genre under investigation.

First, future research using this approach would need to address the issue of sample size. The studies reported here used relatively small samples of texts since the analysis was done by the writer as the sole researcher, although even with these small samples the nature of the type of analysis undertaken represented a relatively formidable task. (For example, the analysis of the Discussion chapters of the five PhD theses involved the close manual analysis and marking up of 157 pages of text.) However, a further development of this approach in future research would involve the use of larger samples of texts belonging to a genre category and the use of multiple researchers to perform the initial analysis to identify the key generic elements. Both developments would lend robustness to the findings by the use of larger data sets and providing the means for the research to establish inter-rater reliability in the analysis.

A second extension to this research approach would be to follow Drew's (2004) suggestion that qualitative inquiry be followed by quantitative. Here I am suggesting that it may be possible to triangulate aspects of the manual genre analysis through the use of corpus methods to provide quantitative data relating to the qualitative findings. This could, for example, involve the use of tagged, genre-specific, micro-corpora to validate the qualitative findings by exploring larger samples of texts. To achieve this would involve investigating the possibilities of tagging and quantifying the use of coherence relations or other discursive features in corpora. It could also involve searching for occurrences of the lower-level features identified, such as metadiscourse devices and metaphors. However, the key issue here would be to gather a sufficiently large number of texts to form a genre-specific micro-corpus to make it possible to perform this type of computer-mediated analysis.

A further development in future research that follows this genre-based approach would be to extend the research beyond a focus on the textual elements used to express critical thinking to include investigations of the discourse processes that relate to the text. This would involve investigating the wider enactment of criticality that takes place around the texts of a particular genre, such as by researching the communicative intentions of writers and the interpretive understandings of readers. This step would involve 'bringing together the rhetor and the receiver and the text and the context' (Rogers, 2000, p. 466). Extending the study to include the enactment of criticality through a genre by the interlocutors would, therefore, involve triangulation of the type of textual analysis undertaken here with further data collection, such as through ethnographic interviews. It would include obtaining the data about the communicative practices and perspectives of writers of the texts of a particular genre category, along with the discursive interpretations of readers of the genre. In this type of ethnographic investigation around a particular genre, consideration would also need to be given to wider contextual factors, such as disciplinary requirements and expectations of the genre that is the object of investigation.

8.5 Some concluding thoughts

Much has been written about critical thinking and its expression, and this volume is yet another contribution to that extensive literature. The motivation for this stream of literature, as I noted in Chapter 1, arises from the fact that undertaking and communicating critical thinking have been central to Western approaches to knowledge creation and to the appropriation of knowledge through formal education. As noted in Chapter 1 (and again at the beginning of this chapter), given its centrality to Western knowledge and learning, critical thinking is considered a core educational value by governments, their policy-makers, ministries of education and educational institutions at all levels. The ability to exercise critical thinking is considered a central skill to be developed by learners as they pass through their school and university systems. Students are expected to exercise this skill as they process new knowledge and manifest these thinking approaches in the productive outcomes of their learning, such as through written and spoken responses to academic tasks. As a result, for educators, the issue of understanding critical thinking, what it is, and how it can be taught and expressed through writing, remains a central concern and a pedagogic challenge, especially since as was mentioned in Chapter 1, there is a wide diversity of definitional and instructional approaches. However, as has also been raised in this volume, the imperatives placed on teachers and university faculty to develop students' critical thinking skills have tended to presuppose a monolithic knowledge base and singularity of pedagogic approach that simply does not exist, as Brookfield (2012) and others clearly demonstrate. These imperatives have also been predicated on the assumption that, once learned, this uniform and transparent type of critical thinking will 'transfer' across domains and subject disciplines, an assumption that has also been largely refuted, such as by Ramanathan and Kaplan (1996) and others.

Yet the issue remains. Authorities demand that students learn these skills, and the same authorities and the media are quick to complain when they perceive a deficit in these skills among graduating students. Therefore, for writing teachers, thesis supervisors and others, this volume has been a small attempt to uncover the types of textual and discursive knowledge involved, and to describe them in a way that they may be considered and developed in pedagogical contexts. The volume represents a shift in focus on critical thinking from one that centres on general principles of logical reasoning and argumentation to the use of genre analysis to explore how it is constructed through the texts of different disciplines. It is hoped that this approach may help to provide a more grounded approach to writing pedagogy, and also to provide a possible way forward for future research in this area.

Appendices

Appendix A: Sociology Essays from the BAWE Corpus

Sociology Text	Assignment Task	Level	Grade	Corpus File
1	Discuss the implications for women, in gender and class terms, of the rise of medicine as a profession	1	Merit	001c
2	Why do women have children? Why do some not do so?	2	Distinction	001d
3	What groups and individuals are most at risk from unemployment and what explains their vulnerability?	2	Merit	001e
4	Outline the social and political factors that led to the development of feminism in Japan	1	Distinction	002b
5	'Having a view about the nature of social reality is not an option'. What is your own view now, towards the end of the course, and what has persuaded you to adopt it?	1	Distinction	004b
6	Critically evaluate the assertion that sporting practices and their associated subcultures bear no relation whatsoever to the social construction of masculine ideals.	2	Merit	004c
7	Foucault's writings went a long way towards challenging the presumption that in the Victorian period 'On the subject of sex, silence became the rule' (Foucault). Explain and evaluate Foucault's views.	3	Unknown	0156d
8	Are all forms of art part of the 'culture industry'?	2	Merit	0179b
9	There are no parallels in life to the concentration camps. Its horror can never be fully embraced by the imagination for the very reason it stands outside of life and death. Discuss.	2	Merit	0179c
10	What factors led to the idea that there could be a science of society?	1	Merit	0179f
11	The social division between man as 'breadwinner' and woman as 'homemaker' is a product of modern society.	1	Merit	0179h

Sociology Text	Assignment Task	Level	Grade	Corpus File
12	What are the distinctive features of 'modern societies'?	1	Merit	0179i
13	Is motherhood a woman's destiny or the source of her subordination?	2	Unknown	0214d
14	Private/independent and state schools are completely different (and separate) entities. Critically discuss.	3	Distinction	0252j
15	What conclusions should one draw about the 'self' from Goffman's work?	2	Distinction	0252k

Appendix B: English Literature Essays from the BAWE Corpus

English Text	Assignment Tasks	Level	Grade	Corpus File
1	How have any two writers that you have read conceived of social identity through the politics of space and/or place?	3	Distinction	301b
2	Discuss the handling of the discourses of religion and the effects of religious and ethical change in the Victorian period.	3	Distinction	3003a
3	The construction of gender and gender roles in *The Good Soldier* by Ford Madox Ford and *Mrs Dalloway* by Virginia Woolf.	3	Distinction	3004b
4	Discursive written analysis.	1	Distinction	3006a
5	With reference to at least two authors, explore the conflict between the public and private 'self' of the Renaissance.	2	Distinction	3006e
6	'Writers that were part of that period of experimentation that is often termed modernism' seem to have lost faith in narrative. Instead of telling interesting stories, they prefer to capture a mood or create a complex character.' Do you agree' Discuss with reference to at least two texts on the course.	2	Distinction	3006g
7	Consider the ways in which Orwell articulates the relationship between power and language in at least two texts.	2	Distinction	3007a
8	'The author's text is only half the story'. In what ways is meaning always mediated through discursive dialogues?	3	Distinction	3007b
9	How does the text reflect the culture, society, ideas or historical events, or a combination of these, of the time in which it was written? What commentary does the text make upon these issues?	3	Distinction	3008e
10	'Women talk: men are silent: that is why I dread women' (Dickinson). How is the question of gender and speech or eloquence rendered in any of the texts?	3	Distinction	3008f
11	Discuss a single stanza, scene or chapter from two texts from different literary genres assessing their significance to their respective narratives overall.	1	Distinction	3080b

English Text	Assignment Tasks	Level	Grade	Corpus File
12	Examine the relationship between language and spectacle in the texts of at least two authors,	2	Distinction	3080c
13	'Writers that were part of that period of experimentation that is often referred to as 'Modernism' seem to have lost faith in narrative. Instead of telling interesting stories, they ...'	2	Distinction	3110a
14	How important is Montaigne's 'To the Reader' for our appreciation of any two or more of the essays?	1	Merit	3110e
15	Discuss the representation of knowledge in English Renaissance literature	2	Merit	3129a

Appendix C: Example of the Analysis: English Essay 7

EC7	Consider the ways in which Orwell articulates the relationship between power and language in at least two texts	
Sections	Content/Structuring	Criticality/Evaluative Devices
Introduction	Context Move – Principal ideas in Orwell's works • Language is used as a tool to uphold power, such as in the two novels about totalitarianism (Animal Farm & 1984) • A conscious objective approach to the use and observation of language was needed to avoid the type of social degradation seen in Stalin's Soviet Union	
Body	*Psychological Manipulation –* Explanation Cognitive Genre	'The relation between physical labour and navet is *important* because … ' (Reason/Result)
		'Like all modernist writers, Orwell hinted at the booming scientific movement as an extension of the government that was attempting to create a sense of 'reality' in the minds of the population.' (Amplification)
		'From the concepts of control described above, it is possible to see another system of control that the party establishes in Nineteen Eighty-Four: the idealisms of conformity and orthodoxy through the constant monitoring of people's language. '(Grounds/Conclusion)

EC7	Consider the ways in which Orwell articulates the relationship between power and language in at least two texts	
	Political Orthodoxy – Explanation Cognitive Genre	'The <u>tyrannical</u> party's use of 'junior spies' to monitor adults language is a necessary extension of their power for them because ...' (Reason Result)
		'Yet what is <u>striking</u> about the way that the party moulds its citizens into the instruments of its power is the manner of ...' (Amplification)
		'The <u>deceitful</u> aspect of this way of treating people is a very simple one.' (Amplification)
	Emotions – Explanation Cognitive genre	'The <u>cruel</u> fact that they allow the majority of the population to become devoid of any real human emotions to become ...' (Amplification)
		'A <u>key</u> use of the language of songs and poems when they are recited as a whole is the ...' (Amplification)
Conclusion	*The Manipulation of Language* – Discussion Cognitive Genre	'Modernist writers continually infer that a unified sense of self is 'unnatural' in a civilised person .... Therefore, Orwell's vision seems to ...' (Grounds Conclusion)
		Nevertheless, as shown in these two novels ... language is inevitably corrupted by anyone that comes into power ...' (Concess./Contraexp.)
		'The extent to which this is shown in the two novels i<u>s not as improbable</u> as it may seem since already we have seen how ... ' (Reason/Result)
		'In both novels Orwell suggests that ... but what is <u>changeable and important</u> is the need for people outside the circle of power to keep [a] conscious objective approach to the use of language.' (Concession/Contraexpectation)

Appendix D: Source Theses of Discussion Chapters

Thesis	Reference	Methodology/Data	Chapter/Number of Pages/Number of Words
1	Cao, Y. (2009). *Understanding the notion of interdependence, and the dynamics of willingness to communicate.* PhD Dissertation, The University of Auckland.	Multiple case study, qualitative data	Chapter 7, pp. 222–34 (13 pages), 4,326 words
2	Jones, J. (2010). *An ethnographic enquiry into the implementation of the Kenyan Language-in-Education Policy (mother tongue as subject and medium of instruction) in the Sabaot Language Group.* PhD Dissertation, The University of Auckland.	Ethnography, qualitative data	Chapter 8, pp. 247–69 (23 pages), 8,528 words
3	Nguyen, L. V. (2011). *Computer-mediated collaborative learning in a Vietnamese tertiary EFL context: Process, product and learners' perceptions.* PhD Dissertation, Massey University.	Multi-method, including quasi-experiment, quantitative and qualitative data	Chapter 9, pp. 220–49 (30 pages), 10,788 words (estimated)
4	Booth, D. (2012). *Exploring the washback of the TOEIC in South Korea.* PhD Dissertation, The University of Auckland.	Multi-method, quantative and qualitative data	Chapter 10, pp. 253–97 (45 pages), 18,521 words)
5	Rodgers, M. P. H. (2013). *English language learning through viewing television: An investigation of comprehension, incidental vocabulary acquisition, lexical coverage, attitudes and captions.* PhD Dissertation, Victoria University of Wellington.	experimental, quantitative data	Chapter 2, Section 2.11 (6 pages), Chapter 3, Section 3.8 (6 pages), Chapter 4, Section 4.9 (8 pages), Chapter 5, Section 5.8 (5 pages), Chapter 6, Section 6.8 (9 pages); 15,232 words (estimated)

Appendix E: Crombie's Interpropositional Relations

Process	Relation	Definition
Associative	Simple Contrast	Involves the comparison of two things, events or abstractions in terms of some particular in respect of which they differ.
	Comparative Similarity (Simple Comparison)	Involves the comparison of two things, events or abstractions in terms of some particular in respect of which they are similar.
	Statement–Affirmation	The truth of a statement is affirmed.
	Statement–Exception	Involves a statement and an exception to that statement.
	Statement–Exemplification	The first member provides a general statement, and the second adds a proposition that is presented as an exemplification of the general statement in the first member.
	Statement–Denial	Involves the denial of the truth of a statement or validity of a proposition.
	Denial–Correction	Involves a corrective non-antonymic substitute for a denial.
	Concession–Contraexpectation	Involves direct or indirect denial of the truth of an inference.
	Supplementary Alternation	Involves two or more non-antithetical choices.
	Contrastive Alternation	Involves a choice between antitheses.
	Paraphrase	Involves the same proposition expressed in different ways.
	Amplification	Involves implicit or explicit repetition of the propositional content of one member of the relation in the other, together with a non-contrastive addition to that propositional content.

Process	Relation	Definition
Logico-deductive	Condition–Consequence	Involves a consequence that depends upon a realizable or unrealizable condition or hypothetical contingency.
	Means–Purpose	Involves an action that is/was/will be undertaken *with the intention of* achieving a particular result.
	Reason–Result	Involves the provision of a reason *why* a particular effect came about or will come about.
	Means–Result	Involves a statement of *how* a particular result is/was/will be achieved.
	Grounds–Conclusion	Involves a deduction drawn on the basis of an observation.
Tempero-contigual	Chronological Sequence	Provides the semantic link between event propositions one of which follows the other in time. .
	Temporal Overlap	The relation of Temporal Overlap links two events which overlap, either wholly or partly, in time.
	Bonding	This is a non-elective, non-sequential relation between two conjoined or juxtaposed propositions. The second member adds at least one new proposition to the first and the members are not connected in an elective, comparative or sequential way.

(Summarized from Crombie. 1985, pp. 18–28, 1987, p. 102)

Appendix F: The Sample of Fund Manager Commentary Texts

Text Number	Name of Fund	Location	Type of Investment	Date of Commentary
1	Tyndall Option and Corporate Bond funds	New Zealand	Share options, corporate bonds	30 June 2011
2	AMP Capital NZ Property Fund	New Zealand	NZ property	March 2011
3	Gareth Morgan Kiwisaver (NZ pension fund)	New Zealand	Ccash, bonds, equities	June 2011
4	Oakmark Fund	United States	US companies, mid- & large-cap	30 June 2011
5	Oakmark Equity and Income Fund	United States	US equities & fixed income securities	30 June 2011
6	MacKay Shields, Convertible Securities Portfolio (Mainstay Investments)	United States	Convertible securities	31 March 2011
7	Investec Cautious Managed Fund	South Africa	Commodities, equities	31 March 2011
8	PIMCO	United States	Municipal bonds	October 2011
9	Schroders Active Managed Fund	United Kingdom	Global equities and bonds	October 2011
10	Wells Fargo Advantage Funds	United States	Bonds, commercial paper	31 October 2011
11	Thornburg Investment Management Equity Funds	United States	International (non-US) equities	Third Quarter, 2011
12	Janus Overseas Fund	United States	International (non-US) equities	Third quarter 2011
13	Lazard UK Alpha Fund	United Kingdom	UK equities	November 2011
14	John Handcock Balanced Fund	United States	Mixed – equity and debt securities	Third Quarter, 2011

Text Number	Name of Fund	Location	Type of Investment	Date of Commentary
15	MitonOptimal Core Diversified Fund	United Kingdom (Guernsey)	Mixed – cash, bonds, equities, alternative strategies	May 2011
16	Aberdeen American Equity Fund	United Kingdom	North American securities	31 January 2011
17	IRP Property Investments Ltd (F&C Investments)	United Kingdom	Property investments	April 2011
18	Blackrock gold and general fund	United Kingdom	Gold mining	August 2011
19	AXA General Trust GBP	United Kingdom	UK, American and Japanese equities	31 October 2011
20	PruFund Cautious Life Fund/Protected Cautious Life Fund	United Kingdom	Global equities and case	30 September 2011
21	Fidelity Equities Fund (Fidelity Worldwide Investment)	Australia	Australian equities	November 2011
22	Ironbark Karara Australian Share Fund	Australia	Australian equities	October 2011
23	Manulife US All Cap Equity Fund	Canada	Over 90% US equities	30 September 2011
24	Educators Dividend Fund (BMO Asset Management)	Canada	Mainly Canadian and some US equities	30 June 2011
25	BT Wholesale Property Securities Fund	Australia	Property investments	September 2011
26	Compass Portfolio Funds	Canada	Equities and fixed-income securities	2011 Third Quarter
27	Manulife Preferred Income Fund	Canada	Fixed-income securities	30 September 2012
28	Momentum Resources Fund	South Africa	Mining equities	Third Quarter, 2011
29	Momentum Bond Fund	South Africa	Bonds, fixed interest	Third Quarter 2011
30	Franklin Natural Resources Fund	South Africa	Commodities	November 2011

Appendix G: Headings Announcing the Four Moves in the Sample of Texts

Move 1 is variously termed *Fund Performance* (Text 3), *Performance Summary* (Texts 8 & 12), *Performance Data* (Text 13), *Fund Results* (Text 14), *Performance Review* (Text 17), *Cumulative Performance* (Text 18), *Performance* (Texts 19, 23 & 26), *Portfolio Overview* (Text 29).

Move 2 is identified as *Portfolio Performance* (Text, 6,) *Portfolio Review* (Texts 7 & 17), *Performance Discussion* (Text 12), *Performance Review* (Text 14), *Portfolio Activity* (Text 19), *Main changes to the portfolio during October, Factors affecting performance during October* (Text 20), *The Portfolio* (Text 22), *Performance review and portfolio activity* (Text 23), *Portfolio Review* (Text 24), *Fund Performance* (Text 26), *Your portfolio* (Text 27), *Portfolio manager commentary* (Text 28) .

Move 3 is called *Market Summary* (Text 3), *Market Review* (Text 7), *Market Commentary* (Text 8), *Money Market Overview* (Text 10), *Investment Environment* (Text 12), *Market Review* (Texts 13, 17, 19, 23, 24 & 26), *Market Environment* (Text 14), *Current Market Influences and Outlook* (Text 20), *Outlook for Interest Rates* (Text 28), *Economic Overview* (Texts 29 & 30), *Overview* (Text 31).

Move 4 is termed *Strategy Notes* (Text 3), *Portfolio Positioning* (Text 7), *Explanation of Portfolio Characteristics* (Text 8), *Fund Profile* (Text 9), *Outlook* (Texts 13, 14, 17 & 22), *Market Outlook* (Text 24), *Investment Strategy* (Text 25), *Strategy and Outlook* (Text 26), *Conclusion* (Text 27), *Portfolio Positioning* (Texts 29 & 30), *Investment Outlook* (Text 31).

Appendix H: Commentary Articles by Polly Toynbee in The Guardian

Bedroom tax: Why you should march against this heartless, pointless 'reform' (15 March 2013). Retrieved from http://www.theguardian.com/commentisfree/2013/mar/15/bedroom-tax-march-heartless-reform

Will Britain's press repent its nasty ways? Don't hold your breath (18 March 2013). Retrieved from http://www.theguardian.com/commentisfree/2013/mar/18/will-britains-press-repent-its-nasty-ways

Do people get Osborne and co yet? Even Thatcher wouldn't have gone this far (21 March 2013). Retrieved from http://www.theguardian.com/commentisfree/2013/mar/21/do-people-get-osborne-even-thatcher

Labour needs to recapture the spirit and nerve of 1945 (25 March 2013). Retrieved from http://www.theguardian.com/commentisfree/2013/mar/25/labour-recapture-spirit-nerve-1945

Benefit cuts: Monday will be the day that defines this government (28 March 2013). Retrieved from http://www.theguardian.com/commentisfree/2013/mar/28/benefit-cuts-monday-defines-government

The latest cure for the NHS really could kill the patient (1 April 2013). Retrieved from http://www.theguardian.com/commentisfree/2013/apr/01/latest-cure-nhs-kill-patient

IDS should try living on £53 a week. Even minimum wage opened my eyes (2 April 2013). Retrieved from http://www.theguardian.com/commentisfree/2013/apr/02/iain-duncan-smith-53-pounds-a-week

Martine White is a product of British welfare not Mick Philpott (4 April 2013). Retrieved from http://www.theguardian.com/commentisfree/2013/apr/04/martine-white-product-welfare-not-philpott

Thatcher's reckless acolytes don't know where to stop (9 April 2013). Retrieved from http://www.theguardian.com/commentisfree/2013/apr/09/thatcher-acolytes-cameron-dont-know-when-to-stop

Benefits don't look quite the electoral winner Cameron presumed (11 April 2013). Retrieved from http://www.theguardian.com/commentisfree/2013/apr/11/benefits-not-electoral-winner-cameron-presumed

Tony Blair is like a loose horse at the Grand National (16 April 2013). Retrieved from http://www.theguardian.com/commentisfree/2013/apr/16/tony-blair-loose-horse-grand-national

George Osborne's case for austerity has just started to wobble (18 April 2013). Retrieved from http://www.theguardian.com/commentisfree/2013/apr/18/debt-error-bombshell-shatters-austerity

Teacher-bashing: A political sport with no winners (22 April 2013). Retrieved from http://www.theguardian.com/commentisfree/2013/apr/22/teacher-bashing-gove-performance-pay

Labour's lesson after Ukip: Put more passion into your politics (7 May 2013). Retrieved from http://www.theguardian.com/commentisfree/2013/may/07/labour-ukip-passi on-politics

Queen's speech: Sound and fury signifying nothing (8 May 2013). Retrieved from http://www.theguardian.com/commentisfree/2013/may/08/queens-speech-no-substance

Labour must stand firm: No to a referendum on Europe (9 May 2013). Retrieved from http://www.theguardian.com/commentisfree/2013/may/09/labour-fears-eu-refere ndum-britain-europe?CMP=twt_gu

The noise on immigration is drowning out real problems (13 May 2013). Retrieved from http://www.theguardian.com/commentisfree/2013/may/13/noise-immigration -drowning-out-real-problems

Amid Tory disarray, Labour's critical moment looms (17 May 2013). Retrieved from http://www.theguardian.com/commentisfree/2013/may/17/amid-tory-disarray-lab our-critical-moment

Mervyn King's housing warning is too little, too late (21 May 2013). Retrieved from http://www.theguardian.com/commentisfree/2013/may/21/mervyn-king-housi ng-warning-fannie-mae

Jeremy Hunt's blundering blaming of GPs makes for bad politics (23 May 2013). Retrieved from http://www.theguardian.com/commentisfree/2013/may/23/nhs-gps

As Labour's iron man, Ed Balls could do the trick (3 June 2013). Retrieved from http://www.theguardian.com/commentisfree/2013/jun/03/labour-iron-man-ed-balls

Snowden's revelations must not blind us to government as a force for good (10 June 2013). Retrieved from http://www.theguardian.com/commentisfree/2013/jun/10/sn owden-government-force-for-good-big-brother

Forget the excuses, here's how Britain can tax the rich (18 June 2013). Retrieved from http://www.theguardian.com/commentisfree/2013/jun/18/heres-how-britain-can-tax-the-rich

Bankers banged up? They need to return to planet Earth first (19 June 2013). Retrieved from http://www.theguardian.com/commentisfree/2013/jun/19/bankers-banged-up -return-planet-earth

Osborne's comprehensive spending review puts society in intensive care (25 June 2013). Retrieved from http://www.theguardian.com/commentisfree/2013/jun/25/osborne -spending-review-intensive-care

Osborne's comprehensive spending review puts society in intensive care (15 June 2013). Retrieved from http://www.theguardian.com/commentisfree/2013/jun/25/osborne -spending-review-intensive-care

Labour's spending worked. Why don't they defend it (2 July 2013). Retrieved from http://www.theguardian.com/commentisfree/2013/jul/02/labour-spending-worked-blai r-brown-stealth

Peter Mandelson's HS2 epiphany has tipped the balance (3 July 2013). Retrieved from http://www.theguardian.com/commentisfree/2013/jul/03/peter-mandelson-hs2-ep iphany-tipped-balance

Falkirk crisis: Labour needs the unions, but both need members (8 July 2013). Retrieved from http://www.theguardian.com/commentisfree/2013/jul/08/falkirk-labour-unions-empty-democracy

Will Labour have the guts to fight our unfair care system (22 July 2013). Retrieved from http://www.theguardian.com/commentisfree/2013/jul/23/labour-unfair-care-system-elderly

Notes

Chapter 2

1. In this section, my discussion of the terms *text, discourse* and *ideology* are an expanded version of the definitions in Section 1.1 of the article (Bruce, 2015b, pp. 45–6).
2. VBDUs, as segments of texts, are identified by a computational method termed *TextTiling* (Hearst, 1997).
3. The social genre/cognitive model was first proposed in detail in an earlier book (Bruce, 2008a). The description of the model presented here is an adapted summary from a more recent article (Bruce, 2018).

Chapter 3

1. Reprinted with permission from Elsevier.
2. 'Grounds' is the evidence that supports a 'claim', an assertion being made, and 'warrant' is the assumption or principle that links the evidence to the claim. For example: The boy was born in Canada (grounds), so he must be a Canadian citizen (claim). Canada is one of the thirty countries that confers birthright citizenship (warrant).
3. Hyland (2005b, p. 49) explains that *endophoric markers* 'refer to information in other parts of the text, for example, noted above; see Fig; in Section 2', and that *frame markers* 'refer to discourse acts, sequences or stages e.g. finally; to conclude; my purpose is'.
4. The data in this study come from the BAWE Corpus, which was developed at the Universities of Warwick, Reading and Oxford Brookes under the directorship of Hilary Nesi and Sheena Gardner (formerly of the Centre for Applied Linguistics [previously called CELTE], Warwick), Paul Thompson (Department of Applied Linguistics, Reading) and Paul Wickens (Westminster Institute of Education, Oxford Brookes), with funding from the ESRC (RES-000-23-0800).

Chapter 4

1. Reprinted with the permission of the Editor of *ESP Today*.

2 Different metadiscourse devices occurred in other parts of the schema. However, two are highlighted here because of their particular role in constructing the critical statements.

Chapter 5

1 Reprinted with permission from Elsevier.

Chapter 6

1 Reprinted with permission from Sage.

Chapter 7

1 Much of this chapter is reprinted from the journal *Discourse, Context & Media*, Volume 10, Ian Bruce, 'Resisting neoliberalism through political and social critique: *The Guardian* column of Polly Toynbee', pp. 45–52, © 2015, with permission from Elsevier.

References

Abrahamson, E. & Park, C. (1994). Concealment of negative organizational outcomes: An agency theory perspective. *The Academy of Management Journal, 37*(5), 1302–34.
Adam, J.-M. (1985). Quels types de textes? *Le Français dans le Monde, 192*, 39–43.
Adam, J.-M. (1992). *Les Textes: Types et propotypes*. Paris, France: Nathan.
Allison, D., Cooley, L., Lewkowicz, J. & Nunan, D. (1998). Dissertation writing in action: The development of a dissertation writing support program for ESL graduate research students. *English for Specific Purposes, 17*(2), 199–217.
Alton-Lee, A. (1998). A troubleshooter's checklist for prospective authors derived from reviewers' critical feedback. *Teaching and Teacher Education, 14*(8), 887–890.
Alvesson, M. & Karreman, D. (2000). Varieties of discourse: On the study of organizations through discourse analysis. *Human Relations, 53*(9), 1125–49. doi:10.1177/0018726700539002
Andrews, R. (2000). Introduction. In S. Mitchell & R. Andrews (Eds), *Learning to argue in higher education* (pp. 1–14). Portsmouth, NH: Boynton/Cook.
Artemeva, N. (2008). Toward a unified social theory of genre learning. *Journal of Business and Technical Communication, 22*(2), 160–85. doi:10.1177/1050651907311925
Atkinson, D. (1997). A critical approach to critical thinking in TESOL. *TESOL Quarterly, 31*(1), 71–94.
Babaii, E. (2011). Hard science, hard talk? The study of negative comments in physics book reviews. In F. Salager-Meyer & B. A. Lewin (Eds), *Crossed words: Criticism in scholarly writing* (pp. 55–77). Bern, Switzerland: Lang.
Babaii, E. & Ansary, H. (2005). On the effect of disciplinary variation on transitivity: The case of academic book reviews. *Asian EFL Journal, 7*(3), 113–26.
Bacha, N. N. (2010). Teaching the academic argument in a university EFL environment. *Journal of English for Academic Purposes, 9*(3), 229–41.
Bailey, S. (2018). *Academic writing: A handbook for international students* (5th edn). London, UK: Routledge.
Bakhtin, M. M. (1986). *Speech genres and other late essays* (M. A. Holquist & C. Emerson, Trans.). Austin: University of Texas Press.
Barnett, C. (2005). The consolations of 'neoliberalism'. *Geoforum, 36*(1), 7–12.
Barron, O. E., Kile, C. O. & O'Keefe, T. B. (1999). MD&A quality as measured by the SEC and analysts' earnings forecasts. *Contemporary Accounting Research, 16*(1), 75–109.
Barsalou, L. W. (1983). Ad hoc categories. *Memory & Cognition, 11*(3), 211–27.

Basturkmen, H. (2009). Commenting on results in published research articles and masters dissertations in language teaching. *Journal of English for Academic Purposes*, 8(4), 241–51. doi:10.1016/j.jeap.2009.07.001

Basturkmen, H. & Von Randow, J. (2014). Guiding the reader (or not) to re-create coherence: Observations on postgraduate student writing in an academic argumentative writing task. *Journal of English for Academic Purposes*, 16, 14–22.

Bawarshi, A. S. & Reiff, M. J. (2010). *Genre: An introduction to history, theory, research, and pedagogy*. West Lafayette, IN: Parlor Press.

Bazerman, C. (1997). The life of genre, the life in the classroom. In W. Bishop & H. Ostrom (Eds), *Genre and writing: Issues, arguments, alternatives* (pp. 19–26). Portsmouth, NH: Boynton/Cook.

Beattie, V., Dhanani, A. & Jones, M. J. (2008). Investigating presentational change in U.K. annual reports: A longitudinal perspective. *Journal of Business Communication*, 45(2), 181–222.

Bennett, J. (2013). Moralising class: A discourse analysis of the mainstream political response to occupy and the August 2011 British riots. *Discourse & Society*, 24(1), 27–45. doi:10.1177/0957926512463634

Berkenkotter, C. & Huckin, T. N. (1995). *Genre knowledge in disciplinary communication: Cognition/culture/power*. Hillsdale, NJ: Erlbaum.

Bhatia, V. K. (1993). *Analysing genre: Language use in professional settings*. Burnt Mill, UK: Longman.

Bhatia, V. K. (1998). Generic conflicts in academic discourse. In T. Dudley-Evans & I. Fortanet Gomez (Eds), *Genre studies in English for academic purposes* (pp. 15–28). Castello de la Plana, Spain: Jaume I University.

Bhatia, V. K. (2002). Applied genre analysis: A multiperspective model. *Ibérica*, 4, 3–19.

Bhatia, V. K. (2004). *Worlds of written discourse: A genre-based view*. New York, NY: Continuum.

Bhatia, V. K. (2008). Genre analysis, ESP and professional practice. *English for Specific Purposes*, 27(2), 161–74.

Bhatia, V. K. (2010). Interdiscursivity in professional communication. *Discourse & Communication*, 4(1), 32–50.

Biber, D. (1989). A typology of English texts. *Linguistics*, 27(1), 3–44.

Biber, D., Csomay, E., Jones, K. & Keck, C. (2007). Introduction to the identification and analysis of vocabulary-based discourse units. In D. Biber, U. Connor & T. A. Upton (Eds), *Discourse on the move: Using corpus analysis to describe discourse structure. Studies in corpus linguistics* (pp. 155–73). Amsterdam, The Netherlands: Benjamins.

Biber, D. & Finegan, E. (1989). Styles of stance in English: Lexical and grammatical marking of evidentiality and affect. *Text-Interdisciplinary Journal for the Study of Discourse*, 9(1), 93–124.

Bitchener, J. (2010). *Writing an applied linguistics thesis or dissertation: A guide to presenting empirical research*. Basingstoke, UK: Palgrave Macmillan.

Bitchener, J. & Basturkmen, H. (2006). Perceptions of the difficulties of postgraduate L2 thesis students writing the discussion section. *Journal of English for Academic Purposes, 5*(1), 4–18.

Blommaert, J. (2005). *Discourse: A critical introduction*. Cambridge, UK: Cambridge University Press.

Boas, T. & Gans-Morse, J. (2009). Neoliberalism: From new liberal philosophy to antiliberal slogan. *Studies in Comparative International Development, 44*(2), 137–61. doi:10.1007/s12116-009-9040-5

Boote, D. N. & Beile, P. (2005). Scholars before researchers: On the centrality of the dissertation literature review in research preparation. *Educational Researcher, 34*(6), 3–15.

Borg, E. (2003). Key concepts in ELT: Discourse community. *ELT Journal, 57*(4), 398–400.

Brookfield, S. D. (2012). *Teaching for critical thinking: Tools and techniques to help students question their assumptions*. San Fransisco, CA: Wiley.

Bruce, I. (2008a). *Academic writing and genre: A systematic analysis*. London, UK: Continuum.

Bruce, I. (2008b). Cognitive genre structures in methods sections of research articles: A corpus study. *Journal of English for Academic Purposes, 7*(1), 38–54.

Bruce, I. (2009). Results sections in sociology and organic chemistry articles: A genre analysis. *English for Specific Purposes, 28*(2), 105–24. doi:10.1016/j.esp.2008.12.005

Bruce, I. (2010a). Textual and discoursal resources used in the essay genre in sociology and English. *Journal of English for Academic Purposes, 9*, 153–66. doi:10.1016/j.jeap.2010.02.011

Bruce, I. (2010b). Evolving genres in online domains: The hybrid genre of the participatory news article. In A. Mehler, S. Sharoff & M. Santini (Eds), *Genres on the Web* (pp. 323–48). Dordrecht, The Netherlands: Springer.

Bruce, I. (2014a). Expressing criticality in the literature review in research article introductions in applied linguistics and psychology. *English for Specific Purposes, 36*, 85–96.

Bruce, I. (2014b). Enacting criticality in corporate disclosure communication: The genre of the fund manager commentary. *International Journal of Business Communication, 51*(4), 315–36.

Bruce, I. (2015a). Use of cognitive genres as textual norms in academic. *Bulletin VALS-ASLA, T2*, 161–75.

Bruce, I. (2015b). Resisting neoliberalism through political and social critique: The Guardian column of Polly Toynbee. *Discourse, Context & Media, 10*, 45–52.

Bruce, I. (2016). Constructing critical stance in university essays in English literature and sociology. *English for Specific Purposes, 42*, 13–25.

Bruce, I. (2018). The textual expression of critical thinking in PhD discussions in applied linguistics. *ESP Today, 6*(1), 2–24. Doi:10.18485/esptoday.2018.6.1.1

Bruce, I. J. (2003). *Cognitive genre prototype modelling and its implications for the teaching of academic writing to learners of English as a second language* (PhD dissertation). University of Waikato, Hamilton, New Zealand.

Bryan, S. H. (1997). Incremental information content of required disclosures contained in management discussion and analysis. *The Accounting Review, 72*(2), 285–301.

Carrell, P. L. (1981). *Culture-specific schemata in L2 comprehension.* Paper presented at the Selected papers from the ninth Illinois TESOL/BE annual convention, First Midwest TESOL Conference.

Carrell, P. L. (1987). Content and formal schemata in ESL reading. *TESOL Quarterly, 21*(3), 461–481.

Casanave, C. P. & Hubbard, P. (1992). The writing assignments and writing problems of doctoral students: Faculty perceptions, pedagogical issues, and needed research. *English for Specific Purposes, 11*(1), 33–49.

Channell, J. (2000). Corpus-based analysis of evaluative lexis. In S. Hunston & G. Thompson (Eds), *Evaluation in text: Authorial stance and the construction of discourse* (pp. 38–55). Oxford, UK: Oxford University Press.

Charles, M. (2006). The construction of stance in reporting clauses: A cross-disciplinary study of theses. *Applied Linguistics, 27*(3), 492–518.

Clark, G., Thrift, N. & Tickell, A. (2004). Performing finance: The industry, the media and its image. *Review of International Political Economy, 11*(2), 289–310. doi:10.1080/09692290420001672813

Clark Williams, C. (2008). Toward a taxonomy of corporate reporting strategies. *Journal of Business Communication, 45*(3), 232–64.

Clarke, J. (2004). Dissolving the public realm? The logics and limits of neo-liberalism. *Journal of Social Policy, 33*(1), 27–48.

Clarkson, P. M., Kao, J. L. & Richardson, G. D. (1999). Evidence that management discussion and analysis (MD&A) is a part of a firm's overall disclosure package. *Contemporary Accounting Research, 16*(1), 111–34. Retrieved from http://search.ebscohost.com/login.aspx?direct=true&db=buh&AN=2323988&site=ehost-live

Coffin, C., Curry, M. J., Goodman, S., Hewings, A., Lillis, T. & Swann, J. (2003). *Teaching academic writing: A toolkit for higher education.* London, UK: Routledge.

Cohen, L., Manion, L. & Morrison, K. (2011). *Research methods in education* (7 edn). London, UK: Routledge.

Cohen, L., Manion, L. & Morrison, K. (2018). *Research methods in education* (8 edn). London, UK: Routledge.

Collins, A., Brown, J. S. & Newman, S. F. (1989). Cognitive apprenticeship: Teaching the crafts of reading, writing and mathematics. In R. Glaser & L. B. Resnick (Eds), *Knowing, learning and instruction* (pp. 453–94). Hillsdale, NJ: Erlbaum

Comte, A. (1974). *The positive philosophy.* New York, NY: AMS Press.

Cone, J. D. & Foster, S. L. (1993). *Dissertations and theses from start to finish: Psychology and related fields.* Washington, DC: American Psychological Association.

Connor, U. & Mauranen, A. (1999). Linguistic analysis of grant proposals: European union research grants. *English for Specific Purposes, 18*(1), 47–62.

Conrad, S. & Biber, D. (2000). Adverbial marking of stance in speech and writing. In S. Hunston & G. Thompson (Eds), *Evaluation in text: Authorial stance and the construction of discourse* (pp. 56–73). Oxford, UK: Oxford University Press.

Cooley, L. & Lewkowicz, J. (1995). The writing needs of postgraduate students at the University of Hong Kong: A project report. *Hong Kong paper in Linguistics and Language Teaching, 18*, 121–3.

Cooley, L. & Lewkowicz, J. (1997). Developing awareness of the rhetorical and linguistic conventions of writing a thesis in English: Addressing the needs of EFL/ESL postgraduate students. *Trends in Linguistics Studies and Monographs, 104*, 113–30.

Cortazzi, M. & Jin, L. (2000). Evaluating evaluation in narrative. In S. Hunston & G. Thompson (Eds), *Evaluation in text: Authorial stance and the construction of discourse* (pp. 102–20). Oxford, UK: Oxford University Press.

Council of Europe. Council for Cultural Co-operation. Education Committee. Modern Languages Division. (2001). *Common European framework of reference for languages: Learning, teaching, assessment.* Cambridge, UK: University of Cambridge.

Council of Writing Programe Administrators. (2014). WPA Outcomes Statement for First-Year Composition (3.0), Approved 17 July 2014. Retrieved from http://wpa council.org/positions/outcomes.html

Craswell, G. & Poore, M. (2011). *Writing for academic success.* Los Angeles, CA: Sage.

Crawford Camiciottoli, B. (2009). Discourse connectives in genres of financial disclosure: Earnings presentations vs. earnings releases. *Journal of Pragmatics, 42*(3), 650–63.

Creme, P. & Lea, M. (2008). *Writing at university: A guide for students.* Maidenhead, UK: McGraw-Hill.

Crombie, W. (1985). *Process and relation in discourse and language learning.* Oxford, UK: Oxford University Press.

Davies, M. & Barnett, R. (2015). *The Palgrave handbook of critical thinking in higher education.* New York, NY: Palgrave Macmillan.

Day, J. F. S. (1986). The use of annual reports by UK investment analysts. *Accounting and Business Research, 16*(64), 295–307. Retrieved from http://search.ebscohost.com/login.aspx?direct=true&db=buh&AN=13813152&site=ehost-live

Del Lungo Camiciotti, G. & Tognini-Bonelli, E. (Eds). (2004). *Academic discourse: New insights into evaluation.* Bern, Switzerland: Lang.

Derewianka, B. (1990). *Exploring how texts work.* Rozelle, Australia: Primary English Teaching.

Devitt, A. J. (2004). *Writing genres.* Carbondale: Southern Illinois University Press.

Diani, D. (2009). Reporting and evaluation in English book review articles. In K. Hyland & G. Diani (Eds), *Academic evaluation: Review genres in university settings* (pp. 87–104). Basingstoke, UK: Palgrave Macmillan.

Dong, Y. R. (1998). Non-native graduate students' thesis/dissertation writing in science: Self-reports by students and their advisors from two US institutions. *English for Specific Purposes, 17*(4), 369–90.

Dörnyei, Z. (2007). *Research methods in applied linguistics: Quantitative, qualitative, and mixed methodologies.* Oxford, UK: Oxford University Press.

Dressen, D. (2003). Geologists' implicit persuasive strategies and the construction of evaluative evidence. *Journal of English for Academic Purposes, 2*(4), 273–90. doi:10.1016/S1475-1585(03)00046-8

Drew, P. (2004). Integrating qualitative analysis of evaluative discourse with the quantitative approach of corpus linguistics. In G. Del Lungo Camiciotti & E. Tognini-Bonelli (Eds), *Academic discourse: New insights into evaluation* (pp. 217–29). Bern, Switzerland: Lang.

Dudley-Evans, A. (1986). Genre analysis: An investigation of the introductions and discussion sections of MSc dissertations. In M. Coulthard (Ed.), *Talking about text* (pp. 128–45). Birmingham, UK: University of Birmingham.

Dudley-Evans, T. (1989). An outline of the value of genre analysis in LSP work. In C. Lauren & M. Nordman (Eds), *Special language: From humans thinking to thinking machines* (pp. 72–79). Clevedon, UK: Multilingual Matters.

Dudley-Evans, T. (1993). Variation in communication patterns between discourse communities: The case of highway engineering and plant biology. In G. M. Blue (Ed.), *Language, learning and success: Studying through English* (pp. 141–7). London, UK: Macmillan.

Dudley-Evans, T. (1994). Genre analysis: An approach to text analysis in ESP. In M. Coulthard (Ed.), *Advances in written text analysis* (pp. 219–28). London, UK: Routledge.

Eggins, S. (2004). *Introduction to systemic functional linguistics* (2nd edn). London, UK: Continuum.

Ennis, R. H. (1989). Critical thinking and subject specificity: Clarification and needed research. *Educational Researcher, 18*(3), 4–10.

Epstein, G. A. (2005). *Financialization and the world economy.* Cheltenham, UK: Elgar.

Evans, D., Gruba, P. & Zobel, J. (2011). *How to write a better thesis.* Melbourne, Australia: Melbourne University.

Facione, P. (1990). *Critical thinking: A statement of expert consensus for purposes of educational assessment and instruction* (The Delphi Report). Retrieved from https://philpapers.org/rec/FACCTA

Feyerabend, P. (1975). *Against method : Outline of an anarchistic theory of knowledge.* London, UK: New Left Books.

Foucault, M. (1984). The order of discourse. In M. J. Shapiro (Ed.), *Language and politics* (pp. 108–38). Oxford, UK: Blackwell.

Freedman, A. & Medway, P. (1994). *Learning and teaching genre.* Portsmouth, NH: Boynton/Cook.

Friedman, M. & Friedman, R. D. (1962). *Capitalism and freedom*. Chicago, MI: University of Chicago Press.

Gee, J. P. (2011). *How to do discourse analysis: A toolkit*. New York, NY: Routledge.

Giannoni, D. S. (2011). 'Don't Be stupid about intelligent design': Confrontational impoliteness in medical journal editorials. In F. Salager-Meyer & B. A. Lewin (Eds), *Crossed words: Criticism in scholarly writing* (pp. 79–98). Bern, Switzerland: Lang.

Gibbins, M., Richardson, A. & Waterhouse, J. (1990). The management of corporate financial disclosure: Opportunism, ritualism, policies, and processes. *Journal of Accounting Research*, 28(1), 121–43. Retrieved from http://www.jstor.org/stable/2491219

Gilbert, G. N. & Mulkay, M. (1984). *Opening Pandora's box: A sociological analysis of scientists' discourse*. Cambridge, UK: Cambridge University Press.

Gillaerts, P. & Van de Velde, F. (2010). Interactional metadiscourse in research article abstracts. *Journal of English for Academic Purposes*, 9(2), 128–39. doi:10.1016/j.jeap.2010.02.004

Glaser, R. (1984). Education and thinking: The role of knowledge. *American psychologist*, 39(2), 93.

Grabe, W. (2002). Narrative and expository macro-genres. In A. M. Johns (Ed.), *Genre in the classroom: Multiple perspectives* (pp. 249–67). Mahwah, NJ: Erlbaum.

Grabe, W. & Kaplan, R. B. (1996). *Theory and practice of writing: An applied linguistic perspective*. New York, NY: Longman.

Gramsci, A. (1971). *Selections from the prison notebooks of Antonio Gramsci* (Q. Hoare & G. Nowell-Smith, Trans.). London, UK: Lawrence & Wishart.

Hale, G., Taylor, C., Bridgeman, B., Carson, J., Kroll, B. & Kantor, R. (1995). A study of writing tasks assigned in academic degree programs. *ETS Research Report Series*, 1995(RR-95-44, TOEFL-RR-54). doi:10.1002/j.2333-8504.1995.tb01678.x

Halliday, M. A. K. (1978). *Language as a social semiotic: The social interpretation of language and meaning*. London, UK: Arnold.

Halliday, M. A. K. (1989). Context of situation. In M. A. K. Halliday & R. Hasan (Eds), *Language, context and text: Aspects of language in a social-semiotic perspective* (pp. 3–14). Oxford, UK: Oxford University Press.

Halliday, M. A. K. & Hasan, R. (1976). *Cohesion in English*. London, UK: Longman.

Halpern, D. F. (1998). Teaching critical thinking for transfer across domains: Disposition, skills, structure training, and metacognitive monitoring. *American Psychologist*, 53(4), 449.

Halpern, D. F. (2001). Assessing the effectiveness of critical thinking instruction. *The Journal of General Education*, 50(4), 270–86.

Harvey, D. (2005). *A brief history of neoliberalism*. Oxford, UK: Oxford University Press.

Hasan, R. (1989). The identity of a text. In M. A. K. Halliday & R. Hasan (Eds), *Language, text and context* (pp. 97–118). Oxford, UK: Oxford University Press.

Hayek, F. A. (1978). *The constitution of liberty*. Chicago, MI: University of Chicago Press.

Hearst, M. A. (1997). TextTiling: Segmenting text into multi-paragraph subtopic passages. *Computational Linguistics, 23*(1), 33–64.

Hewings, M. (2010). Materials for university essay writing. In N. Harwood (Ed.), *English language teaching materials: Theory and practice* (pp. 251–78). New York, NY: Cambridge University Press.

Hirst, P. H. (2009). The logical and psychological aspects of teaching a subject. In R. S. Peters (Ed.), *The concept of education* (pp. 31–42). Florence, KY: Routledge.

Hoey, M. (1979). *Signalling in discourse*. Birmingham, UK: English Language Research, University of Birmingham.

Hoey, M. (1983). *On the surface of discourse*. London, UK: Allen & Unwin.

Hoey, M. (1991). *Patterns in lexis in text*. Oxford, UK: Oxford University Press.

Hoey, M. (1994). Signalling in discourse: A functional analysis of a common discourse pattern in spoken and written English. In M. Coulthard (Ed.), *Advances in written text analysis* (pp. 26–45). London, UK: Routledge.

Hoey, M. (2000). Persuasive rhetoric in linguistics: A stylistic study of some features of the language of Noam Chomsky. In S. Hunston & G. Thompson (Eds), *Evaluation in text: Authorial stance and the construction of discourse* (pp. 28–37). Oxford, UK: Oxford University Press.

Hoey, M. (2001). *Textual interaction: An introduction to written discourse analysis*. London, UK: Routledge.

Holmes, R. (1997). Genre analysis, and the social sciences: An investigation of the structure of research article discussion sections in three disciplines. *English for Specific Purposes, 16*(4), 321–37.

Hood, S. (2016). Systemic functional linguistics and EAP. In K. Hyland & P. Shaw (Eds), *The Routledge handbook of English for academic purposes* (pp. 193–205). London, UK: Routledge.

Hopkins, A. & Dudley-Evans, T. (1988). A genre-based investigation of the discussion sections in articles and dissertations. *English for Specific Purposes, 7*(2), 113–21.

Huber, C. R. & Kuncel, N. R. (2016). Does college teach critical thinking? A meta-analysis. *Review of Educational Research, 86*(2), 431–68. doi:10.3102/0034654315605917

Humphrey, S. & Hao, J. (2011). Deconstructing written genres in undergraduate biology. *Linguistics & the Human Sciences, 7*, 29–53.

Hunston, S. & Sinclair, J. (2000). A local grammar of evaluation. In S. Hunston & G. Thompson (Eds), *Evaluation in text: Authorial stance and the construction of discourse* (pp. 74–101). Oxford, UK: Oxford University Press.

Hunston, S. & Thompson, G. (2000). *Evaluation in text: Authorial stance and the construction of discourse*. Oxford, UK: Oxford University Press.

Hyland, K. (1998a). Persuasion and context: The pragmatics of academic metadiscourse. *Journal of Pragmatics, 30*(4), 437–55. doi: 10.1016/S0378-2166(98)00009-5

Hyland, K. (1998b). Exploring corporate rhetoric: Metadiscourse in the CEO's letter. *Journal of Business Communication, 35*(2), 224–45. Retrieved from http://search.ebscohost.com/login.aspx?direct=true&db=ufh&AN=1310707&site=ehost-live

Hyland, K. (1996). Writing without conviction? Hedging in science research articles. *Applied Linguistics, 17*(4), 433–54.

Hyland, K. (2004). *Genre and second language writing*. Ann Arbor: University of Michigan Press.

Hyland, K. (2005a). Stance and engagement: A model of interaction in academic discourse. *Discourse Studies, 7*(2), 173–92. doi: 10.1177/1461445605050365

Hyland, K. (2005b). *Metadiscourse: Exploring interaction in writing*. London, UK: Continuum.

Hyland, K. (2009). *Academic discourse: English in a global context*. London, UK: Continuum.

Hyland, K. & Diani, G. (2009). *Academic evaluation: Review genres in university settings*. Basingstoke, UK: Palgrave Macmillan.

Hyon, S. (1996). Genre in three traditions: Implications for ESL. *TESOL Quarterly, 30*(4), 693–722. Retrieved from http://www.jstor.org/stable/3587930

Jameson, D. A. (2000). Telling the investment story: A narrative analysis of shareholder reports. *Journal of Business Communication, 37*(1), 7–38. doi:10.1177/002194360003700101

Jenkins, S., Jordan, M. K. & Weiland, P. O. (1993). The role of writing in graduate engineering education: A survey of faculty beliefs and practices. *English for Specific Purposes, 12*(1), 51–67.

Johns, A. M. (1997). *Text, role and context: Developing academic literacies*. Cambridge, UK: Cambridge University Press.

Johns, A. M. (2001). The future is with us: Preparing diverse students for the challenges of university texts and cultures. In M. A. Hewings (Ed.), *Academic writing in context: Implications and applications* (pp. 30–42). London, UK: Continuum.

Johns, A. M. (Ed.). (2002). *Genre in the classroom: Multiple perspectives*. Mahwah, NJ: Erlbaum.

Johns, A. M. (2008). Genre awareness for the novice academic student: An ongoing quest. *Language Teaching, 41*(2), 237–52. doi:10.1017/S0261444807004892

Johnson, M. (1987). *The body in the mind: The bodily basis of meaning, imagination, and reason*. Chicago, MI: University of Chicago Press.

Jordan, R. R. (1997). *English for academic purposes: A guide and resource book for teachers*. Cambridge, UK: Cambridge University Press.

Judd, V. C. & Tims, B. J. (1991). How annual reports communicate a customer orientation. *Industrial Marketing Management, 20*(4), 353–60. Retrieved from http://www.sciencedirect.com/science/article/pii/0019850191900114

Kanoksilapatham, B. (2003). *A corpus-based investigation of scientific research articles: Linking move analysis with multidimensional analysis*. (Unpublished doctoral dissertation). Georgetown University, Washington, DC.

Kanoksilapatham, B. (2012). Research article structure of research article introductions in three engineering subdisciplines. *IEEE Transactions on Professional Communication, 55*(4), 294–309.

Knapp, P. & Watkins, M. (1994). *Context - text - grammar: Teaching the genres and grammar of school writing in infants and primary classrooms*. Broadway, Australia: Text Productions.

Knapp, P. & Watkins, M. (2005). *Genre, text, grammar: Technologies for teaching and assessing writing*. Sydney, Australia: University of New South Wales Press.

Knorr Cetina, K. (1999). *Epistemic cultures: How the sciences make knowledge*. Cambridge, MA: Harvard University Press.

Knott, A. & Sanders, T. (1998). The classification of coherence relations and their linguistic markers: An exploration of two languages. *Journal of Pragmatics, 30*(2), 135–75.

Koutsantoni, D. (2011). 'I felt that the proposal had some promise, but was hampered by lack of specificity': Personal attribution and mitigation in grant proposals review reports. In F. Salager-Meyer & B. A. Lewin (Eds), *Crossed words: Criticism in scholarly writing* (pp. 99–126). Bern, Switzerland: Lang.

Kuhn, T. S. (1962). *The structure of scientific revolutions*. Chicago, MI: University of Chicago Press.

Kwan, B. S. (2006). The schematic structure of literature reviews in doctoral theses of applied linguistics. *English for Specific Purposes, 25*(1), 30–55.

Kwan, B. S. C., Chan, H. & Lam, C. (2012). Evaluating prior scholarship in literature reviews of research articles: A comparative study of practices in two research paradigms. *English for Specific Purposes, 31*(3), 188–201. doi:10.1016/j.esp.2012.02.003

Labov, W. & Waletzky, J. (1967). Narrative analysis: Oral versions of personal experience. In J. Helm (Ed.), *Essays on the verbal and visual arts* (p. 44). Seattle, WA: University of Washington.

Lackstrom, J., Selinker, L. & Trimble, L. (1973). Technical rhetorical principles and grammatical choice. *TESOL Quarterly, 7*(2), 127–36. Retrieved from http://www.jstor.org/stable/3585556

Lakoff, G. (1987). *Women, fire, and dangerous things*. Chicago, MI: Chicago University Press.

Laskin, A. V. (2009). A descriptive account of the investor relations profession. *Journal of Business Communication, 46*(2), 208–33. doi: 10.1177/0021943608328078

Latour, B. & Woolgar, S. (1986). *Laboratory life: The construction of scientific facts*. Princeton, NJ: Princeton University Press.

Lave, J. & Wenger, E. (1991). *Situated learning: Legitimate peripheral participation*. Cambridge, UK: Cambridge University Press.

Lea, M. R. & Street, B. V. (1998). Student writing in higher education: An academic literacies approach. *Studies in Higher Education, 23*(2), 157–72.

Lea, M. R. & Street, B. V. (2006). The 'academic literacies' model: Theory and applications. *Theory into Practice, 45*(4), 368–77.

Lee, J. J. & Casal, J. E. (2014). Metadiscourse in results and discussion chapters: A cross-linguistic analysis of English and Spanish thesis writers in engineering. *System, 46*, 39–54.

Lee, S. H. (2015). Evaluative stances in persuasive essays by undergraduate students: Focusing on appreciation resources. *Text & Talk, 35*(1), 49–76.

Lee, T. A., Tweedie, D. P. & Institute of Chartered Accountants in England Wales Research Committee. (1977). *The private shareholder and the corporate report: A report to the Research Committee of the Institute of Chartered Accountants in England and Wales*. London, UK: Institute of Chartered Accountants in England and Wales.

Levitas, R. (2005). *The inclusive society?: Social exclusion and New Labour* (2nd edn). Basingstoke, UK: Palgrave Macmillan.

Lewin, B. A. & Fine, J. (1996). The writing of research texts: Genre analysis and its applications. In G. Rijlaarsdam, H. Van den Bergh & M. Couzjin (Eds), *Theories, models and methodology in writing research* (pp. 423–44). Amsterdam, The Netherlands: Amsterdam University Press.

Lewin, B. A. & Perpignan, H. (2011). Mind the gap: Criticism in literary criticism. In F. Salager-Meyer & B. A. Lewin (Eds), *Crossed words: Criticism in scholarly writing* (pp. 127–51). Bern, Switzerland: Lang.

Lovitts, B. E. (2007). *Making the implicit explicit: Creating performance expectations* for the dissertation. Sterling, VA: Stylus.

Martin, J. R. (1984). Language, register and genre. In F. Christie (Ed.), *Children writing: Reader* (Vol. 1, p. 984). Geelong, Australia: Deakin University.

Martin, J. R. (1986). Intervening in the process of writing development. In C. Painter & J. R. Martin (Eds), *Writing to mean: Teaching genres across the curriculum* (pp. 11–43). Woolongong, Australia: Applied Linguistics Association of Australia.

Martin, J. R. (1992). *English text: System and structure*. Philadelphia, PA: Benjamins.

Martin, J. R. (1994). Macro-genres: The ecology of the page. *Network, 21*, 29–52.

Martin, J. R. (1995). Text and clause: Fractal resonance. *Text, 15*, 5–42.

Martin, J. R. (1997). Analysing genre: Functional parameters. In F. Christie & J. Martin (Eds), *Genre and institutions: Social processes in the workplace and school* (pp. 3–39). London, UK: Cassell.

Martin, J. R. (2000a). Design and practice: Enacting functional linguistics. *Annual Review of Applied Linguistics, 20*(1), 116–26.

Martin, J. R. (2000b). Beyond exchange: Appraisal systems in English. In S. Hunston & G. Thompson (Eds), *Evaluation in text: Authorial stance and the construction of discourse* (pp. 142–75). Oxford, UK: Oxford University Press.

Martin, J. R. & Rose, D. (2008). *Genre relations: Mapping culture*. London, UK: Equinox.

Martin, J. R. & White, P. R. R. (2005). *The language of evaluation: Appraisal in English*. Basingstoke, UK: Basingstoke : Palgrave Macmillan.

McPeck, J. E. (1981). *Critical thinking and education*. Oxford, UK: Robertson.

Mei, W. S. (2006). Creating a contrastive rhetorical stance: Investigating the strategy of problematization in students' argumentation. *RELC Journal, 37*(3), 329–53.

Miller, C. R. (1984). Genre as social action. *Quarterly Journal of Speech, 70*(2), 151–67. doi:10.1080/00335638409383686

Mitchell, S. (2000). Putting argument into the mainstream. In S. Mitchell & R. Andrews (Eds), *Learning to argue in higher education* (pp. 146–54). Portsmouth, NH: Boynton/Cook.

Moore, T. & Morton, J. (1999). Authenticity in the IELTS Academic Module Writing Test: A comparative study of Task 2 items and university assignments. *IELTS Research Reports, 2,* 64–106.

Moore, T. & Morton, J. (2005). Dimensions of difference: A comparison of university writing and IELTS writing. *Journal of English for Academic Purposes, 4*(1), 43–66.

Moreno, A. I. & Suárez, L. (2009). Academic book reviews in English and Spanish: Critical comments and rhetorical structure. In K. Hyland & G. Diani (Eds), *Academic evaluation: Review genres in university settings* (pp. 161–78). Basingstoke, UK: Palgrave Macmillan.

Murphy, G. L. & Medin, D. L. (1985). The role of theories in conceptual coherence. *Psychological Review, 92*(3), 289–316. doi:10.1037/0033-295x.92.3.289

Murray, N. (2012). *Writing essays in English language and linguistics: Principles, tips and strategies for undergraduates.* London, UK: Cambridge University Press.

Navarro, F. (2011). The critical act as a pragmatic unit for studying academic conflict: A methodological framework. In F. Salager-Meyer & B. A. Lewin (Eds), *Crossed words: Criticism in scholarly writing* (pp. 23–52). Bern, Switzerland: Lang.

Nesi, H. & Gardner, S. (2006). Variation in disciplinary culture: University tutors' views on assessed writing tasks. In R. Kiely, G. Clibbon & P. Rea-Dickens (Eds), *Language, culture and identity in applied linguistics* (pp. 99–117). London, UK: Equinox.

Nesi, H. & Gardner, S. (2012). *Genres across the disciplines: Student writing in higher education.* Cambridge, UK: Cambridge University Press.

North, S. (2005). Disciplinary variation in the use of theme in undergraduate essays. *Applied Linguistics, 26*(3), 431–52.

Nwogu, K. N. (1991). Structure of science popularizations: A genre-analysis approach to the schema of popularized medical texts. *English for Specific Purposes, 10*(2), 111–23. Retrieved from http://www.sciencedirect.com/science/article/B6VDM-465D8GK-19/2/3c76408f9433568e8a6708bb36073168

Oldroyd, D. R. (1986). *The arch of knowledge: An introductory study of the history of the philosophy and methodology of science.* Kensington, Australia: New South Wales University Press.

Oller, J. W., Jr. (1995). Adding abstract to formal and content schemata: Results of recent work in Peircean semiotics. *Applied Linguistics, 16*(3), 273–306.

Oshima, A., Hogue, A. & Lê, H. L. (2006). *Writing academic English* (4th edn). White Plains, NY: Pearson/Longman.

Paltridge, B. (2002). Genre, text type and the English for Academic Purposes (EAP) classroom. In A. M. Johns (Ed.), *Genre in the classroom: Multiple perspectives* (pp. 73–90). Mahwah, NJ: Erlbaum.

Paltridge, B. (2004). The exegesis as a genre: An ethnographic examination. In L. J. Ravelli & R. A. Ellis (Eds), *Analysing academic writing: Contextualized frameworks* (pp. 84–103). London, UK: Continuum.

Paltridge, B. & Starfield, S. (2007). *Thesis and dissertation writing in a second language: A handbook for supervisors*. London, UK: Routledge.

Paltridge, B., Starfield, S., Ravelli, L. & Nicholson, S. (2012). Doctoral writing in the visual and performing arts: Two ends of a continuum. *Studies in Higher Education*, *37*(8), 989–1003.

Paltridge, B., Starfield, S., Ravelli, L. J. & Tuckwell, K. (2012). Change and stability: Examining the macrostructures of doctoral theses in the visual and performing arts. *Journal of English for Academic Purposes*, *11*(4), 332–44. doi: 10.1016/j.jeap.2012.08.003

Parkinson, J. (2011). The discussion section as argument: The language used to prove knowledge claims. *English for Specific Purposes*, *30*(3), 164–75.

Peacock, M. (2002). Communicative moves in the discussion section of research articles. *System*, *30*(4), 479–97.

Pilegaard, M. & Frandsen, F. (1996). Text type. In J. Verschueren, J.-O. Ostaman, J. Blommaert & C. C. Bulcaen (Eds), *Handbook of Pragmatics* (pp. 1–13). Amsterdam, The Netherlands: Benjamins.

Polanyi, K. (1957). *The great transformation*. New York, NY: Rinehart.

Popper, K. R. (1965). *Conjectures and refutations; The growth of scientific knowledge* (2nd edn). London, UK: Routledge.

Posteguillo, S. (1999). The schematic structure of computer science research articles. *English for Specific Purposes*, *18*(2), 139–60.

Prior, P. A. (1998). *Writing/disciplinarity: A sociohistoric account of literate activity in the academy*. Mahwah, NJ: Erlbaum.

Quinn, J. (1993). A taxonomy of text types for use in curriculum design. *EA Journal*, *11*(2), 33–46.

Ramanathan, V. & Kaplan, R. B. (1996). Some problematic 'channels' in the teaching of critical thinking in current L1 composition textbooks: Implications for L2 student-writers. *Issues in Applied Linguistics*, *7*(2), 225–49.

Riddle, M. (2000). Improving argument by parts. In S. Mitchell & R. Andrews (Eds), *Learning to argue in higher education* (pp. 53–64). Portsmouth, NH: Heinemann.

Ridley, D. (2012). *The literature review: A step-by-step guide for students*. Thousand Oaks, CA: Sage.

Rogers, P. S. (2000). CEO presentations in conjunction with earnings announcements: Extending the construct of organizational genre through competing values profiling and user-needs analysis. *Management Communication Quarterly*, *13*(3), 426–85.

Rogers, P. S., Gunesekera, M. & Yang, M. L. (2011). Language options for managing: Dana Corporation's philosophy and policy document. *The Journal of Business Communication*, *48*(3), 256–99.

Rosch, E. H. (1978). Principles of categorization. In E. H. Rosch & B. B. Lloyd (Eds), *Cognition and categorization* (pp. 27–47). Hillsdale, NJ: Erlbaum.

Rudestam, K. & Newton, R. (2007). *Surviving your dissertation: A comprehensive guide to content and process* (3rd edn). Thousand Oaks, CA: Sage.

Rumelhart, D. E. & Ortony, A. (1977). The representation of knowledge in memory. In R. C. Anderson, R. J. Spiro & E. Montague (Eds), *Schooling and the acquisition of knowledge* (pp. 99–135). Hillsdale, NJ: Erlbaum.

Rutherford, B. (2005). Genre analysis of corporate annual report narratives: A corpus linguistics-based approach. *Journal of Business Communication, 42*(4), 349–78. doi:10.1177/0021943605279244

Salager-Meyer, F. & Lewin, B. A. (Eds). (2011). *Crossed words: Criticism in scholarly writing*. Bern, Switzerland: Lang.

Salancik, G. R. & Meindl, J. R. (1984). Corporate attributions as strategic illusions of management control. *Administrative Science Quarterly, 29*(2), 238–54. Retrieved from http://www.jstor.org/stable/2393176

Sampson, V. & Clark, D. B. (2008). Assessment of the ways students generate arguments in science education: Current perspectives and recommendations for future directions. *Science Education, 92*(3), 447–72.

Samraj, B. (2002). Introductions in research articles: Variations across disciplines. *English for Specific Purposes, 21*(1), 1–17.

Sanford, A. & Garrod, S. C. (1981). *Understanding written language: Explorations of comprehension beyond the sentence*. Chichester, UK: Wiley.

Schroeder, N. & Gibson, C. (1990). Readability of management's discussion and analysis. *Accounting Horizons, 4*(4), 78–87. Retrieved from http://search.ebscohost.com.ezproxy.waikato.ac.nz/login.aspx?direct=true&db=bth&AN=9604010100&site=ehost-live&custid=s4804380

Schryer, C. F. (1993). Records as genre. *Written Communication, 10*(2), 200–234. doi:10.1177/0741088393010002003

Selinker, L., Todd-Trimble, M. & Trimble, L. (1978). Rhetorical function-shifts in EST discourse. *TESOL Quarterly, 12*(3), 311–20. Retrieved from http://www.jstor.org/stable/3586057

Shaw, P. (1991). Science research students' composing processes. *English for Specific Purposes, 10*(3), 189–206. doi:10.1016/0889-4906(91)90024-Q

Shaw, P. (2003). Evaluation and promotion across languages. *Journal of English for Academic Purposes, 2*(4), 343–357. doi:10.1016/S1475-1585(03)00050-X

Shaw, P. (2004). How do we recognise implicit evaluation in academic book reviews. In G. Del Lungo Camiciotti & E. Tognini-Bonelli (Eds), *Academic discourse: New insights into evaluation* (pp. 121–40). Bern, Switzerland: Lang.

Shaw, P. (2009). The lexis and grammar of explicit evaluation in academic book reviews, 1913 and 1993. In K. Hyland & P. Shaw (Eds), *Academic evaluation: Review genres in university settings* (pp. 217–35). Basingstoke, UK: Palgrave Macmillan.

Silva, T. (1990). Second language composition instruction: Developments, issues and directions in ESL. In B. Kroll (Ed.), *Second language writing: Research insights for the classroom* (pp. 11–23). Cambridge, UK: Cambridge University Press.

Simon, S. (2008). Using Toulmin's argument pattern in the evaluation of argumentation in school science. *International Journal of Research & Method in Education, 31*(3), 277–89.

Sinclair, J. M. (1988). Mirror for a text. *Journal of English and Foreign Languages, 1*, 15–44.

Smart, G. (1998). Mapping conceptual worlds: Using interpretive ethnography to explore knowledge-making in a professional community. *Journal of Business Communication, 35*(1), 111–27. Retrieved from http://search.ebscohost.com/login.aspx?direct=true&db=ufh&AN=167660&site=ehost-live

Stanton, P. & Stanton, J. (2002). Corporate annual reports: Research perspectives used. *Accounting, Auditing & Accountability, 15*(4), 478–500.

Stapleton, P. & Wu, Y. A. (2015). Assessing the quality of arguments in students' persuasive writing: A case study analyzing the relationship between surface structure and substance. *Journal of English for Academic Purposes, 17*, 12–23.

Starfield, S., Paltridge, B. & Ravelli, L. (2014). Researching academic writing: What textography affords. In J. Huisman & M. Tight (Eds), *Theory and method in higher education research II* (pp. 103–20). Bingley, UK: Emerald.

Stotesbury, H. (2003). Evaluation in research article abstracts in the narrative and hard sciences. *Journal of English for Academic Purposes, 2*(4), 327–41.

Swales, J. M. (1981). *Aspects of article introductions*. Birmingham, UK: The University of Aston.

Swales, J. M. (1988). Discourse communities, genres and English as an international language. *World Englishes, 7*(2), 211–20.

Swales, J. M. (1990). *Genre analysis: English in academic and research settings*. Cambridge, UK: Cambridge University Press.

Swales, J. M. (1998). *Other floors, other voices: A textography of a small university building*. Mahwah, NJ: Erlbaum.

Swales, J. M. (2004). *Research genres: Explorations and applications*. Cambridge, UK: Cambridge University Press.

Swales, J. M. & Feak, C. B. (2012). *Academic writing for graduate students: Essential tasks and skills* (3rd edn). Ann Arbor: University of Michigan Press.

Thompson, J. B. (1990). *Ideology and modern culture: Critical social theory in the era of mass communication*. Stanford, CA: Stanford University Press.

Thompson, P. (1999). Exploring the contexts of writing: Interviews with PhD supervisors. In P. Thompson (Ed.), *Issues in EAP writing research and instruction* (pp. 37–54). Reading, UK: University of Reading.

Thompson, P. (2012). Achieving a voice of authority in PhD theses. In K. Hyland & C. Sancho Guinda (Eds), *Stance and voice in written academic genres* (pp. 119–33). Basingstoke, UK: Palgrave Macmillan.

Thompson, G. & Hunston, S. (2000). Evaluation: an introduction. In S. Hunston & G. Thompson (Eds), *Evaluation in text: Authorial stance and the construction of discourse* (pp. 1–27). Oxford, UK: Oxford University Press.

Thompson, G. & Zhou, J. (2000). Evaluation and organization in text: The structuring role of evaluative disjuncts. In *Evaluation in text: Authorial stance and the construction of discourse* (pp. 121–41). Oxford, UK: Oxford University Press.

Toulmin, S. E. (2003). *The uses of argument*. Cambridge, UK: Cambridge University Press.
Toynbee, P. (2003). *Hard work: Life in low-pay Britain*. London, UK: Bloomsbury.
Toynbee, P. & Walker, D. (2008). *Unjust rewards: Exposing greed and inequality in Britain today*. London, UK: Granta.
Tse, P. & Hyland, K. (2009). Discipline and gender: Constructing rhetorical identity in book reviews. In K. Hyland & G. Diani (Eds), *Academic evaluation: Review genres in university settings* (pp. 105–21). Basingstoke, UK: Palgrave Macmillan.
Tucker, P. (2003). Evaluation in the art-historical research article. *Journal of English for Academic Purposes*, 2(4), 291–312. doi:10.1016/S1475-1585(03)00047-X
Tucker, P. (2004). Evaluation and interpretation in art-historical discourse. In G. Del Lungo Camiciotti & E. Tognini-Bonelli (Eds), *Academic discourse: New insights into evaluation* (pp. 161–79). Bern, Switzerland: Lang.
Van Dijk, T. A. (1980). *Macrostructures: An interdisciplinary study of global structures in discourse, interaction, and cognition*. Hillsdale, NJ: Erlbaum.
Van Dijk, T. A. (1997). *Discourse as structure and process*. London, UK: Sage.
Van Dijk, T. A. (1998). *Ideology: A multidisciplinary approach*. London, UK: Sage.
Van Dijk, T. A. (2008). *Discourse and power*. Basingstoke, UK: Palgrave Macmillan.
Van Leeuwen, L. (2008). *Discourse and practice : New tools for critical analysis*. New York, NY: Oxford University Press.
Verhoeven, L. & de Jong, J. H. A. L. (1992). *The construct of language proficiency: Applications of psychological models to language assessment*. Amsterdam, The Netherlands: Benjamins.
Virtanen, T. (1992). Issues of text typology: Narrative - a 'basic' type of text? *Text - Interdisciplinary Journal for the Study of Discourse*, 12(2), 293–310. Retrieved from http://dx.doi.org/10.1515/text.1.1992.12.2.293
Webber, P. (2004). Negation in linguistics papers. In G. Del Lungo Camiciotti & E. Tognini-Bonelli (Eds), *Academic discourse: New insights into evaluation* (pp. 181–202). Bern, Switzerland: Lang.
Werlich, E. (1976). *A text grammar of English*. Heidelberg, Germany: Quelle and Meyer.
West, C. (1982). *Prophesy deliverance!: An Afro-American revolutionary christianity*. Philadelphia, PA: Westminster Press.
Widdowson, H. G. (1983). *Learning purpose and language use*. Oxford, UK: Oxford University Press.
Widdowson, H. G. (2000). On the limitations of linguistics applied. *Applied Linguistics*, 21(1), 3–25.
Widdowson, H. G. (2004). *Text, context, pretext: Critical issues in discourse analysis*. Malden, MA: Blackwell.
Widdowson, H. G. (2007). *Discourse analysis*. Oxford, UK: Oxford University Press.
Wingate, U. (2012). 'Argument!' helping students understand what essay writing is about. *Journal of English for Academic Purposes*, 11(2), 145–54.

Yang, R. & Allison, D. (2003). Research articles in applied linguistics: Moving from results to conclusions. *English for Specific Purposes, 22*(4), 365–85.

Yuthas, K., Rogers, R. & Dillard, J. F. (2002). Communicative action and corporate annual reports. *Journal of Business Ethics, 41*(1), 141–57. doi:10.1023/a:1021314626311

Zhu, W. & Cheng, R. (2008). Negotiating the dissertation literature review: The influence of personal theories. In C. P. Casanave & X. Li (Eds), *Learning the literacy practices of graduate school: Insiders reflections on academic enculturation* (pp. 134–49). Ann Arbor: University of Michigan Press.

Index

academic literacies 11
American pragmatism 8
Andrews, R. 51, 63–5
annual report (of publicly listed companies) 112–14
appraisal theory 24–5, 151–2, 155
Aristotle 4
Artemeva, N. 28, 32
Atkinson, D. 9–10, 12
attribution (Sinclair) 79
averral (Sinclair) 79

Bacon, Francis 4–5
Basturkmen, H. 73, 77, 79, 85
Bakhtin, M. M. 40
Bakhtinian dialogism 24
Bhatia, V. K. 26–8, 30–2, 34, 36, 40, 73, 107, 113–15, 124
Biber, Douglas 28, 37, 41
Bitchener, J. 70, 72, 92–3, 107
Blommaert, J. 18
British Academic Written English (BAWE) Corpus 11, 48, 51, 53
Brookfield, S. D. 2–10, 160

Carrell, P. L. 22, 34–5, 40
CARS move structure 95–6, 99, 109, 147
categorization theory 36–8, 41
cognitive genre, *see* genre
Comte, Auguste 5
Concession Contraexpectation, *see* interpropositional relations
construct validity 15, 27–8, 33, 36–7, 45
corporate disclosure 112–14
 communication 111
 genre 113
corpus methods 24, 115, 151, 153–4, 159
counterclaiming 64, 105
critical discourse analysis 6, 8, 18
critical statements (in essays) 53–68
critical statements (in PhD Discussions) 76, 79–88

Critical Theory School (Frankfurt School) 6, 8
 Institute for Social Research 6
critical thinking (definition) 2
 as logical argument 10
 as social practice 10
Crombie, W. 23, 41–2, 44, 55, 57–9, 63–4, 75–6, 79–80, 82–3, 98, 103–4, 107–9, 147, 152, 157, 170

deductive reasoning 4–5
Descartes 5
dialectic 4
discourse (definitions) 5, 17–19, 131
discourse communities 31–3

empiricism 4–5, 8
enacting criticality 2–3, 16–17
engagement 44, 125, 157
essay genre, *see* university essay genre

Fabian Society 134
falsifiability, principle of 8
falsification, theory of 6
Feyerabend, Paul 6, 16
financialization 132–3
fund manager commentary (FMC) genre 111

genre (definitions) 26–43
 ESP approach to genre 30–2
 SFL-influenced approach to genre 29–30
 NR/RGS approach to genre 32–3
 social/ cognitive genre model 38–43
genre-based pedagogy 125, 155
 analysis phase 125–6, 156–7
 synthesis phase 126, 157
Grounds Conclusion, *see* interpropositional relations

Guardian, The (newspaper) 129–30, 134, 144

hegemony 129, 130, 133, 142
Halliday, M. A. K. 22, 29
Hasan, R. 27–30, 35, 40
Hirst, P. H. 2, 11
Hoey, M. 22, 25, 27, 41–2, 151, 153
Hood, S. 28–9
Hume, David 6
Hyland, K. 17, 19, 26, 35–6, 40, 44, 52, 55, 60–3, 75–6, 79, 83, 85–6, 98, 101, 107, 113–15, 117, 125, 137–8, 147–9, 151, 157

ideology (definition) 18, 130–3
interpropositional relations 23, 170–1
   Concession Contraexpectation 59–60, 82, 103–6
   Grounds Conclusion 57–9, 82–3
   Reason Result 58–9, 80–2

Johns, A. M. 26, 28, 49
Johnson, M. 34, 41–2

Kuhn, Thomas 6

literature reviews (RA) 92–5
logical atomism (Russell) 5
logical grammar 2, 11
logical positivism 5–6

McPeck, J. E. 2, 16
Martin, J. R. 25, 27–30, 35
metadiscourse devices 40, 60–1, 83–4
   attititude markers 62, 83–4, 101–3, 120–2, 138
   hedging 60–1, 84, 148–9
   self mention 60–1, 117, 120–3
metaphor 121, 123, 126–7
Miller, C. R. 20–2, 28, 32, 39

narrative structure 101, 151
neoliberalism 129, 132–4, 139, 143

Paltridge, B. 27, 32, 34, 38, 49, 73, 92
paradigm 6–7
PhD Discussion chapter 70–1
Popper, Karl 6, 8

Prior, Paul 145
procedural knowledge 21–2, 34–5, 38–41, 65
prototype theory 34

Reason Result, *see* interpropositional relations
register 29–30, 34–6
rhetoric 4
rhetorical shifts 50, 52, 64, 66
rhetorica nova 4
Royal Society 4, 8

schemata 21
   content schemata 22, 40
   formal schemata 22, 35
   image schemata 41–2
schematic knowledge 21, 34, 39, 118–19, 135–6
scientific method 5–6
semantic prosodies 117, 121, 123, 126, 148–9
Sinclair, J. M. 79
situatedness 6–7, 10, 16
sociolinguistics 18
sociology of science 7
stance 24, 40, 44, 60, 75, 83, 93, 120–3, 137–8
Swales, J. M. 27–8, 30–2, 34–6, 40, 72, 94–6, 98–9, 103, 107, 109, 119, 138, 147
syllogism 4
systemic functional linguistics 28–9

teaching critical thinking (in writing) 10–13, 65–6, 86–7, 107–8, 125–6, 155–8
   cognitive apprenticeship approach 11–12
   teachable skills approach 10–11
teaching critical thinking (skill) 7–9
   criticality movement 9
   critical pedagogy movement 9
   critical thinking movement 9
text (definition) 3, 17
Toulmin's argument pattern (TAP) 50–1, 63–5
Toynbee, Polly 129–30, 134

university essay genre 48

Van Dijk, Teun 17–18, 34, 130
Vienna circle 5–6

Widdowson, H. G. 3, 12, 17, 19, 21, 33, 39, 124, 130, 153
Writing Program Administrators' (WPA) Outcomes Statements for First-Year Composition 48

www.ingramcontent.com/pod-product-compliance
Lightning Source LLC
Chambersburg PA
CBHW072109010526
44111CB00037B/2131